THE BOOK OF
MANATON

• PORTRAIT OF A DARTMOOR PARISH •

Compiled by
Jean Baldwin, Simon Butler, Bryan Harper,
Jane Hewitt, Ray Hugo, Maggie Kapff,
Kathleeen Perkins, Colin Stewart, Andrew Taylor

HALSGROVE

First published in Great Britain in 1999

British Library Cataloguing-in-Publication Data
A CIP record for this title is available from the British Library

ISBN 1 84114-038-4

HALSGROVE
PUBLISHING, MEDIA AND DISTRIBUTION

Halsgrove House
Lower Moor Way
Tiverton, Devon EX16 6SS
Tel: 01884 243242
Fax: 01884 243325
email www.halsgrove.com

Printed and bound in Great Britain by Bookcraft Ltd, Midsomer Norton

Contents

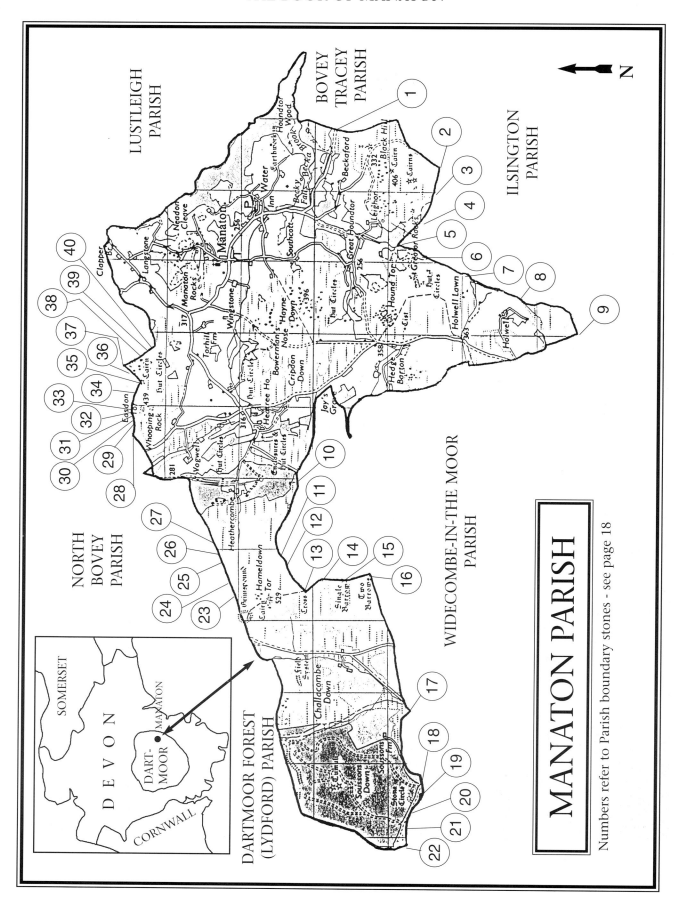

MANATON PARISH

Numbers refer to Parish boundary stones - see page 18

Foreword

The opportunity for Manaton parishioners to publish a pictorial outline of its history was presented to the Parish Council late in 1998. Since that time a group of us have endeavoured to record those aspects of the Parish that have made it a community. Thus the book is about people and events, mostly past but some present. Our early fears that there would be little response to our appeals for information proved groundless as memorabilia of all sorts poured in, and continues to do so even after the printer's ink is dry!

Although the final book is much larger than planned, it contains but a small part of the many contributions received from far and near. The book was never intended to be a comprehensive survey of the Parish but more an opportunity to look back on Manaton's past, with the photographs leading what has been written. Our aim has been to produce a book that will have something for everyone to enjoy and, whereas every attempt has been made to make it factually correct, no claim is made for its academic status. However all the material collected, including over a thousand photographs, will be kept safely to serve as a superb Manaton archive for the use of future historians. If readers have any comments, or new information and photographs, we would welcome them for inclusion in the archive.

As always with books of this sort it is impossible to thank individually all those who have provided information and photographs. However, some have shown such generosity and faith in our ability to use their memories and family photographs to good purpose, that we must acknowledge them here. To all others we extend our most grateful thanks.

Our particular thanks go to: Captain N. Bearne; Phyllis Bickham; Susan Brewer, Ruby and Doris Brown; Lang Burrell; Jeremy Butler; Jim Churchward; Barbara and Peter Clarke; Evelyn Clark; Joyce Cross; Charles Crout; Peter Daw; Miss R. Everard; John Frost; Francis Germon; Dorothy Harris; Francis Heath; Tom Heath; Bill Howe; Betty Hunt; Paulie James; Sylvia Needham; Frank, Norman and Pat Perryman; Tom and Viv Pollard; Alison Simpkins; Cyril Skerrett, Susan Smith; Rev Robin Taylor; Michelle Thomas; Mrs H. Tremain; Anne Wadham; Freda Wilkinson; Mr and Mrs R. Willcocks; Dick Wills; Stephen Woods.

The Manaton Book Group, formed in 1998 in order to collect and present the information included in this book. From the left: Jean Baldwin, Maggie Kapff, Kathleen Perkins, Simon Butler, Jane Hewitt, Ray Hugo, Andrew Taylor, Bryan Harper (Chairman). Colin Stewart, also a member of the group, is not in the photograph.

Almost every inch of the parish bears some evidence of early settlement. This aerial photograph of Easdon shows clearly the reaves, field boundaries and hut circles that were all part of the prehistoric community's settlement.

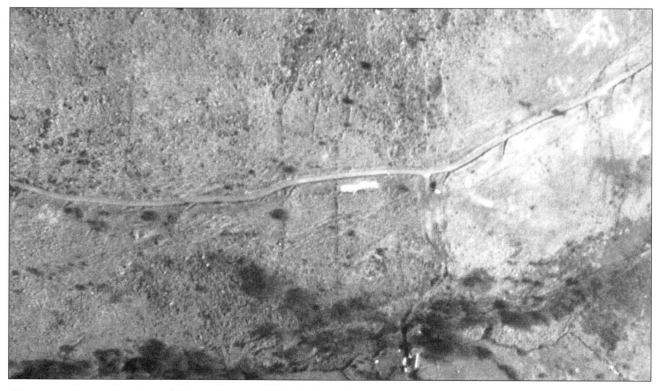

Blissmoor lies at the foot of Hayne Down which is littered with evidence of early occupation. Prehistoric field walls and hut circles can be found in abundance. (Photos courtesy Jeremy Butler)

1 - Earliest Times

We know that the area of Dartmoor in which Manaton parish now lies was first settled in Mesolithic times – that is about 8000 years BC. These earliest inhabitants were hunter-gatherers, who wandered the thick pine and birch woodland of the river valleys, and the heather-clad slopes of the upland areas. Evidence of their occupation comes from stone and flint tools found on the moor. Although flint is not naturally found here, it is not unusual to find pieces of it in ploughed fields locally. Such pieces have been recovered from the Church Field and elsewhere. All this flint was carried to the moor in times past and is the primary evidence for original human presence on Dartmoor.

The first people to settle the moor arrived around 4000BC. This was the Neolithic period in which the first farmer began to clear areas in the dense oak woodland, and cultivate areas on the moorland edge for the growing of cereal crops. Hunting remained an important part of their lives and it is easy to imagine herds of deer living in the woodland around Becky Falls, much as they do today. Wolves, bears and wild boar also inhabited Dartmoor, and remained until comparatively recent times, certainly into the early centuries AD.

It is likely that these people were also nomadic, migrating from the coastal areas of Devon to look for food during the summer months, erecting temporary shelters for themselves and their stock. In his excellent series of books, *The Dartmoor Atlas of Antiquities* (Vols 1–5), Dr Jeremy Butler, drawing on the evidence of his fieldwork, paints a vivid picture of how Dartmoor was settled at this time.

Rather than attempt to reproduce all that has been written about the prehistory of Dartmoor in general, and of Manaton in particular, this chapter draws a conjectural day in the life of a Manaton villager of 3–4000 years ago.

It is early morning, just before sunrise, and already there is movement in the scatter of huts on Hayne Down. A woman, dressed in a loose-fitting coarsely woven dress, stoops to avoid the low beam over the hut door and looks out over the landscape. To her left, Bowerman's Nose stands black against the purple sky, and the view eastwards, towards the high slopes of Dartmoor, reveals dense, dark woodland, sweeping as far as the eye can see, with only the higher slopes bare of trees. A dog barks in the neighbouring hut, and thin streams of smoke drift from the conical thatch roofs of each dwelling.

The woman checks the thorn hedge that overlies the low stone walls running around her home, looking for signs of intruders. But there are no signs of deer, or of other wild animals, breaking in to devour the precious crops. The walls of the garden plot are joined directly to the hut walls, while further fields spread out on the downslope, the thin soil, cleared of stones, supporting a struggling crop of grain.

From a decorated stoneware pot, the woman takes a handful of corn and feeds some grains into the quernstone that she revolves by turning a wooden handle. The ground 'flour' trickles out into a flat stone beneath. A tiny naked child totters from the doorway behind her and blinks as the first rays of the sun lighten the landscape.

Her husband also appears, a wolfskin cloak tugged around his shoulders. In his hand he holds a flint knife and he bends to begin to cut thin strips of hide from a deerskin. These will later be used to bind a flint spearhead to its wooden shaft.

A cry from the summit of the hill alerts the hut-dwellers who look towards the sound, shielding their eyes from the sun. But it is only one of the shepherds calling to his dog.

The farmers carry on with their tasks, some carrying water in skin bags from the little stream running near Blissmoor, others hacking at the dry earth with antler picks, clearing the ground for replanting. The women gather at a communal fire, outside the largest hut of the settlement, set a little aside from the rest. They sing as they bake small cakes made of flour and water; children cry for food or play in the dust at the doorway of the hut.

It is a blue summer day, much as the days we know on Dartmoor. The landscape they look out upon is much like the landscape we see today.

A view looking towards the summit of Hayne Down. The double stone row is possibly a prehistoric 'droveway', leading to the hilltop enclosure. It is conjectured that such passages allowed cattle to be driven through the existing settlements and on to higher ground for grazing, without disturbing the crops of the hillside farmers. The summit of Hayne Down contains a great many puzzling archaeological features. (Photos courtesy Jeremy Butler)

The familiar peak of Easdon Tor, the huge shoulder of Hameldown to the west. Though prey to wild animals, and subject to drought and famine, the life of these people is a settled one.

The shepherd, from his lookout on the summit of Hayne, is not of the same people as the hut dwellers. His people are from the lowland slopes, farmers for the most part, who have cleared the woodland in the soft rolling hills close to the sea in south Devon. Each summer, as they have done for centuries, the shepherds bring their flocks out from the lowlands and on to the high slopes of Dartmoor, where the summer grass is rich, and the flocks are free to wander, safer from wolves and bears that haunt lowland forests.

The shepherds and the hut dwellers co-exist during the summer months but live in separate communities. Droveways have been built between the hut settlements through which the flocks are driven up to the higher ground, avoiding damage to the crops. The shepherds build their own temporary shelters, constructed much like the permanent huts but dismantled at the end of each summer, or left to fall into decay and repaired again at the start of each season.

On this day the shepherd has arranged to slaughter one of his barren ewes, and half the meat will be taken down to the hut dwellers and exchanged for grain. The shepherd also has some cherts of flint that he purchased from a trader passing through the lowlands. This too he will use for trade. The hut dwellers make good cloth on their looms, strong and warm – as it has to be to withstand the moorland winter.

The shepherd's view takes in the whole of the surrounding moor – even to the sea – close to his own village. Nearer at hand are the slopes of Trendlebere across which he trekked a few days earlier, bringing his flock up the narrow trackway, past the double stone row. This is part of the religion of the hut dwellers, and the shepherds take care not to intrude upon or disturb these sites. The shepherd recalls the other monuments nearby – the burial chest at Hound tor and the many standing stones and cairns – all part of the hut-dwellers' community.

He stands upon a rock, against both sides of which abut a double bank of stone walls. These form part of the droveway, and complete the enclosure around the whole of the summit of Hayne down. Up to the edge of this runs one of the massive banks, or reaves, which delineates a clear boundary between the tribal regions of Dartmoor. The reave runs up the slope of Hayne

© Dartmoor National Park Authority

Above: A spindle whorl - used from prehistoric times as a weight on the loom for clothmaking.

Left: A reconstruction of a hut circle - home to prehistoric people of the moor. The remains of thousands of these can be found across Dartmoor, often associated with field and boundary walls.

Above: These chisel-shaped arrowheads are typical of those used in the Mesolithic period. In later periods they were to take on a characteristic leaf shape.

Right: A granite quern, used for grinding corn. These are found in many variations throughout the world and date from prehistoric times up to the medieval period. (Photos courtesy Stephen Woods)

north-west from Cripdon down, and continues eastwards down towards the modern-day village of Manaton. The shepherd knew that the reave ran over the western horizon towards the massive settlement of Grimspound, where many hut circles lay grouped within a single protective compound.

Over many centuries these scenes of life in prehistoric times would have been as commonplace to the people of those times, as our lives are to us today. From around 1700–600BC, climate change and the introduction of bronze for tools and weapons brought fundamental changes to the lives of these people. Their ceremonial monuments also took on a more sophisticated character, with cairn circles, multiple stone circles, and ring cairns being built.

From 600BC–AD 43 the Iron Age brought a further gradual change to the lives of these moor-land dwellers. The building of massive hillforts suggests a need for defensive settlements, perhaps as tribal competition increased. These form a circuit around the eastern edge of the moor, standing on prominent hilltops, often within sight of each other. One such fort, at Hunters Tor in Lustleigh, overlooks the Cleave, while a sister fort, now hidden by woodland, stands at the head of Hound Tor Wood.

Though these early people relied entirely upon their own devices for the essentials in life – their whole world was encompassed by the landscape they could see around them – they nevertheless were bound by the communality of existence; with grief, caring, loss and laughter, as much part of their lives as of ours. These people, living thousands of years ago, are a direct link into our past – and the evidence of their life abounds in Manaton parish today.

The photographs on this page are from Robert Burnard's albums dated from around the turn of the nineteenth century. Here is Grimspound, perhaps the best known prehistoric settlement site on the moor, which was 'renovated' by Burnard and a group of his friends in the 1890s. (Photos courtesy Lady Sayer)

Right: *George French stands at the reconstructed entrance to Grimspound 28 April 1894. The work was overseen by the Rev. Sabine Baring-Gould, a keen amateur archaeologist and composer of the hymn 'Onward Christian Soldiers'.*

Left: *The Rev. Sabine Baring-Gould looks on as his workmen complete the rebuilding of one of the massive walls at Grimspound, 26 May 1894.*

Right: *Burnard's photograph of the kistvaen below Hound Tor, taken on 13 August 1889. Kists are prehistoric graves, a coffin made up of slabs of granite standing on their edge, with a lid of granite covering the interment. Excavation of kists often recovers cremated remains in an urn, pottery fragments, beads, etc.*

An aerial view over Greator. This is an area of prehistoric occupation but on the centre right is the site of the medieval village. Thought to have been abandoned in the fourteenth century, possibly due to the Black Death, this settlement (below right) contains longhouses, corn-drying barns and evidence of strip lynchets and ridge-and-furrow agriculture. (Photos courtesy Jeremy Butler)

HOUND TOR MEDIEVAL VILLAGE

The climate changes over the passing centuries made Dartmoor a harsher environment in which to live. People now lived in longhouses - narrow rectangular single-storey buildings divided in two, with animals housed in the downslope end. Many of these survive in the parish, although the term 'longhouse' today is applied to almost any ancient farm dwelling.

Hound Tor medieval village is a Scheduled Monument. It is thought to be the site referred to in Domesday as belonging to Tavistock Abbey:

A wintry view across the deserted medieval village at Hound Tor. (Photo courtesy Jeremy Butler)

> *Reginald holds Houndtor from the Abbot. Abbot Sihtric held it before 1066. It paid tax for 1/2 hide. 4 ploughlands. In lordship 1 plough, 2 slaves, 1 virgate. 2 villagers and 4 small holders have 1 plough and 1 virgate. 9 acres of meadow, 2 acres of woodland and 1 league of pasture. 7 cattle, 28 sheep and 18 goats. Value 20s.*

The site was excavated in the 1960s and much of what can be seen there today results from the work done at that time. The settlement was occupied over several centuries with original turf buildings eventually being replaced by stone. In all there are eleven distinct buildings: eight are dwellings and the remaining three are corn-drying barns, built towards the end of the site's occupation. The generally deteriorating climate meant that crops no longer dried naturally in the fields and artificial means were employed to dry the seed corn. A pair of kilns for this purpose can be seen within each of the platforms constructed across the upper end of the barns.

This type of building is mirrored throughout the parish and remained largely unchanged up until the nineteenth century when, among other things, mechanisation in farming brought about the need for new styles of farm building.

MISSING STONES MYSTERIES

Anyone looking into Manaton's history will come across the reference to a 'cyclopean' stone circle that once stood in the fields to the right of the road between the village centre and the church crossroads. This it seems was once Manaton's answer to Stonehenge.

There are references to this 'elliptical stone circle' in a number of early books, and one or two academic papers have been written in more recent times. The circle stood at the junction of three fields – Lower Manaton Hills, Lower Top Field and Furze Close – according to one source, or in a field called Hookaway, according to another. The Tithe Map refers to field No. 710 as Lower Manaton Hills, 712 as Hookacre (Hookaway?), 707 as Furze Park and 708 as Lower Top Field. There is also a reference to 709 as 'Pound' (possibly a reference to the elliptical circle).

In *A Guide to the Eastern Escarpment of Dartmoor* (no date but circa 1860) there is the following reference:

At some distance below the village in a field called Hookaway, was a noble circle or cyclopean inclosure of stone, considered by Colonel Hamilton Smith as one of the finest in England. In 1849 it was partly destroyed for the purpose of making a wall, and in 1850 it was wholly destroyed to make a partition between two fields, leaving only six stones to denote its once venerated site.'

In the notebook compiled by Miss Everard ('Little Silver') in the 1950s there is a sketch of the position of the circle (opposite). The notebook contains a further description from the last century:

One half is left of the so-called pound at Lower Manaton Hills, on Town Barton Farm - the diameter (or perhaps it would be more correct to say the chord) is now about a hundred and twenty feet, but in 1828 it had an elliptical form, and was very perfect, with a diameter of a hundred and thirty eight feet by one hundred. The wall is of large rough blocks, very carefully set, and has a height of about four feet. I was however informed that stones of a greater size existed in the section destroyed, their dimensions being six feet in height and about three feet in breadth and thickness. Formerly a row, consisting of thirty or forty stones, four feet high, extended up the field to the east of the enclosure, these stone touched each other - But two are left standing about seventy feet apart.

(There is also remains of an enclosure in Hookacre consisting of stones six or seven feet high) - it should be added, that what remains of the existing enclosure now forms part of a hedge, and is only with difficulty detected.

The compiler of the notebook records: 'Evelyn and I searched and eventually found what could have been the remains of a pound in the corner of the field in 1953.' She also refers to another published work: 'March 1964. *Investigations on Dartmoo*r, borrowed from the Devon County Library Transactions of the Plymouth Institution, printed and published by Rowe - sold by Baldwin and Craddock, London, 1830':

In a small pasture field about a furlong SE of Manaton church, adjoining a parish road, is an inclosure of an elliptical form in an exceeding perfect condition - the stones of which the fence is composed are from 4 to 6 feet high, placed in a double row set closely together. One stone however is so large that it fills the whole breadth of the fence, being six feet wide and five feet thick - the diameters of the area are 100 and 138 feet, and there are no vestiges of any druidical relic within the precincts. It will instantly be distinguished from the sacred circles of Gidleigh and the Grey Wethers by the position of the stones which are without lateral intervals.

I conjecture this inclosure to have named the village of Manaton, or rather Maen-y-Dun - the inclosure of erect stones (page 195) - Note by Major C.H. Smith.

Miss Everard concludes with the note: 'I seem to have this on my mind!! Large elliptical pound. Ruthlessly destroyed in 1849 by the Rector!! It is situated in the middle of several fields on Town Barton. We have found this - but no one is in the least interested - March 1957. Strange but true.'

And finally: 'Anyone interested in finding the Manaton ELLIPTICAL POUND better go into the field in LATE EVENING says I....'

The truth appears to be that the vicar of Manaton, in 1849 (see opposite), employed workmen to break up the stones in order to make new fields, using the stone in the hedges. And there is little likelihood of this structure giving its name to Manaton - but who knows?

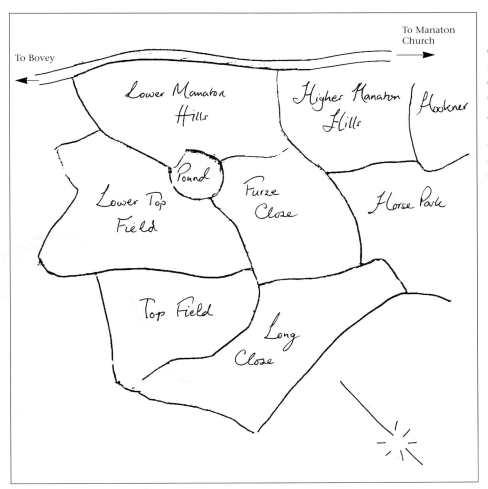

The map, dated 15 June 1843, showing the position of the fields and the pound in the area in which the elliptical stone cricle once exisited. The map is taken from a notebook compiled in the 1950s and includes a contemporary note: 'The Elliptical Pound - ruthlessly destroyed in 1849.'

MANATON CHURCHYARD CROSS

This cross provides every Dartmoor guidebook with a good tale. As the Rev. Sabine Baring-Gould (see his photo on page 10) wote in *A Book of Dartmoor*, published in 1900:

In the churchyard was a fine granite cross. A former rector, the Rev. C. Carwithen, wantonly destroyed it in the night. The people had been wont at a funeral to carry the corpse the way of the sun thrice round the cross before interment. He preached against the custom ineffectually, so he secretly smashed the cross.

The dates suggest that this was the same reverend gentleman that took to the elliptical stone circle with a sledgehammer.

The Rev. John C. Carwithen arrived in Manaton in 1841 – one of a long line of incumbents of that family – being the eighth of that name to have held office. His objections to the pagan practices of his flock may appear to have some merit although his destruction of the cross seems, today, to have been an act of desecration in itself.

It is said that the rector was at once suspected but no sign of the cross could be found despite a thorough search – only the socket stone remained.

Let the local historian Harry Starkey, in his book *Dartmoor Crosses*, now complete the story:

One day, in 1908, a local man whose name I have been unable to discover, was working in the church at Manaton, attending to the bells, I was told. At mid-day, having had his lunch, he went for a short walk along the lane near the church. He eventually came to a spot where a wall was carried across a stream upon a long post of granite. He noticed that the granite post had a cross cut in it at one end and on closer examination found that the post was indeed a cross, complete except for one arm, which had been broken off and was missing. The story of the missing churchyard cross was then remembered and the then rector, thinking that the newly found cross was the missing one, had it erected in the empty socket-stone in the churchyard where we see it to-day.

The identification was faulty of course, the newly found cross is quite unlike the kind of cross that would have belonged to the carefully made socket-stone; in any case it does not fit, as examination will show. There is no doubt that the cross now standing in Manaton churchyard originally came from some track or lane nearby where it acted as a waymark. It is equally true that the real Manaton churchyard cross has yet to be found, if it has not been utterly destroyed.

Local accounts have it that the replacement cross was found half-buried near Mill Farm before being elevated to its churchyard position.

2 - The Parish Boundaries

The Norman and medieval period saw the increasing effects of ecclesiastical influence on Dartmoor. Great power lay in the hands of the Abbeys and Monasteries; many parish churches date from this time, or at least were rebuilt on earlier foundations, and parish boundaries were firmly established. The stone crosses found alongside many of the ancient trackways also mainly date from this period, as do many bridges.

BOUNDARIES AND BOUNDARY STONES

Manaton parish has a main East to West axis of about eleven kilometres or 6.5 miles, stretching from the river Bovey in the east to the far side of Soussons Wood to the west (see map page 4). The length of the boundary is in excess of 41 kilometres or 25 miles on the map, but boundary beaters would find it difficult to keep to these figures because of the terrain.

Starting at the north-east corner of the parish at Clapper Bridge (753828) the boundary follows the river Bovey to the lowest point of about 80 metres or 250 feet above sea level where the Becka Brook enters the Bovey (7790 8015). Turning west along the brook for about .5km the boundary turns south and ascends a steep gully which crosses the old leat before meeting the road from the village to Bovey Tracey on Trendlebere Down. The first stone marking the Manaton–Lustleigh boundary is on the south side of the road. Continuing in this direction to the edge of Yarner Wood (7700 7893) the route turns south-west passing North Lodge and on to Black Hill, to the three parish stone marking the boundary with Ilsington and Bovey Tracey parishes.

At this point the walker has climbed some 310 metres or 1000 feet above the river Bovey. The line of the old reave (282 metres) leads to the Duke of Somerset (DS 1853) stone named 'Prince of Wales' before the descent to the Hole stone.

A rough-hewn stone stands just above the bridle path while the Horseshoe stone lies in the Becka Brook below the clapper bridge. Thence south-west up the line of the Becka Brook passing Long Pool (LP) stone and later a new stone placed opposite the lower field gate to Holwell farm. This stone commemorates the well-known writer

The 'First Stone' marked M/L, stands beside the road on Trendlebere Down (76870 79720).

and inveterate walker Harry F. Starkey. Near the headwaters of the Becka the boundary turns west to a further meeting of three parishes (Manaton, Widecombe and Ilsington) along the wall line to the north of Hemsworthy or White gate.

The line of the stone wall between Holwell farm and Bone Hill Down stretches north-west before the trail crosses the stream on the southern boundary of Hedge Barton farm. Climbing to the top of Hedge Down the spring and stream lead the boundary down into the yard, effectively placing the farm in two parishes. Following the stream for a further 500 metres the boundary then runs north-east before turning west just to the south of Jay's Grave.

The bridle path westward from the grave now forms the boundary to Natsworthy Gate where the Pit Stone shows the line up the East Webburn river past Blue Jug and Grey Wethers to Hameldown Cross and Broad Barrow. At an elevation of 532 metres, or 1750 feet, this is the highest point in the parish.

MANATON BOUNDARY STONES

*Three parish stone (M/ILS/BOV)
7663 78325*

*The gully and boundary stone
on Trendlebere 7685 7970*

*'Prince of Wales' (DS) 75996
78401*

*Hemsworthy-Holwell Lawn BS
W/M/ILS 74046 76436*

*Hameldown Cross 70420
80105*

*Fallen boundary stone at
Hameldown 70820 81220*

*On field wall below Easdon Tor
72666 82423*

*Near summit of Easdon Tor
7348 8251*

*On the reave running south-east
on Easdon Tor 7369 8231*

Beyond Single Barrow to Two Barrows the trail turns west along the wall-line descending and crossing the two roads below Challacombe farm to the first of the Spitchwick stones, erected by Mr Jack Simpson, owner of Spitchwick Manor. The boundary then turns westward along the leat and wall-line skirting the southern boundary of Soussons Wood, on to the road, along the track past the three Cator boundary (CB) stones before a further Spitchwick stone on the river bank below Runnage Bridge.

Following the Constituency boundary north along the edge of Soussons to its north-east corner the boundary turns east following the wall across Challacombe Down to Firth Bridge. Over the road the line continues on to Hameldown, to the north of Grimspound, passing the linestones running north-east before descending the steep gully above Heathercombe.

After passing through enclosed land around Kendon farm and Vogwell cottage the trail crosses Long Lane to the first of the thirteen stones stretching across the summit of Easdon Tor. The most westerly stone is set into a field wall while the rest run in an easterly direction to the summit before continuing in a peculiarly zig-zag fashion along a number of intersecting ancient reaves, then picking up the line of a boundary wall running eastward and downhill to the roadside bridge below Luckdon. Here the boundary follows the line of the stream, and crosses the Bovey to a three-parish unmarked boundary point just above Clapper Bridge.

Circumnavigation of the parish boundary is an historic activity which was of importance when the title to land was not always well recorded or the area well delineated. Supposedly the term 'beating' referred to the custom of bumping the children on the stones to ensure that following generations would not easily forget the limits of the parish. In general, stones were placed in open countryside where the topograhical features were insufficient to mark the boundary line. In other areas natural features, ancient reaves, or boundary walls were used. Some 36 stones are marked on the OS map but 40 are known to exist – perhaps others have yet to be revealed.

The incised letters represent either the name of the stones or the initials of the bordering parishes or manor. In the case of the Duke of Somerset stones, DS marks the limits of Natsworthy Manor, and CB Cator Manor. Some stones are dated 1853 or 1854.

The regularity of beating the bounds is uncertain but the most recent was in 1997. This perambulation was led by parishioner Stan Fitton, ably assisted by Paulie James and a local expert, Jim Churchward. It took place over several weekends with a number of parishioners walking, helping to refresh the memories of those who had walked on previous occasions.

To ensure that future generations do not 'lose sight' of the stones and the parish heritage they represent, an accurate position of each known stone has been recorded and is included on the following page:

Bryan Harper, who did much of the work for this chapter, and who took many of the contemporary photographs used in this book, at the Duke Stone, 1999.

MANATON PARISH BOUNDARY STONES
GRID REFERENCES (All Sheet SX)

1. FIRST STONE M/L 76870 79720 to south of road.
2. THREE PARISH STONE, M/ILS/BOV 76337 78325.
3. PRINCE OF WALES (DS) 75996 78401.
4. HOLE STONE, one marker and adjacent stone with hole 75573 78435.
5. ROUGH HEWN STONE. 75m below, east of large oak tree just above bridle path 75430 78680.
6. HORSESHOE STONE in the Becka brook about 150m below the clapper bridge 75250 78850.
7. LONG POOL on the east bank and to the SW of the stream joining the Becka 74940 78120.
8. THE DUKE STONE/ Harry F. Starkey stone. Below Holwell House about 30 m south-east of gate leading to bottom field. Inscription to F. H. Starkey on east side 74600 77390.
9. THREE PARISH STONE, WID/M/ILS NNW of Hemsworthy gate along wall 74046 76436.
10. PIT STONE Left inside Natsworthy Gate 72127 80197.
11. BLUE JUG At the source of the East Webburn 70860 80386.
12. GREY WETHERS 70720 80320.
13. HAMELDOWN CROSS 70420 80105.
14. BROAD BARROW 70569 79960.
15. SINGLE BARROW 70533 79541.
16. TWO BARROWS 70666 79273.
17. FIRST SPITCHWICK MANOR STONE west bank of river 68801 78762.
18. 'STONE' Not on boundary line 67683 78615 Marked 'CB'.
19. 'CB' STONE on track - 67531 78511 then along old bank to...
20. SECOND 'CB' STONE 67361 78688.
21. THIRD 'CB' STONE 67170 78730.
22. SECOND SPITCHWICK STONE/ THREE PARISH BOUNDARY, Wid/Man/Lyd boundary, on south bank 150m downstream from bridge 66902 78684.
FIRTH BRIDGE 6974 8086 then follow stream on bearing 076 deg. mag.
23. BS 70285 81037 B on stream bank.
24. BS 70473 81067 B Leaning N to S.
25. BS 70820 81220 B Fallen.
26. BS 70925 81239 B.
27. BS 71044 81288 B Large slab N to S.
28. BS 72666 82423 B Against field wall, in boggy area.
29. BS 72750 82408 B fallen along E-W reave.
30. BS 72798 82469 unmarked but cuts on side, fallen.
31. BS 72875 82445 B in boggy area.
32. BS 72905 82448 B on reave line.
33. BS 73056 82425 B lm high, on reave line.
34. BS 73262 82363 B broken top, on reave line.
35. BS 73385 82343 B on reave line.
36. BS 73438 82432 B on reave line.
37. BS 73488 82525 B (faint) large, leaning.
38. BS 73538 82431 B on reave running SE.
39. BS 73695 82350 B on reave running SE lm high.
40. BS 73760 82210 B on reave running SE to wall 100m W of wood.

Cator Boundstone - Soussons

OTHER STONES OF NOTE

SWALLERTON GATE CROSS

One of many wayside crosses in the area, this cross head is built into the road side wall at Swallerton Gate, Hound Tor having-been rediscovered in a load of rubble in 1987. It was fortunate that the late Harry F. Starkey, a well known expert on Dartmoor and its wayside markers and crosses, was passing the cottage at precisely the time when the new owner was sorting out some stone for a foundation and remarked on the fact that it was indeed a cross head with an incised cross on one side. Apparently the cross had been found in a hedge row some years before but mislaid. A shaft for the cross was not found, hence the decision to set it into the wall. Its origin is unknown but is likely to have been placed at the junction of the three roads for the benefit of travellers. The fact that the cottage was an inn frequented by drovers and travellers in the seventeenth and eighteenth centuries may have had something to do with the loss of the cross for many years. Grid Reference SX 7390 7920.

Cross-head in the wall at Swallerton Gate.

THE HEATHERCOMBE CROSSES

Three granite posts were erected between 1969 and 1977 by Claude Pike OBE, the owner of the Heathercombe estate. Each bears an inscription taken from the Lord's Prayer and a carved relief of three fishes. The first post was erected in 1969 at the junction of the road from Widecombe through Natsworthy where it intersects the road from Heatree to Heathercombe. The second

(1971), stands on the right of the winding lane that leads from Heathercombe to Heathercombe Brake. The third is just inside the moorgate to Heathercombe Newtake.

The grid references of the crosses, along with the inscriptions are: SX 72450 80840 'Thine is the Power'; SX 71790 81280 'And The Kingdom'; SX 71900 80920 'And The Glory'.

'And The Glory' stone at Heathercombe.

CORN LAW STONE AT HEDGE BARTON FARM

A large inscribed granite rock stands on the south side of the private drive from East Lodge to Hedge Barton House bearing the inscription 'Free Trade in Corn' and a date 1848. The date is a little confusing as the Corn Laws were repealed in 1846. At this time the estate was in the ownership of James Bryant, younger brother of William, who in partnership with a Mr May started the match making firm of Bryant & May around 1840 in Plymouth.

The Corn Law stone at Hedge Barton.

Cecil Hunt's painting of Manaton church, the Church and Ivy Cottages c. 1900. The painting was made for Eden Phillpotts as part of a souvenir folder for the 300th performance of his play, The Farmer's Wife.

Manaton church from a postcard, early 1900s. The picture shows some interesting changes: the boundary hedge on the left was removed in 1950 to extend the graveyard, while the little hut on the west wall has also gone. The tower, unrendered at this date, also has no clock face – this was not installed until 1934. The granite war memorial is absent.

3 - Manaton Church

The Church is one of the focal points in Manaton, occupying a prominent site in the upper part of the village on the north side of the village green. Lying in the lee of Manaton Rocks and thus sheltered from the north, to the south the view is across to Hayne Down and Bowerman's Nose, a marvellous vista of the moor as you leave out of the south porch.

The present church probably dates from the fifteenth century but there was almost certainly a place of worship in the parish before then. By the time of Domesday, manors were known to exist at Manaton, Langstone, Neadon and Hound Tor, the last named being held by the Abbot of Tavistock before, and probably for a time after the Norman conquest. This would suggest that a place of worship existed at Hound Tor though there is no evidence as to where any chapel might have been. The oldest parts of the present granite-built church are the nave and chancel built early in the fifteenth century and later that century were added the north and south aisles, with the tower also being built then or at least soon after.

The origins of the church's dedication to St Winifred are also shrouded in some uncertainty. Bowerman, who lived at Hound Tor in William the Conqueror's time (and gave his name to the 'Nose') reputedly had a daughter called Winifred. On the other hand the source of the dedication might have been Winifreth, a Devon-born priest and missionary who was murdered in Germany in AD755. He was later canonized, but not as St Winifred, rather as St Boniface, so links with this source seem unlikely.

Most probably the dedication can be ascribed to St Winifred who lived in the seventh century in Wales, where she founded a community of Christian women and became known as St Winifred the Abbess. Her shrine is in Shrewsbury Abbey and her feast day is on 3 November. Not one of the better known saints perhaps (in fact only six churches in Britain are dedicated to her), but she was of great faith and is credited with many good works. She is someone to whom the church in Manaton can happily turn to for inspiration and example.

The church from Manaton rocks c.1920, Hay Tor distant. The dressed stone of the tower shows how handsome this was before rendering was undertaken in the 1930s.

Top left: *The interior of the church, from a postcard c.1920. The pulpit is shown in its original position on the north side of the nave.*

Above: *Robert Falcon's drawing of the church c.1900.*

Left above: *A view of the church from Cross Park c.1910. Note the thick hedge surrounding the churchyard – and no car park!*

Left: *A drawing from Lizzie Walter's sketchbook of the 1880s. She was the daughter of Rev. Walters, one time tenant at Foxworthy.*

A recent photograph of the sixteenth century rood screen. It is one of the church's greatest treasures.

THE ROOD SCREEN

For the first 150 years or so of the present church, Catholicism prevailed, and during this time, around AD1500, the rood screen was built, with its Tudor Rose and Fleur de Lis decorations, commemorating many Christian saints and martyrs. When the Reformation came to England towards the middle of the sixteenth century a decree from the Privy Council in 1548 ordered all superstitious (ie Catholic!) images to be taken down or defaced. It was almost certainly at this time that all the figures on the screen at Manaton were defaced and statues on the top removed – acts of vandalism done in the name of the religious correctness of the time.

We can only be thankful, however, that the whole screen was not taken down and destroyed. What has been left to us may have been devalued by the deeds of intolerance, but the screen remains one of the treasures of the church.

Much later, in 1900, the screen was restored, and again in 1980–1 it was cleaned and restored by a team of experts led by Miss Anna Hulbert.

She listed some twenty-four saintly images, many recognised by their accoutrements: St Paul with sword and book; St Thomas with a spear; St Andrew with a X-cross, and so on. On the central doors are the four doctors of the Church, Gregory, Jerome, Ambrose and Augustine.

Sadly we do not have as many records of the church as we would like, especially prior to the nineteenth century. This may be due to the fact that, though many Diocesan records were removed during the Second World War from the Cathedral precincts in Exeter and deposited in Crediton, those relating to Manaton (and no doubt some other churches as well) were accidentally left behind and destroyed in the blitz.

We do know, however, that the church was severely damaged in a violent storm in 1779. The tower was split from top to bottom, destroying much of the belfry and bell wheels; the east front of the chancel was demolished; and a pinnacle, suppposed to be 'a thousand pounds weight' was hurled through the nave roof – all of which puts the present problems of lead roofing and tower rendering into some sort of perspective.

Above: *The rood screen – a photograph taken before the major restoration in the 1920s. Compare with the modern photograph on the previous page the position of the pulpit and the priest's lectern, the pews and the wall script.* Right: *Figures defaced at the time of the Reformation,* from left: *St James, St Bartholomew and St Paul.* Inset above: *St Paul's defaced image on the rood screen.*

Repairs were in due course carried out and over the years the fabric of the building has generally been well looked after. There have nevertheless been times when major costly repairs were needed. Though we read that in 1859: 'a new roof has been placed on the chancel by the Rector' such skills were not normally a requirement for the position, and as befits a Grade 1 listed building professional experts are invariably used.

CHURCH RESTORATION

The last major restoration of the church occurred in 1924 and was supervised by the London architect Sir Charles Nicolson. Little was left untouched. There was a new roof put on the South aisle and porch while the rest of the roof, over the nave, north aisle and chancel was thoroughly repaired. There was new flooring over much of the interior and, not forgetting the comfort of church-goers, the old box pews with doors were all replaced, while the oak screen which still divides the tower from the nave was built, thus forming a vestry at the rear of the church. Even more obvious to the congregation was the mov-

ing of the pulpit from the north side of the nave to the south, where it is today, for reasons which are not entirely clear, but possibly the sun shining through the windows on the south wall made it difficult for preachers in the pulpit's original position. The old staircase at the north end of the screen was opened up and biblical texts on the ceiling of the chancel were removed.

All the structural work cost about £2500 at the time and gave rise to a major appeal for funds. 'Manaton is but a poor, moorland parish' it was claimed, and with generous assistance from outside the Church the necessary funds were raised. During all the restoration work services were held in St Winifred's Room (an earlier building on the site of the present parish hall) and the re-opening service was conducted by the Bishop of Exeter on 14 April 1925. In 1927 the Rural Dean was able to write 'the church is in excellent order'.

The work of maintaining and improving the fabric of the church, however, never ceases, and in the years since the 1920s many changes have taken place. Both chapels on the north and south of the chancel were refurbished in 1950, the latter as a Lady chapel and the former as a children's corner. The organ, which in 1904 had been exchanged for an American instrument, was again changed in 1922 when Richard Champernowne, one of the churchwardens at the time, donated a chamber organ which had come from Dartington, and this was installed in the north-east corner of the nave, presumably for acoustic reasons. This organ is still used in the church today and its musical qualities have been much appreciated by those who have played or heard it. When electricity was brought to the church in 1950 the organ was fitted with an electric motor, much to the relief no doubt of those who had previously had to operate the manual organ blower. but on the other hand there was no longer the 13 shillings per quarter, the going rate for organ blowing! Not only did the arrival of electricity improve conditions significantly inside the church but the heating system has been steadily upgraded, as when the solid fuel boiler was replaced in 1960 by oil heating, a gift from the Smerdon family.

STAINED GLASS WINDOWS

St Winifred's is adorned with five stained glass windows. The window at the eastern end behind the altar was given in 1860 in memory of Dorothea Vavasour, a considerable benefactor and major contributor to the village school. Her grave lies beneath the yew tree in the old churchyard. Two windows on the north wall (one now sadly hidden by the organ) were given in memory of the Nosworthy family who lived and farmed at Ford. There are also several wall plaques in that area of the church to members of the family, and Albert Nosworthy who died in 1905 left £100 to the choir and bell-ringers. But perhaps the most interesting member of the family is the Rev. John Nosworthy (1612–77) whose name does not appear in the list of Rectors, but who, during Cromwell's Protectorate in 1659 and following the sequestration of the Rector, James Hill, for drunkeness and debauched living , seeing that the living was vacant, and with an eye for an opening, installed himself. Such opportunism, however, was too much for the authorities and he was ejected unceremoniously.

On the south side of the Chancel there is a bright and beautiful window given in memory of William Carwithen and his wife. He was Rector from 1824–1841. Sadly this fine window is not visible to many seated in the congregation who may not even realise that it is there.

The newest stained glass window is on the

The Hunt Window.

south-west corner of the nave and is known as the Hunt window. It was installed in 1929 in memory of Esmond Moore Hunt who died in 1927, aged 19. Designed by Sir Frank Brangwyn RA, the glasswork was produced in Hammersmith, West London by Silvester Sparrow using a technique in which there is little surface colouring. Rather the colour is embedded in molten glass at the time of manufacture, producing a remarkably bright glow.

We are indebted to the Hunt family for the heraldic details of the window. Centre: Hunt shield borne by Esmond Moore Hunt, traceable back to Alderman Thomas Hunt of Exeter (d.1548), whose arms are displayed in the Guildhall, Exeter. Shield contains two labels showing that E. M. Hunt was born in the lifetime of father and grandfather. Left: Hunt arms, borne by Cecil A. Hunt quartered with Gumbleton of

The church tower and clock, seen from the green. This photograph was taken in the summer of 1999, shortly following the sale of Church Cottage, the thatch of which was then repaired.

County Waterford, Moore of Moore Abbey (Drogheda) and Brenchley of Benenden. Right: Lucas family shield borne by mother of E. M. Hunt

TOWER AND CLOCK

At the west end of the church stands the tower, 76 feet high and about 500 years old. For visitors and villagers alike the tower clock, installed in 1934 in memory of Charlotte Kitson, strikes every hour and can be heard in all parts of the village. In 1966 the clock faces were repainted and the west face repaired, the necessary funds being raised through a private donation. Twenty-three years later both faces were replaced and an automatic winding system was installed, the latter paid for by Deaconess Kristeen Macnair.

For many years the tower suffered from damp and in 1931 a fund was started to provide a rendering for the whole tower and the Western end of the South wall. To those admirers of the aesthetic qualities of granite this was no doubt a retrograde step but it achieved its end and damp in the tower was not a serious problem after this – for which the bell-ringers at least are very grateful!

Much older than the clock and even more audible is the set of bells, housed within the tower. In fact in the set of six bells there are three which are as old as or older than the tower itself. The Tenor was probably cast at Robert Norton's Exeter

foundry around 1500, while the Fourth and Fifth, cast by Johanna Hill, widow of a London bell-founder, are likely to date from the 1440s. The former is dedicated, as only a few were at that time, to St Catherine (Sancta Katerina ora pro nobis) and the latter to St George (Sancte George ora pro nobis), an even rarer dedication possibly associated with tin-mining in the area.

In 1934 all the bells were taken down, repaired, retuned and rehung on strengthened frames – a very necessary operation every so often, considering the bells together weigh 33cwt.3qtrs.11lbs! They were rededicated by the Archdeacon of Totnes in May 1934.

With bells go bell-ringers, practising an ancient and traditional skill, proclaiming imminent services in the church as well as marking times of celebration and, with muffled peal, sadness. With the depopulation of many villages teams of bell-ringers, let alone good ones, can be hard to muster, and in many villages such teams no longer exist and the bells remain silent. Not so in Manaton happily.

As far as we are able to tell a local team of bell-ringers has existed without interruption and peals have been regularly rung. Manaton is very proud of its bell-ringing tradition. In years gone by bell-ringers turned up in smart uniforms. Though sartorial elegance is no longer the first quality one associates with bell-ringers the fellowship and

BELL-RINGING

Manaton bell-ringers c.1910.

Rededication of the bells prior to being rehung in May 1934.

Manaton bell-ringers October 1999, l-r: Mike Baker, Brian Moss, Stan Fitton, Jane Ducker, Doreen Smith, Pam Shilston, Brian Warne, Jim Crout.

The restoration of the bells in 1934. Inset: *John Hutchings, of Water, was Captain of the Tower for many years in the 1970s and 80s. He also wound up the weights on the clock, and cut the grass in the churchyard.*

team spirit is clear to see. Competitions are entered with enthusiasm and the annual bell-ringers' outing is an occasion when bell-ringing and revelry are equally important. The present team under Captain of the Tower Brian Warne fully maintains Manaton's bell-ringing traditions, and also helps out in neighbouring churches when asked.

THE CHURCHYARD

The interest in St Winifred's, however, lies not only in the building and its interior but in the churchyard and the surrounds of the church. Approaching from the Green, one passes through the lychgate, built in 1866, where biers tradition-ally rested prior to burial. Inside on the right stands a magnificent yew tree about which a recent report suggested that it was probably the largest (and therefore the oldest?) on Dartmoor. It is estimated that it was planted some four hundred years ago – not long after the rood screen was desecrated!

Inside the lychgate just in front of the flagstaff given in memory of Brigadier Welchman (Churchwarden 1948–66) stands the village war memorial erected in 1921 to commemorate origi-nally those who fell in the Great War. Later were added the names of those who fell in the 1939–45 war – together including names from many well-known local families. There, in the shadow of the ancient church, those who gave their lives in two world wars are remembered annually early in November at the service of Remembrance, led by

the local branch of the British Legion, at which a roll of honour is read and a wreath is laid at the foot of the War Memorial.

Undoubtedly some burials in earlier days took place inside the church. There is a tablet on the chancel floor marking the burial place of Richard Eastchurch who was Rector for 37 years until 1698

The churchyard cross, from a postcard c.1900. Compare this view with the modern photograph on page 14. The cross appears to have been turned around, and there is no sign here of the socket stone.

These early incumbents clearly used buildings which predate our present church which may, or may not, have been on the present site.

A cursory glance at this board will show the extent to which the history of St Winifred's has been dominated by one or two families, and among the patrons, the family of Kirkham is the first to stand out. The first Kirkham patron, Sir Nicholas, in 1323, was apparently the brother-in-law of the first mentioned patron, Sir Robert Deneis, and he began a period of Kirkham patronage lasting, with only one or two short breaks, for 375 years, ending in 1698.

In 1698 the last Kirkham patron appointed the first Carwithen rector, one Thomas, who was the beginning of a family involvement, nay domination, of Manaton which was to last, certainly until 1848, though there was one more Carwithen rector to come later who retired in 1894. The influence of the Carwithens was the more striking for the fact that for 112 years members of the family occupied the posts of both rector and patron simultaneously. Though the reign of the Carwithens was undoubtedly nepotistic (in 1766 George Carwithen appointed George Carwithen Jr. as Rector!) there is no evidence that the church

The lychgate, built in 1866, from a photograph taken c.1920.

and all the stone tablets in the Nave are believed to date from the seventeenth century.

But the vast majority of burials are in the churchyard, to the north of the church to begin with, until pressure on space led to an extension to the south in 1950, thus removing the hedge that used to grow on the south side of the path to the church porch. The adjacent Church Field was left to the Church for further burial space when needed as well as for recreational activities of the village. Thus in the summer it provides a fine setting for the MCC, the Manaton Cricket Club.

At the Western end of the churchyard is an old granite cross, the story of which is told on pages 13 and 14.

PERSONALITIES

Inside the church on the southern wall of the tower, near the entry to the vestry, is a remarkable wooden board listing all the rectors and patrons of the parish of Manaton from the year 1265, when Sir Robert Deneis appointed Richard de Bosco as Rector.

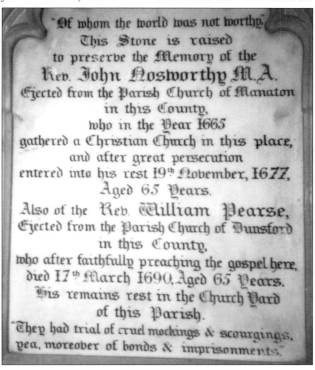

"Of whom the world was not worthy."
This Stone is raised
to preserve the Memory of the
Rev. John Nosworthy M.A.
Ejected from the Parish Church of Manaton
in this County,
who in the Year 1665
gathered a Christian Church in this place,
and after great persecution
entered into his rest 19th November, 1677,
Aged 65 Years.
Also of the Rev. William Pearse,
Ejected from the Parish Church of Dunsford
in this County,
who after faithfully preaching the gospel here,
died 17th March 1690, Aged 65 Years.
His remains rest in the Church Yard
of this Parish.
"They had trial of cruel mockings & scourgings,
yea, moreover of bonds & imprisonments."

A commemorative plaque to John Nosworthy who was born in Manaton in 1612. A Dissenter, he was ejected from the living of Manaton in 1660 and later started a congregation at a meeting house in Ashburton.

A remarkable and awful event happened on Monday morning early December 13th 1779. A terrible thunderstorm attended with large hail and lightning fell on the Chancel and Church.

The East front of the Chancel was demolished as likewise a handsome new Altar Piece and Communion Table.

A large stone hurled into the Parsonage Seat which broke some part of it. The Tower was split from the top to almost the bottom.

One of the Pinacles 4' 8" in length, 21" in diameter and 5'3" in circumference, supposed to be a thousand pounds weight, broke in the roof of the Northern sides of the Church and crushed some seats in the fall, near the singing seats.

In short a sight shocking to all beholders. The Northern side of the Tower.

The wheels of three if not four of the Bells are in pieces and since the storm the top or lead floor of the Tower is likewise sunk.

Just over the Altar Piece it broke up the roof for some feet, broke in the large Chancel Window with its stone-work and several parts of the Altar Piece were shattered leaving marks as if done by gun-powder and the glass of several other windows at the East end of the Church all broke. Several stones were carried from the Tower about 6 yards North into a field beyond the Church-yard.

All accounts agree that the storm came from the North West and directed its course to the South East.

Left: *A facsimile of the memorandum written by the Rev. Thomas Carwithen in 1779 recording the thunderstorm which damaged the church tower. This extract was provided by Mr Eales of 'Pillars'.*

Below: *A poster for a nativity play performed in 1954-5 by the parishioners of Manaton and North Bovey*

Sunday School group c,1939. Back row l-r: Norman Perryman, Frank Perryman, Mr Aery, Cyril Skerrett, Pat Perryman. Front row: Mary Ridd; Hazel Perryman, Rev. Hamilton, Grace Heath, Betty Perryman. Mary Ridd was daughter of the farm manager at Town Barton, living at Rose Cottage.

Two Performances
of a
Nativity Play
will be given
by Parishioners of
North Bovey and Manaton
in
North Bovey Church
(by permission of the Bishop)
on Sunday, December 23rd
at 3.30 p.m. and 6.30 p.m.
Cast of 30 : : Seven Scenes

With the Music specially arranged for the Play

A Bus Service will be provided for CHAGFORD and MORETONHAMPSTEAD Friends which will leave The Square, Chagford at 3 p.m., Moretonhampstead at 3.10 p.m. returning to both places immediately after the performance

The Willcocks of Wingstone at a family gathering near Manaton church in the 1930s.

or the parish suffered as a result. John Carwithen wrote *A History of the Church of England* in 1829 and though Rural Deans' reports are not available for most of this period, in the case of William Henry Carwithen, Rector 1887–1904, the last of the Carwithens, the Archdeacon (no less) was able to write: 'much pleased with this church which is in excellent order'. Many of the Carwithens are buried in the family vault in the churchyard and several are commemorated by plaques in the Chancel, while William Carwithen (1784–1850) and his wife are remembered by the stained glass window mentioned above.

One of the less noteworthy periods in the history of Manaton church was during the rectorship of John Charles Burch Sanders, a period of 26 years from 1894 to 1920. Not only in affairs of the Church did problems arise. Mary Stanbrook in her *Old Dartmoor Schools Remembered* relates how the Rev. Sanders became Chairman of the Managers' Committee of Manaton school but how he and his wife 'engaged in a continual series of rows with the parishioners'; how he posted a notice on the church door saying, 'I do as I like in this parish'; and how Mrs Sanders wrote insulting postcards and letters (often anonymously) 'to all and sundry'.

As far as the church was concerned all seemed to go according to plan for the first few years of his rectorship but problems then arose – and seemed to take some time to put right! In 1907

William John 'Jack' Howe, who died in 1962, was sexton at St Winifred's for over 35 years. Among his many duties was the lighting of the oil lamp outside the lychgate before electricity came to the village.

DEVON AND EXETER GAZETTE. FRIDAY. JANUARY 16, 1920.

DEVON CLERGYMAN CHARGED.

Newspaper cutting from the Devon and Exeter Gazette, *16 January 1920 reporting on the case of the Rev Sanders who was to leave Manaton in disgrace. The caption to the picture reads: 'Sir Francis Newbolt KC, Chancellor of the Diocese of Exeter, who presided over a Consistory Court yesterday to investigate a charge against the Rev. J. C. B. Sanders, Rector of Manaton'.*

the Rural Dean was forced to comment, 'this church requires considerable and immediate repairs', and it was not until 1912 that he was able to report that these had been carried out. But no sooner had the structural defects of the church been seen to than the problem moved elsewhere –to the Rectory (the house now known as Manaton Gate). In 1917 the Dean wrote, 'the Rectory is in a neglected condition' and a year later the situation had not improved; in fact 'the Rectory continues to deteriorate – the general state is deplorable'. On several occasions we are told the Rector prevented visitors from entering – perhaps we can understand why!

In 1919 Sanders failed to make an appearance at the time of the Rural Dean's visit. Perhaps he could feel the net closing in, because in January, 1920 his 26 years as Rector were brought to an abrupt end when he appeared at a consistory court in Exeter, charged with selling an Elizabethan chalice belonging to the parish of

Manaton to a jewellers in Torquay. A silver paten and pewter flagon were also missing. Being adjudged guilty, the Bishop deprived him of his benefice, and he left in disgrace. Thus ended one of the most eventful, stormy and ultimately demoralising periods in the history of Manaton church. It says much for the resilience of the Church members that within a short space of time after Sanders' departure so much valuable restoration work had been carried out to put the church back on its feet.

Though not Sanders' immediate successor as Rector, John Archibald Kitson was Rector between 1927 and 1930. Such a short period does not adequately reflect, however, the beneficial influence which the Kitson family had on the local community. John Kitson never actually lived in the Rectory because his family home was just down the road at Heatree, a property which had been purchased in 1863. A photo of John Kitson still hangs in the Parish Hall and a brass plaque in the

Reverend David Evans

church records how the clock in the tower was donated by the family in memory of his mother, with the clock faces on the east and west sides of the tower because, it is thought, the latter could be seen from Heatree! Though Kitson's rectorship only lasted some four years, it certainly wasn't the last contribution the family made to Manaton church, because about fifty years later his nephew the Rev. David Evans retired to Manaton and for 17 or 18 years after that regularly took services in St Winifred's.

CHURCH GOVERNMENT

Dramatic changes have occurred in the last fifty years in the administration of the church in Manaton. Using the board of Rectors in the church, we can see that for 688 years since Richard de Bosco in 1265 and during 43 rectorships, Manaton was looked after by its own priest, as an independent parish. The problems of clerical recruitment and population shifts since the Second World War, however, have necessitated numerous mergers in the Church of England and much consolidation among rural parishes in particular. Manaton was inevitably caught up in these changes. In 1953, during Thomas Dixon's time, Manaton and North Bovey joined forces to share the Rector's services, an arrangement which lasted until 1978 when we joined up with Moretonhampstead to form a United Benefice of the three parishes. This became four parishes in 1996 when Lustleigh was added to the group.

THE RECTORY

Clearly life is very different for the Rector today, looking after four united but independent parish-

es, compared to the situation before 1953 when his duties rarely took him beyond the parochial boundaries. In the years up to 1953, and indeed while Manaton and North Bovey were together, the Rector lived in Manaton. The Rectory, since early in the nineteenth century at least, had been what is now called Manaton Gate, an elegant building with several acres of surrounding land. In historical terms it is remembered for Manaton's role in the Civil War as a royalist enclave surrounded by Cromwellian troops. On the hill above is a group of rocks known as the 'Garrison' from which, the story goes, the King's supporters kept watch in case Roundhead soldiers should be advancing up the valley from Bovey Tracey.

Early in the twentieth century we have seen how during John Sanders' time the Rectory was almost totally neglected and fell into extreme disrepair. Fortunately for Manaton, Viscount Hambleden became patron of the parish soon after the turn of the century, a position he was to hold until he passed the patronage on to the Bishop of Exeter in the 1930s. He was a considerable benefactor and in 1917 acquired the Parish Room, a stone and corrugated iron construction built in 1898 which he then entrusted to a local committee for parochial use. At that time it was known as St Winifred's Room and an entrance to it was made from the road, the site of the present Parish Hall. Having done that Viscount Hambleden turned his attention to the Rectory, and in 1922 at his own expense he thoroughly restored and partly rebuilt it.

Some 45 years later in the Church of England's obsession to dispose of old buildings in their keep this was sold, and the Rector, then Charles Green, and later his successors Robin Taylor and Leo Sherley-Price lived further up the road in the 'new' Rectory, a modern house, now known as Oak Wood. When the United Benefice was formed in 1978 this too was sold, and from then on all rectors lived in Moretonhampstead. The change of Rectors in 1974 involved an interesting and very unusual procedure, namely an exchange of benefices – Robin Taylor and Leo Sherley-Price swapping their parishes at Manaton and Dawlish. Such an exchange requires the consent of the Bishop and the respective patrons but is perfectly legal, if extremely rare.

Though the Church no longer has a rectory in the parish it still owns Ivy Cottage, the attractive thatched cottage adjacent to the lychgate, which was left in 1597 to the Church, as feoffee, by John Southcott (Southcote) whose family was Lord of the Manor of Manaton in the sixteenth and

Right: *Manaton Rectory in 1830 from plans in the Devon Record Office.*

Below: *Manaton Gate, as the Rectory became known when it was sold by the Church in 1967.*

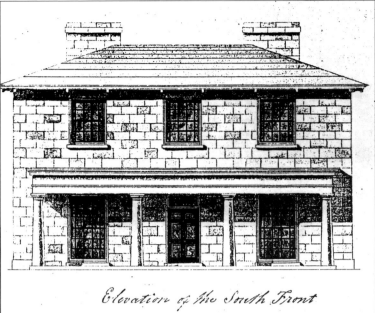

Elevation of the South Front

priest who had three and, since 1996, four other parishes to look after. It became a matter of great importance then whether there were licensed or ordained people, usually retired, living in the parish.

Deaconness Kristeen Macnair came to the village from Lee Abbey. She was licensed in 1971, gave great assistance to St Winifred's right up to her death in 1987, and is commemorated by a small engraved glass pane in one of the north windows of the church. Manaton was equally fortunate, as mentioned above, in being able to call on the Rev. David Evans who retired to Manaton and helped the work of the Benefice by officiating regularly at Manaton services.

CHURCH ORGANISATIONS

A most important role of the church has been with the people of Manaton and their involvement together in a number of joint activities. Since 1920 parishes and their churches have been run by Parochial Church Councils and the first Manaton PCC was formed in that year. The current membership is twelve in number, elected from the church's electoral roll over a rolling three year period. Mention has been made of the bell-ringers and their contribution to the church and the village. Though choirs have come and gone in the past there is currently a large and flourishing choir. This was started and run for a number of years by Alan Jeffs who was succeeded in 1999 by John Wellingham, a professional musician who now lives in the village. It sings at

seventeenth centuries. For some time after this it is thought that the property was run as an inn, but in 1818 it was adapted as a workhouse by the Overseers of the Poor who paid the Church £5 per annum for its use. After 1836 the rooms were let (during the Great War at 10 shillings per week) and the property was looked after by a caretaker. In 1969 the house was divided and the southern half nearest the lychgate, since known as Church Cottage, was sold to Deaconness Macnair. After her death it passed to the Diocese of Exeter but the other half, still known as Ivy Cottage, remains in the Church's possession and is the home of Ruby and Doris Brown, who have lived in the parish all their lives and are an integral part of much of the history covered in this book.

The last 20 years have thus seen major changes in the life of the church in Manaton. No longer do we have an exclusive claim on a Rector of our own, but rather have to share the services of one services twice a month and at the major festivals, as well as representing the parish at the Diocesan Choral Festival each year. Numbers naturally vary but have ranged from around a dozen to over twenty, a remarkable achievement for a small village such as Manaton.

The Church has always been involved with the young and the Sunday School has been an important feature. The problems of keeping a Sunday School going in a village the size of Manaton, however, have been experienced for many years. Numbers ebb and flow and different arrangements have been tried at various times. Deaconness Macnair held a successful Bible class for older children on Sunday afternoons, while there used to be a group of young servers in the church and the Friday Club for the Under 11's.

A Sunday School has been going more often than not, thanks to the efforts of people like May Towning, Linda Warne, Yvonne Crout and currently, Ros Carr. There was a time when instead of a Sunday School the Rector used to take a 'withdrawal class' in Moretonhampstead school. This was arranged by Rector Robin Taylor in the early 1970s along with the Rector of Moretonhampstead, John Benton, and together they overcame the opposition of the then headmaster of the school by using the provision of the 1944 Education Act which allowed parents to request that their children be withdrawn for religious education. The school premises were not allowed to be used (but the church was next door!) and 30 minutes was the maximum time allowed. Enough parents, however, decided to take advantage of this legal provision for a decent sized class to be formed and a three-year course was organised. At other times too the Sunday School has been put in abeyance when numbers of children fell very low, but other activities have also been promoted by the Church such as a Toddlers' Group and a Junior Badminton Club. More recently in the 1980s the PCC had a Youth subcommittee which sought to join with the Parish Council to get a Manaton Youth Club going but this sadly never got off the ground.

The church has in the past promoted fellowship for other age groups as well. For many years there was a Mothers' Union which in 1967 numbered 19 members and met regularly to do useful practical work, maintain links with contacts abroad and help to strengthen Christian family life in Dioceses in developing countries. Declining numbers obliged it to join with North Bovey, before it was put in abeyance and succeeded for a time by a Young Wives group which met

Stalwarts of the Mothers' Union in the 1950s. From the left: Mrs Creber, Evelyn Andrews and Mrs Howe.

each month in the Rectory. There was also in the 1970s and 80s a flourishing playgroup, founded by Anna Butler and Julia Oliver which met in the Parish Hall and, later, also at Homelands.

The Church has held two full-scale Flower Festivals in recent years, in 1972 and 1990 (with a Festival of Talents planned for 2000), and on a regular basis people volunteer to provide flowers for the church (once given the more formal title of the Flower Guild), and also offer to clean the church each week. Neither group consists simply of churchgoers but includes a wider circle of people living in Manaton who wish to see that our beautiful church is looking at its best. One of the most significant decisions taken by the PCC some time ago was to maintain an 'open church' policy, and so during daylight hours local people and visitors alike can enter and enjoy the peace and tranquillity which it offers.

Through all the vicissitudes of life over the past six centuries or more the church has been a constant and continuing feature of Manaton, a much loved asset of the village and the moor which we are happy to share with all those who find themselves in Manaton. As a recent visitor to the church wrote: 'My last visit was 32 years ago – still unchanged – beautiful church, lovingly cared for, in a beautiful area'.

WEDDING BELLS

Manaton church, with its idyllic setting, has seen many
local people 'tying the knot' over the centuries.

Top: *Richard and Maude Willcocks' wedding, Manaton,
7 April 1920.*

Centre left: *Charles Perryman and the former Miss
Annie Rose Leaman in their decorated wedding car on
the Green c.1920. The car belonged to C.A. Hunt of
Foxworthy.*

Left: *Pollard wedding group at Wingstone.*

Above: *The wedding of Mr and Mrs John Peters 1947.*

Above: *Mr and Mrs Clements, 1941.*

Right: *After weddings - births. Cyril Skerret's baptismal certificate from St Winifred's, 1925.*

MANATON DISCOVERS ITS *TITANIC* LINKS THROUGH MARRIAGE

The quartermaster of the *Titanic*, and the person who had his hand actually on the wheel the night she struck the iceberg, was Robert Hitchens from Newlyn. He married a Manaton girl, Florence Mortimore. She was born at Barracott in 1885 of a long-standing Manaton family, and the marriage took place at Manaton Church on 23 October 1906. The family had by then moved to Neadon Cottage where they lived from 1891 to 1906. The marriage certificate shows the witness to be Emily Matilda Brown, the older sister of Doris and Ruby Brown, who still live at Ivy Cottage. She was born in 1887 and died in 1967.

Robert Hitchens survived the disaster. He commanded lifeboat 6 and was picked up by the *Carpathia*, but was thenceforth considered unlucky as a crewman and mariners refused to sail with him. He got a job in South Africa, but by the 1930s was back in Torquay, where he was involved in a shooting incident and sentenced to five years in prison. He and Florence were believed to have moved to Southampton on his release.

Florence Mortimore's brother, John, married Ivy Edwards in 1920 and one of their children was Barbara, now living at Buckfastleigh. She has many childhood memories of Manaton. By the time Barbara was born, in 1925, John and his family had moved to Coffinswell, and later to Widdecombe Farm near Marldon, and so Barbara's memories are of personalities or holiday visits to Manaton. Barbara's husband, Peter Clarke, is a keen family historian and he has kindly provided much of the information in this section.

Barbara's father, John, was born in 1892, probably at Neadon Cottage, and worked at Deal and Mill farms as a young lad. He loved ponies and horses, and broke his thigh at 13 while breaking in a pony, but this didn't prevent him joining the Coldstream Guards at the beginning of the First World War. His attestation papers show he joined up from Gratnor (Gratnar) January 1915 at the 'apparent age' of 24, and that he was wounded in June 1917. He looked after John Galsworthy's horses at Wingstone.

Barbara remembers going to tea at Wingstone – the long scrubbed kitchen table was laden with good things to eat. She remembers the Endacotts (who owned the farm and still worked it at the time the Galsworthys rented the house) coming in from the yard with leggings on. She also remembers John Galsworthy picking up her older sister Marie and saying he'd like to take her home with him, which made Barbara jealous!

Barbara recalls holidays at Water in the 1930s with her granny Susan Neck (who on remarriage had become Mrs Stevens). She used to travel with her father by train from Newton Abbot to Bovey Tracey, and they then cycled to Manaton, Barbara at the time being only four or five years old.

Barbara also remembers William Neck, Susan's son, who used to call at Manaton with a mobile grocer's van which, she recalled, smelt of paraffin.

Top: *Marriage Certificate of Titanic survivor Robert Hitchens and his wife Florence Mortimore. The vicar was the Rev. Sanders (see page 32).*

Left: *Army Attestation form John Mortimore who signed up for the Coldstream Guards in 1915. He lived at Gratnor and later at Deal Cottage.*

Above: *Susan Neck [later Stevens], grandmother to Barbara whose father was John Mortimore.*

A superb photograph of Water cottages c. 1930. Although this photograph was provided for use in the book through a different source, it seems appropriate to place it here as it is possible that one of the women in the picture is Susan Neck. Is it possible that the little girl on the steps is Barbara Mortimore?

Louis Creber (left), caretaker and harmonium player at the Wesleyan Chapel, with Bill Heath at Deal Farm in the 1940s.

The site of the old Wesleyan Chapel in Chapel Lane. Today, now known as The Post House, not much is recognisable of the original single storey chapel building and few records of its past have come to light.

4 - The Wesleyan Chapel

While St Winifred's has always been the parish church of Manaton, there was for a period of about a hundred years another religious establishment in the village in the form of a Wesleyan Chapel. This stood in Chapel Lane in the house now known as the Post House, because after the chapel closed the Post Office moved to that building. The chapel was the culmination of Methodist activity in the early part of the nineteenth century by two denominations of Methodism, the Wesleyans whose circuit was based in Newton Abbot, and the smaller Bible Christian group from Chagford.

Before the building of the chapel various houses in the village were licensed for services, some by the Wesleyans, in 1816 and 1830 for instance, and one by the Bible Christians in 1820, in a house in Water occupied by a certain George Sheres.

In 1840 the Manaton Wesleyans were able to build a chapel of their own, as local groups were encouraged to do at that time and as happened in other Dartmoor parishes such as North Bovey, Bovey Tracey, Moretonhampstead, Chagford (2 chapels), Throwleigh and South Tawton (also 2 chapels).

It is hard to envisage the house today as it was in the days of the chapel. This occupied the whole of the ground floor (the only floor!) of the original house and seated 89 people on fixed pews either side of a central aisle, with the table and harmonium at the front.

In 1851 there was a national census of religion in which the Manaton chapel was included and on that Sunday in March there were three services, morning, afternoon and evening, with congregations of 22, 34 and 20 respectively, though the afternoon meeting may have been a Sunday school.

Manaton took time to find a settled home within the Methodist circuit system. In its early days it was part of the Ashburton circuit, but in the 1870s it joined the Moretonhampstead group (unsuccessfully) before settling, in 1888, in the Newton Abbot circuit.

This meant that ministers came up to take services since Manaton did not have a minister of its own. By the 20th Century these services were reduced to one each Sunday, usually at 6pm. Recorded membership of the chapel was never high, invariably in single figures, though, as the 1851 figures show, congregations were often much larger.

In its heyday the chapel flourished, particularly on special occasions such as Harvest services and Good Friday when congregations were boosted by visitors from further afield outside the village. The pillar of the Methodist community in the period up to the Second World War was Louis Creber who lived in Water Cottages and was not only caretaker of the chapel but the harmonium player as well – and what he couldn't play he sang!

It was perhaps not entirely a coincidence that he left the village soon after the end of the war and, in 1949, the chapel closed – now just a fading memory and a note on older Ordnance Survey maps.

Residents recall that it was in 1952 that the then sub-postmistress, Mrs H. Wreford, began alterations at the Old Chapel in order to transfer the Post Office there. The site was not ideal, as Chapel lane was notoriously difficult to negotiate. There were many complaints, not least that, as the Post Office was now so close, the post box was removed from Freelands. By 1955 the Chapel was up for sale and the repairs to the lane were temporarily forgotten!

The Green in high summer – a photograph by Robert Burnard taken on 13 August 1889. The scene reveals many changes in the past century or so, although much remains the same. Carriages stand outside Half Moon Inn at the top of the Green, the left-hand side of which, at this date, still has a simple stable door. Note also the absence of trees on the hillside behind the inn on the right. Contrast this with the view below, taken twenty years or so later. New buildings stand on the left at Ivy Cottage, while the shop and Post Office occupies the left-hand side of the inn which now sports a verandah. A large tree grows on the green on the right and other trees cast their shade over the foreground.

5 - Manaton Green

Manaton Green is perhaps taken for granted by those who pass by it daily, but it remains one of the treasures of the parish. Writing in 1905, William Crossing records: 'The village of Manaton possesses a green, and there is no village on the Dartmoor borders that has a more pleasing appearance...'.

As with most villages, the Green in Manaton began life as a patch of common land (at least for common use) in the centre of the village. It was here that people met, children played and, by royal command, men practised archery (although there is no evidence of this in Manaton). No doubt wandering stock kept the grass short in times past.

With both the church and the pub bordering the Green, it no doubt attracted people in search of both spiritual and physical sustenance. And, for most people, it must have seemed that the Green was as immovable a part of Manaton as

Bowerman's Nose. However, this incomparable patch of ground at the heart of Manaton might have been lost to the parish had it not been for the foresight of the Rev. John Kitson of Heatree.

When the estates of the late Viscount Hambleden were broken up, nearly 400 acres of land, in 23 lots, were auctioned in August 1929. Lot 13 was described as follows: 'All the Rights possessed by the Vendor in over and under the plot of land known as MANATON GREEN.'

At the same time, Lot 5, the field adjacent known as Lower Foreberry, was advertised as 'Ripe for building'! The Rev. Kitson knew that in the future an extension to the churchyard would be required, and also that Manaton might lose its Green if 'all the rights possessed by the Vendor' fell into the wrong hands. He therefore made successful bids of £450 for Lower Foreberry - later known as the Church Field - and £75 for the rights to the Green, paying £200 from his own

The Green c. 1920. Here the avenue of trees is seen in full leaf, lining the hedge on what was to become the car park. The road is unmetalled, while on the left is a relic of old Dartmoor farming life, a sledge. These were used on rough terrain instead of wheeled carts. This one is piled with brushwood.

Left: *The Green in the early 1900s. Although this snapshot is indistinct, it shows some objects of interest: the pram with a hooded cover, in which Penny (Keogh) or Peter Ripman lies, stands outside the wicket fence of Half Moon, the doorway and sign of which is overhung with ivy. The muddy track in the foreground shows the effects of horse-drawn traffic.*

Below: *A photograph of the hunt taken in the 1920s from the same position as the picture above. What a picturesque scene this must have made.*

Right: *A snapshot taken in the 1920s from the gateway of Cross Park, now Susan Smith's home.*

Left: *The Green decorated with bunting and flags for the Coronation of King George VI in 1937.*

The Green in the 1930s. The large beech tree in the foreground is no longer there, while some of the granite posts remain. The road is still unmetalled at this time.

pocket. A public subscription was set up to fund the remainder, with some people paying a small weekly sum over a period of time.

In the conveyance, the Churchwardens were named as Trustees, and the Green was to be managed by the Trustees and the Rector as 'public ground for the purposes of the Recreation Grounds Act 1859.' This Act states that such grounds shall be held as open public grounds for the resort and recreation of adults and as playgrounds for children and youth, or either of such purposes.

The Green was later provisionally registered under the Commons Registration Act 1965, in March 1967. However, in 1974 the Green was vested with the Charity Commission under a scheme dated 28 January, in which the management was to remain with the Trustees. This arrangement continued for fifteen years, and money for the upkeep was provided, as before, by the Show and Fair Committee from its funds.

In 1989, the Chairman of the Green Trustees, Robert Perkins, suggested to the Parish Council that the number of trustees should be reduced from 6 to 3, with one or more being councillors. He also asked if the costs of the Green, up to £150, could be underwritten from the parish precept.

The Parish Council thought 4 trustees appropriate, two being councillors, and agreed to the financial arrangement.

It is no secret that in recent years who owns what on the Green has been a matter of considerable, and sometimes heated, debate. Whereas some believe that all the Green belongs in Trust to the village, some residents have placed a physical delineation on which part they feel belongs to them.

In 1992 it was suggested that the Parish Council should take ownership of the Green. The Chairman of the Green Trustees at that time, although wishing to resign, agreed to remain as Chairman until the transfer was complete. Due to the difficulties in defining the boundaries (still not defined satisfactorily), and the initial refusal of Devon County Council to accept responsibility for the road at the side, the Chairman remained in post until February 1996.

Since then, the management of the Green has been under the auspices of the Parish Council and, with the help of grants from the Show and Fair, the escalating costs of upkeep have been paid from the parish precept. Although the idea was for the Parish Council to own the Green, the Charity Commissioners retained the freehold,

The Green is planted with mature small-leaved limes, although some have fallen or been felled as they became dangerous over the years. The oak tree at the lower end was planted in 1935 to commemorate the Silver Jubilee of George V and two further oak trees on the right side were planted for the Diamond Jubilee of the Devon Girl Guides in 1970. The horse chestnut by the wall of Manaton Gate was planted by Mick and Ann Moreton at the time of their wedding in 1970.

There are five seats on the Green where people may sit to enjoy the beauty of the scene. The two metal seats were placed there in commemoration of Queen Victoria's Diamond Jubilee in 1897, and one of the wooden seats for the Coronation of George VI in 1937. The other two wooden seats were given in memory of two great friends, May Towning and Greta Matthews, who died in 1993 within a few weeks of each other.

At one time, when the village pub was at Half Moon, the road went completely around the Green. Devon County Council has now accepted responsibility for the road to the church lychgate, but the short stretch beyond is privately owned. The rest was filled in many years ago.

The centre of Manaton has now been designated a Conservation Area, and that, together with the twin safeguards of the Charity Commission and Parish Council, will ensure that the Green continues to be a delightful venue for parish events and a haven of tranquillity and peace for all time.

Lamp standard commemorating the Coronation of King George V, 1911.

and the Custodial and Management Trusteeship, with the Parish Council as Sole Trustee, was transferred on the 10 April 1995.

A maypole dance on the Green in the 1930s. All the smaller children were attending Manaton School at that time.

6 - School Days

Early history of schooling in the village is not clear, although a church school was started in 1828, held possibly in Church House. By the early 1850s, there appeared to be a school in the Freelands area of the village, as a diocesan inspector described 10–15 children being taught in a shed near the blacksmith's shop (presumably the building still called Forge), taught by the blacksmith's wife.

A purpose-built school was built beside the Green in 1859, followed by a school-house for the teachers alongside in 1893. Both these buildings are still there, opposite the church, and are in private occupation.

The school log book entries, as quoted by Mary Stanbrook in her excellent book *Old Dartmoor Schools Remembered*, make intriguing reading:

- *1908 Freddie Frost ill through having swallowed a marble.*
- *1912* Titanic *Disaster has affected all, and as many lessons as possible have been founded upon it.*
- *1919 children decorated the Green for peace celebrations. Welcome to our Heroes. Infants modelled elephant in plasticine.*

The *Titanic* reference is of particular interest due to Manaton's close connection with the tragedy (see page 37). An inspector's report in the 1920s states 'the procedure in this school is casual and unmethodical. Children exceptionally frank and self-reliant.' (Cause and effect?).

In the early 1900s the Kitsons of Heatree were great benefactors, as were John Galsworthy and his wife who came to live at Wingstone in 1905. They provided summer outings for the children to Paignton and Teignmouth, and one year Mrs Galsworthy provided a teacher of morris dancing. For two weeks the children had lessons on the Green – the log book records: the girls have done very well but their heavy boots are a great drawback to the springiness required. On May Day a maypole would be set up on the Green and the children would dance around it (see opposite).

Mr Cyril Skerrett's father attended the school from 5 to 13, and left just after the end of the First World War. The headmistress was at that time Mrs Jones, and she used to bring in her husband to help her maintain discipline, not always easy in an all-age school. When Cyril started school in 1930, conditions had changed little since his father's day:

'*Mrs Jones had been replaced by Mrs Prowse as headteacher with another teacher in the small room where the infants started. The same coke stove heated the big room and water was still brought in from the pump outside. Mrs Prowse would boil eggs brought by the children or heat up their pasties for lunch. She would also make us a cup of cocoa for a charge of only 1¹/2d per week. The school-leaving age was now 14 and there were about 35 children when I was there. There was no question of school transport in those days, so from the age of five Joyce Webber (from Ford Farm) and I joined a little group of other children to walk the two miles to and from school. I cannot recall that it was ever a hardship. On the return journey I would often go into Ford Farm with Joyce and Phyllis and enjoy some of Mrs Webber's fruit cake.*

On Ascension Day, after attending church, we were each given a sixpenny piece by Major Champernowne and allowed the rest of the day off school. The war memorial was kept tidy by older pupils with wild flowers in the vases, picked by the children on their way to school. The school had visits from a school dentist – I remember the paper cup provided for us to rinse out our mouths – and health visitors who kept a check on our health. The teachers tried to give us the opportunity to play cricket and football but with such small numbers in any one age group it was not easy.

As Christmas approached each child would be called out by Mrs Prowse to ask what present he or she would like for Christmas. Nothing elaborate or extravagant probably a ball or skipping rope. Money to buy these presents was raised by whist drives and social evenings throughout the year. The children would make programmes for a Christmas party, which included a concert and a Christmas meal, and would walk miles to sell them to people in the outlying parts of the village. When the great day arrived, children

One of the earliest known photographs of Manaton School, taken in 1913, when the headmaster was Mr Jones. During the compilation of this book a letter was received from his grand-daughter, Mrs Bryony Cullum of Northamptonshire. She wrote: 'My grandparents are buried in the north-west corner of the churchyard and my father was born in the school house where my mother, father and sisters taught. Mr W.H. Jones (pictured standing left) and Mrs H.C. Jones died before I was born but I have quite a large collection of paintings that my grandfather painted.'

Playing marbles in Manaton School yard in 1912. From left: Harold Mortimore (Great Hound Tor Farm); unknown; Tom Marsh (Barrow House); Arthur Brown (about 7 years old – brother to the Misses Brown); George Hole (Swallerton Gate).

Manaton School in 1928. Originals of this photograph were provided by both Cyril Skerrett and Bill Howe.

Views of the schoolyard in the 1930s. The Miss Browns identified the pupils as (left to right): Ivy Ford; Winnie Webber; Lewis Hern; Peggy Crout; Gladys Hutchings; Phyllis Webber; Joyce Brown, Helen Hern, Vera Blatchford; Margaret Hill. The school itself remains today, largely unchanged.

who lived some distance from the school were allowed to bring their best clothes, and after school would be allowed to change into them in Mrs Prowse's school house and she would give them tea. Then to the Parish Room for the concert and the Christmas meal, with the children all the while scanning the Christmas tree and speculating whether the presents hanging there included their requests.'

In 1936 senior pupils were transferred to Chagford, and numbers went down to about 17 (Pat Perryman remembers a heavy snowfall when the Manaton children were dropped off by the bus from Chagford at Beetor Cross and then had to walk four miles home through heavy snow in their school shorts). But evacuees swelled the roll in 1940 and the school was crowded until the end of the war.

Manaton School 1930. Back row left to right: 1. Mrs Prowse; 2. Joan Andrews; 3. Jack Harvey; 4. Norman Hern; 5. Harold Jeffrey; 6. Lewis Hern; 7. Ken Dixon; 8. Charles Jeffrey; 9. Bill Howe; 10. Jack Grimsby; 11. Winnie Webber; 12. Miss Follett. Standing: 13. Margery Skerrett; 14. Amy Hern; 15. Marjorie Brown; 16. Phyllis Webber; 17. Daisy Hill; 18. Emma Hill; 19. Margery Hill; 20. Hetty Howe; 21. Peggy Crout; 22. Marjorie Hutchings; 23. Phoebe Hill; 24. Betty Hannaford; 25. Muriel Cole. Kneeling: 26. Phyllis Hutchings; 27. Frank Willcocks; 28. Jimmy Hern; 29. Ivy Wreford; 30. Nora Webber; 31. Helen Hern; 32. Joyce Brown; 33. Rosemary Underhill; 34. Roy Skerrett; 35. Gideon Webber. Sitting: 36. Jack Piper; 37. George Germon; 38. Ronald Perryman; 39. Charles Crout; 40. Jim Hutchings; 41. Claude Perryman; 42. Francis (?); 43. Jack Skerrett; 44. Joan Jago.

Manaton School photo c. 1932:

Manaton School Treat - an outing to Teignmouth in the 1920s. Included in the photo are J. Endacott; L Cuming; G. Dunning; F. Perryman; J. Pethybridge; J. Crout; W. Crout; A. Brown; A Skerrett; W. Neck; H. Skerrett; W. Webber; P. Webber. Some of these trips were funded by local benefactors, including the Galsworthys of Wingstone and the Kitsons of Heatree. Cyril Skerrett remembers these trips as 'a highlight of the year, an excursion to a different world, for few of us had the opportunity to visit the seaside.'

Manaton School outings to Teignmouth in the late 1920s (above and below): The boys include Gideon Webber; William Howe; Claude Perryman; Lelsie Prowse; Roy Greenaway; Ronald Perryman. The girls include: Helen Hern (Heath); Amy Hern (Mumford); Phyllis Bickham (Webber); Joyce Webber (Cross); Joan Andrews (Pollard); Lucy Winsor (Blowes); Muriel Ball (Heale); Nancy Winsor (Cleave); Emma Hill; Daisy Hill; Rose Hill; Mary Webber; Beatrice Squires; Mrs Skerrett; Mrs Dunning; Mrs W. Howe; Ruby Osborne; Mrs W. Crout; Mrs A. Crout; Mrs L. Crout; J. Winsor.

In 1947, with only 14 children remaining, the school closed and the children went to North Bovey. Miss Wadland, the schoolteacher for five years in the 1930s, bought the school and the school-house. She ran a shop in the school building for some years, became clerk to the parish council, and then a councillor. She remained a well-known local character until her death in 1983.

These days the youngest children begin pre-school days at much earlier ages. There are a number of nursery schools locally, the nearest in Lustleigh. 'Rising fives' and those of school age attend a number of state infant and primary schools. On the closure of North Bovey School in the 1950s, most Manaton children went to Moretonhampstead and this continues as the most likely place for state education. However, children no longer have to make long walks along country lanes in all weathers such as Cyril Skerrett endured. Today they are picked up by bus, often only a short walk, or car ride, from their homes.

Because of the healthy numbers of younger children, at the time of writing, some are obliged to attend other schools in the area: Widecombe, Bovey Tracey or Blackpool.

Most of those students attending Secondary School, unless they are fee-paying, are transported to South Dartmoor Community College in Ashburton. On schooldays they can be seen at the pick-up point at the Kestor, eagerly awaiting the arrival of the coach to take them to school. Those in outlying areas are taken by minibus to the pick-up point, and many children thus walk shorter distances to get to school than those who live in towns.

Even so, attending school for Manaton children requires special disciplines and provides unique experiences. Anyone who has followed a school bus down to Bovey Tracey, windows steamed up and a hive of activity within, will appreciate the importance that this hour a day has upon the social mix of our youngsters.

Manaton parents with one child or more at school or college will also reflect upon the hours they spend ferrying children hither and thither to extra-curricular events.

Miss Katy Wadland, schoolteacher at Manaton for five years in the 1930s, eventually retired to Manaton, living in the old schoolhouse. She fully participated in parish activites, played the organ in church, and is warmly remembered by all who knew her.

Manaton women gather in readiness for a school outing in the 1930s. 1. Lang Crout; 2. Helen Hern (Heath); 3. Emma Hern; 4. Annie Dunning, from Deal Farm

SCHOOL MATES

Above: *Charlie Crout, Muriel Coll, Pat Perryman and friend, 1930s.*

Above right: *Peter and Mike Daw, Hayne 1956.*

Right: *Mellowmead girls, early 1980s, taking a census for a school project. They are sitting on the milk churn stand at Deal Cross opposite the Kestor. They are l-r: Emma Baker; Clare Baker; ?, Vanessa Crout; Rachael Baker; Tina Crout.*

Below: *The school bus morning run at the Kestor, 1999. In the photograph are Tim Warne; Jim Goddard; Harry Butler; Matthew Fisher; Sarah Fisher; Peter Weaving.*

When Manaton School closed in 1947, the children were transferred to North Bovey School, until that too closed in the 1950s. This photograph shows the school around that time with many familiar names and faces from Manaton and neighbouring parishes. They are: 1. Margaret Daw; 2. Susan Brackenbury; 3. unknown; 4. Mike Eveleigh; 5. unknown; 6. Brian Rolands; 7. Linda Shirkie; 8. unknown; 9. George Chapman; 10. Jennifer Greenaway; 11. unknown; 12. Kay Crout; 13-17. unknown; 18. James Hern; 19. Norman Warne; 20. unknown; 21. Gary Carpenter; 22. Ian Brackenbury; 23. David Hole; 24-27. unknown; 28. Gerald Brock; 29. Bert Cuming; 30. Arthur Cuming; 31. Nicky Crout; 32. Tom Pollard; 33. Michael Daw; 34. Maureen Thompson; 35. Mildred Dymond; 36. Diana Hole; 37. unknown; 38. Brian Warne; 39. Wendy Brock; 40. unknown; 41. John Harvey; 42. Mike Clark; 43. unknown; 44. Valerie Hines; 45. Christine Hern; 46. Jim Crout; 47. Celia Leaman; 48. Bill Tooth; 49. Carol Eveleigh; 50. unknown. 51. unknown.

Foxworthy in the 1880s. This photograph is one of many taken by A.R. Hunt who owned Foxworthy at that time. His passion for photography when it was still relatively new has left a legacy of images, many of which appear in this book courtesy of Betty Hunt. This picture shows the use of the sledge on Dartmoor farms – a mode of transporting rocks etc more practical on narrow rocky tracks than a wheeled cart. The barn is now one of the terrace of cottages at Foxworthy.

A sight less common than it once was, swaling is nevertheless an important part of good farming practice on Dartmoor. This is Lustleigh Cleave, above Foxworthy c. 1880.

7 - Farms and Farming

Farming is central to life on Dartmoor. Since prehistoric times people have looked to the moor to provide them with the necessities of life, and ample evidence of this activity survives within the parish. Field walls built thousands of years ago show where crops were grown. Circular pounds remain where stock was once kept. The basics of farming changed little over the centuries and even the introduction of mechanised farming was slow to take effect on Dartmoor due to the terrain. The pictures on page 43 and opposite of the sledge are a reminder that moorland farming required specialized techniques, and wheeled transport was not always an advantage.

Perryman children on a grass mower at Barracott, c.1940.

Packhorses were used well into the twentieth century and evidence of this is seen in the Foxworthy photograph. The narrow, steep little bridges over Dartmoor streams are made just wide enough to accommodate the ponies and their loads. Well into the 1930s and 40s, it was not unusual to see horse-drawn machinery at work in the fields around Manaton, as many of the photographs show. It was the Second World War that was a watershed in farming as far as Dartmoor was concerned. Not only were tractors cheaper and more widely available, but many men had experience of mechanics as a result of military service, and this they used to good effect. It is interesting to note how many farmworkers in the photographs from the late 1940s are wearing items of battledress.

Manaton is an upland farming area, lying between 500 and 1000 feet above sea level and encompassing typical edge-of-the-moor country. Hardy sheep and cattle run on the open moor where ancient 'common rights' are still held. The adjoining patchwork of small fields provides good grazing and ample shelter for livestock. Traditional small family farms are still the norm, and the main products are beef from suckler herds, lamb, wool, and hardy breeding stock, with local breeds such as South Devon cattle and Whiteface Dartmoor sheep still well represented.

The local farmer's year still reflects the traditional cycle – spring lambing, spring and autumn calving, silage and hay making, autumn sales of lambs and suckled calves – and the slog of winter feeding. In the past arable and dairy farming played a larger part, as self-sufficiency was the wellspring from which our farms have grown.

One Manaton story more than any other perhaps demonstrates the feelings that changes in farming brought to those whose life had been spent upon the land. In the late 1970s Dickie Perryman related that he always worked with horses, and had two favourite animals with which he worked in perfect partnership. One evening they were making their way towards Leighon when, used to the road being open, the animals walked on to the newly laid cattle grid, one of them breaking its leg. Dickie never worked with horses again.

Thus the needs of the age of the motor car brought about the end of the farm horse.

This book is not intended to provide an account of agriculture on Dartmoor. The aim of the authors is to give a glimpse of farming times gone by in Manaton. The photographs speak for themselves and provide an eloquent testimony to the hard work and sense of community that farming brought to the parish. They are mute witness to an age that, regrettably, we may be the last generation to observe. At the time of writing there is a crisis in farming. But it is a crisis whose outcome will affect the lives of all who live on Dartmoor. The very nature of the landscape, each lane and hedgerow, each barn and granite gatepost, is there because of farming. Little wonder that we look at these wonderful pictures of the past with some regret.

It would be a Herculean task to attempt to write a history of all the farms in the parish, and some have more records available than others. In the following pages we look at just a selected number of dwellings and settlements in Manaton.

FARMS AND FARMING

This superb sequence of photographs was taken at Foxworthy in the 1880s. They were provided for use in the book by Mrs Dorothy Harris of Sidmouth whose grandfather, the Revd Walters, was a tenant of Foxworthy in the 1870s.

The process known as 'Devonshiring', or beat-burning, used only in the westcountry, involved taking the turf off the field, leaving it to dry, and then breaking up it with a harrow. It was then raked into piles to be burnt, the ash spread over the field as fertiliser.

George Ellis and John Brown worked at Foxworthy in the 1880s. Brown was a boatman at the Hunt's Torquay home, and part time labourer for them at Foxworthy. Here a rest is taken from the arduous work of raking and burning the turf, preparing the field for sowing. The photograph (page 60) reveals the purpose of the implement on which they are resting. The centre picture shows Ellis driving the horse-drawn seed drill over the cleared field.

FARMS AND FARMING

Left: *The sawpit at Foxworthy in 1890. Sawn timber was a valuable commodity and farmers harvested trees for their wood, felled them, and left them to season before sawing them into planks. Before the days of steam-power saws, most timber would have been cut in this way, with a cross-cut saw. One man pulled the saw from above, another from below (the worst position because of the enclosed space and falling sawdust).*

Below left: *A pack saddle, from a photograph taken at Foxworthy in the 1890s. This suggested that, even at that date, they had become objects of antiquarian interest.*

Below: *Sam Scarr, who lived at Foxworthy in the 1920s, with a fine crop of marrows and melons.*

FARMS AND FARMING

Right: *John Brown and George Ellis take a rest from their labours. Brown sits on a harrow which has been used to break up the turf, while Ellis rests on a heavy granite horse-drawn roller, typical of those used on Dartmoor farms.*

Left: *The ash house at Leighon. These were found on most Dartmoor farms, but this is unusual insofar as it uses two natural boulders as walls - most of them are round. Ash from the domestic fireplace was scraped out and stored here for use as a fertiliser on the farm.*

Right: *Miss Needham at Southcott with a working horse. Before the days of tractors these animals were vital to the farmer and a high value was put on a good working team of heavy horses.*

Left: *Rabbits were an essential part of the countryman's diet. The skins were sold to furriers and the meat used in pies and stews. Labourers were often given a concession to catch so many rabbits on the farm for their own consumption, but poaching was commonplace. Here Paulie James' brothers show off their day's catch at Latchel.*

FARMS AND FARMING

Left: *Geese on the spring outside Cross Park, early 1900s.*

Below: *A barrel is taken by cart to the fields near Town Barton c.1920. Possibly cider for the Fair?*

Left: *Bracken was harvested for use as winter bedding. These two men have gathered a cartload and are ready to head back home.*

Below: *A horse rake turning hay near Water in the 1930s.*

FARMS AND FARMING

Many people have the mistaken idea that farming life was idyllic, whereas in fact for many people, particularly between the wars, and into the 1950s, it was a hard life, with hours of work for little reward. Summer work at least had the compensation of the warm weather, but in winter the Dartmoor climate was harsh and cruel.

Above: *Jim Dunning of Deal working with a binder in the fields where Becky Falls car park now lies.*

Right: *Mr Warne carting firewood at Southcott.*

Below: *Norman Perryman and Frank Howe bringing in hay at Horsham.*

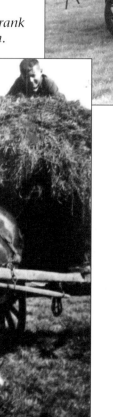

Farm dogs are a vital part of country life. This sheepdog belonged to Penny Keogh in the 1940s

FARMS AND FARMING

Left: *Frank Perryman and 'Ginger' at Horsham in the 1930s. The contraption on the wall is a relic of former days – his father's rope-maker. Straw rope was wound on to the spindle and used for tying down thatch. This kind of rope was also used for trussing hay and so on.*

Top right: *Mick Moreton at Hound Tor Farm on his Quad bike. These handy little machines have been adopted by farmers all over the moor as a general workhorse. Above: Brian (right) and Ben Warne with some rather more serious mechanical gear. Well known in farming circles, and for his agricultural contracting business, Brian's family have farmed at Southcott for many years.*

Two views of Foxworthy, taken in the 1880s. To those who know the place today, these pictures reveal many of the changes that the house has undergone in the past century. This was before the new wing was built by Cecil Hunt. The girl in the doorway (below) is one of the Hunt family members. Opposite: *A sketch by Lizzie Walters dated 14 June 1883. She was the daughter of the Rev. Walters who was then a tenant of Foxworthy.*

FOXWORTHY AND NEADON

Foxworthy, situated on the southerly side of Lustleigh Cleave is of Saxon origin and in fact is in the parish of Lustleigh. However, as its main access is through Manaton, and thus many of those working on the farm in the past were from that parish, it is duly 'claimed' for this book.

Few records exist telling us about the earliest times as a settlement although in his superb journal *Foxworthy- My Saxon Farm,* Cecil Hunt includes records from the time of Elizabeth I and James.

One of the earliest recorded names was Verkisworthy Ford, and it is likely that as this crossing point on the Bovey was subject to frequent flooding, the clapper bridge was eventually built. A parapet was added to the bridge c.1887 when the bridge was strengthened for vehicular traffic.

Being on the river it was natural that there should be a mill a little downstream. This almost certainly also served Neadon, at least at a later date.

During the hundred years in which it was owned by the Hunt family many gentle improvements were made at Foxworthy, including the building of a modern farmhouse in 1939. In the late 1970s the Hunt family moved from Foxworthy to Neadon.

Neadon is a Domesday farm and the earliest house extant is Neadon Upper Hall, said to be late fifteenth century. Its beautifully constructed ashlar stones and carved wooden window frame, speak of an elegance absent from other early moorland buildings. Curious too, is the fact that it was built to house animals on the ground floor, with living accommodation above, reached by an outside stairway. This is in direct contrast to the typical Dartmoor longhouse design where the animals were housed at the downslope end of single storey dwellings. The living accommodation includes a fine granite fireplace, a garde-robe (medieval privy), and a piscina (washing shelf), suggesting ownership by someone of some standing.

The farmhouse opposite dates from the late eighteenth century and replaced the Hall which reverted to use as a barn for animals below and a hay loft above. The Hall's prestige was restored in 1983 when Vernon Hunt CBE was invited by the Department of the Environment to rehabilitate it as a dwelling. The Upper Hall now stands as a lasting memorial to his remarkable endeavour.

Neadon Farmhouse has been home to several families and an early twentieth century census shows 29 people under the roof on a particular night. 'Under the roof' is probably quite literally the case as it is huge, and it is said that children quite often slept under the thatch!

A notable owner for many years until 1976 was Miss Catherine Haines who farmed and also ran a riding stable. This redoubtable lady also filled the house with evacuees during the Second World War. Miss Haines was also a keen huntswoman, revered by her friends.

Tom and Mairi Hunt, with their children Ben and Daisy, now farm Neadon. Mairi is a sculptor whose work in bronze, mainly of animals, upholds the artistic traditions of the family started by Cecil Hunt.

Neadon and Foxworthy have shared many exchanges of land over the years to suit the respective owners - and the River Bovey frontages have been enjoyed likewise. The river provides a unique environment to both farms. Sadly the population of trout, so depleted by disease in the 1970s, has never recovered its strength, but the river itself captivates all who explore the acres of the two ancient Dartmoor farms.

Left: *Foxworthy Bridge c. 1880, when it was a simple clapper bridge, and before the parapet was built.*

Below: *A.R. Hunt, who purchased Foxworthy in the 1880s, seen here smoking out bees from straw bee skips. These skips, or 'skeps', were kept in alcoves in barn walls, or specially constructed bee boles, a number of which can still be seen on Manaton farms.*

Above: *Ann Derges in 1907. She and her husband worked at Foxworthy in the years before the Great War. She lived at The Mount, dying aged 93.*

Right: *C.A. and Mrs S.E. Hunt at Foxworthy c.1930.*

Above: *A.R. Hunt and Henry Leaman on a rabbit shoot in 1914.*

Left: *The Rev. Walters and his daughters, Elizabeth Ann and Katherine Mary, at the door of Foxworthy 1884. He was a Wesleyan minister and President-elect of the Wesleyan Ministry, but a severe railway accident prevented him taking up this post. In 1873, due in part to his wife's poor health, he went to South Africa as the first non-conformist Naval Chaplain. His wife died there aged 40 and he returned to England, renting Foxworthy from the Nosworthy family in 1878 where he and his daughters lived until 1885 when it was purchased by Arthur Hunt.*

Right: *George Derges, George Ellis and John Derges building hayricks at Park Pool field, Foxworthy, in the 1890s.*

Below: *Dolph Leaman and Esmond Hunt getting in the hay in the 1920s.*

Right: *C. A. Hunt, the internationally renowned artist, and his son Vernon setting out for a fishing expedition on the Bovey c. 1915.*

Left: *Vernon Hunt in the hayfield c. 1915.*

FOXWORTHY PEOPLE

Above: *Hunt family members outside Foxworthy 1942*

Above: *Mrs Henry Leaman (Alberta Georgia) c.1920.*

Above: *Henry Leaman* (right) *and Mr Kerswell 1913.*

Above: *Mrs Sam Scarr (Annie Derges) c.1930*

Mr and Mrs Courtier, 1910.

Left: *Phyllis Collett, milkmaid at Foxworthy, 1907.*

FOXWORTHY MILL

There is little doubt that a mill has existed at Foxworthy since the earliest settlement there. The pictures below and on the right are from a hundred years ago and show the mill in a poor state of repair, although thatching has begun on the roofs on the right. The mill wheel is overgrown on the picture below.

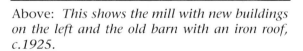

Above: This shows the mill with new buildings on the left and the old barn with an iron roof, c.1925.

Above: Myfanwy, Charlie Crout's second wife, and her father relaxing outside the mill in the 1930s.

Above: The new farmhouse at Foxworthy, built in 1939 by the Hunt family. For many years it was the home of Terry and Beryl Turner and their family.

NEADON FARM

Right: *Neadon Farm before the First World War. Note the magnificent trees in the meadow.*

Left: *Neadon Farm c. 1939. It was still thatched at this time, a huge span.*

Right: *Neadon Farm c. 1929.*

Below: *Robert Earle and his family at Neadon Farm c.1910.*

Above: *An early motor car outside Neadon Farm in the 1920s.*

NEADON UPPER HALL

Neadon Upper Hall is one of the parish's most intriguing buildings. Fifteenth century in origin, it was rescued from its use as a barn by Vernon Hunt who restored it for modern use, but retained all its medieval features and character. Above left, right and centre: *carved window tracery, the original door to the shippen, and the main building before restoration.* Left: *Work on the Upper Hall roof c.1983.*

HEDGE BARTON FARM

The existence of Hedge Barton is suggested in the Survey of Lord Dynham's Lands in 1566, although at that time likely to have been known as Brockadon Hedge after a tenant of Natsworthy Manor who rented part of a Newtake on the Manaton–Widecombe boundary.

The parish boundary runs through the present farmyard, with the house in Manaton and many of the outbuildings in Widecombe parish. The present farmhouse and cottages were constructed over a number of years, around 1846, and are known to have been in the ownership of William Bryant (of Bryant & May 'Swan Vestas' match-making fame) around 1850. Bryant also owned Heathercombe and Heatree farms, and Jay's Grave which he had excavated to establish the truth of the story of Kitty Jay. The bones were reinterred in their present roadside grave close to the Manaton–Widecombe boundary. Subsequently the farms were sold to the Kitson family, in 1863. Hedge Barton estate was sold to John Kitson in 1908 for £4500 and included 358 acres, with common rights on Bonehill and Hameldown.

Claude Whitley bought the estate from the Kitsons in 1955 and he farmed here until his death in 1989. Claude was for many years Chairman and Clerk of Newton Abbot Racecourse and was master of the South Devon Hunt for 42 years.

Today, Tim Whitley farms Hedge Barton which comprises 550 acres with 216 cattle and 385 sheep. Like his father he is a keen country sportsman and ran the North Dartmoor beagles for number of years.

An inscribed rock (see photograph on page 19) within the estate records the end of the Corn Laws. Although strangely it has a date of 1848, the law itself was repealed in 1846.

Looking down on Hedge Barton Farm from Hedge Tor.

VOGWELL FARM

Vogwell or Bogwell, was earlier known as *Foghille*, meaning Foggy hill-pasture. In fact Vogwell is an ancient settlement and Vogwell lake is referred to in a Saxon document in Exeter Cathedral library. In medieval place names, *Foghille* appears as a settlement site in 1333.

The farmhouse, modernised earlier this century, was probably built in the sixteenth century with string courses of bricks still remaining on two of the chimneys. An old building opposite the house, now derelict, could be the relic of the medieval longhouse. A large barn facing the ruin contains a doorway arch typical of fourteenth or fifteenth century style.

In the eighteenth century John, and then Elizabeth Nosworthy, owned Vogwell between 1780-1790, and let it to John and then James Mudge. It is possible that the

Nosworthys owned it well before this, as they also owned several other Manaton properties, notably Heathercombe and Foxworthy.

John Pethybridge bought Vogwell in 1800, and also lived there, leaving the property to Thomas Pethybridge who also occupied it. The Heatree sawmills were sited here, powered by a large water-wheel fed from the East Webburn leat; this leat fed another wheel at Heatree House. In 1842 when Thomas paid tithes for the farm, two of his fields were called 'Wash', and 'Mill Pitts'. The first indicates a sheep wash, and the last probably a blowing house and tinner's pit.

In the 1843 Tithe map, three fields indicating possible tin-mining were Mill Pits, Pitts and Pitty Park, and a field adjacent to some prehistoric hut circles called Yelland – usually a derivation of 'old lands', indicating early cultivation.

The brothers Walter and William Irish were at Vogwell in 1870, probably as tenants, because the Kitsons bought it from Thomas Pethybridge in 1872, when Thomas was living in Dittisham.

Vogwell was then let to a succession of farmers: 1874 Elizabeth May; 1902 Joseph Shorrock and George Hawkins Hext; 1914 Charles Wills and Edwin Cuming. In the 1920s and 30s the Kitsons had a farm manager living at Vogwell for a while, Trelawny Lowe.

When the Rev. John Kitson died in 1947, the farm was sold to James and Mabel Greenaway for £2250. The Greenaway family, including their sons Roy and Geoff and daughter Lily, had been renting Langdon, and were offered that farm to buy but had always wanted Vogwell. James died in 1952, and the next generation took responsibility for running the farm. The partnership was dissolved when Geoffrey married and went to work for Claude Whitley at Hedge Barton; Roy continued to run the farm with his sister Lily.

Geoff's son Derek and daughter Jennifer came to live at Vogwell in 1958; their Uncle Roy was like a second father to them, helping with homework, and giving them jobs to do. Originally Vogwell was a mixed farm, but later Roy was to concentrate on a South Devon herd. He was a practical man and could turn his hand to most things. He was a good stonewaller, and there are some fine examples of his work at the farm.

His solution to problems could be quite basic, as when a hang glider got caught up in a tree on the farm, Roy rescued the man by cutting the tree down with a chain saw! He was always willing to help other farmers, especially at hay time.

He was courteous and polite, and never said a bad word about others. He also loved dropping in for a chat, and left with a cheery: 'Well, I'd better find my way home.'

Sadly, Lily died in 1984, and Roy kept things going for another twelve years, although coping with angina. He was a farmer through and through, and ended his days doing what he had always done.

When Roy died in 1996, his nephew Derek and niece Jennifer inherited the farm and they are now running a small suckler herd of South Devons, and gradually renovating the old buildings.

They have found a 'Good Luck Stone' in the shippon, built into the wall when a previous owner brought it from another farm for luck.

Right: *Vogwell Down showing the field patterns from earlier settlements; both prehistoric and medieval field systems are to be found here. Vogwell farm lies off to the right of this aerial view.* (Photo courtesy Jeremy Butler)

Left: *The linhay at Vogwell Farm prior to restoration. The huge upright granite pillars originally supporting the roof of the linhay are typical of this type of building on Dartmoor.*

Right: *Vogwell Farm today.*

FORD FARM

Ford farm is an ancient longhouse and it retains its original paved central passageway. The ash house still exists and there are bee boles in good condition in the granite walls of the kitchen garden. There is a rectangular pig trough built into the thickness of the pigsty wall to facilitate feeding without entering the sty; also a boar pen and duck houses.

The feeding trough in the pigsty at Ford. This allowed one to feed the pigs from the yard without entering the sty itself. (Photo courtesy Stephen Woods)

Ford came under the Manor of Little Manaton, which included Torhill, Cripdon, the Barracotts, Canna, the Easdons, Vogwell, Heatree and the Heathercombes, and was in the extensive Manor of Kenton, so named by the Courtenays who owned the area from early times.

Ownership or tenancy can be traced back to William Nosworthy of Ford. Born in 1709, he married Elizabeth Nosworthy of Greator in Manaton; a succession of Nosworthys named William or John continued to hold it until William who died in 1820. In his will he left a great deal of land to his sons and daughters, including some of the Challacombes, the Barracotts, the Beckhams and Canna. His son, John of Cripdon, was trustee, and his wife Mary died at Eastdown or Easdon in 1832. An interesting social record exists:

1763. Complaint by Edward Nosworthy of N. Bovey (also Ford) that his apprentice Susannah Spry has committed sundry misdemeanours. She is committed to the house of Correction for one months hard labour.

Even though Nosworthys were paying the land tax until 1830, the farm appears to have been sub-let to William, Edward and Nicholas Merdon in the Kenton survey of 1764, when the rent was seven shillings and sixpence for 50-plus acres. The Merdon family had been associated with Manaton since 1629, when Edward married Margaret Nosworthy.

Although these farms were owned by the Nosworthys, they were still paying 'chief rent' to the Lords of the Manor; this was for the 'waste' of the moor, or commonland. From 1780–1830 William and Robert Nosworthy were paying £1.19s land tax.

JAMES BRYANT

James Bryant (of the Bryant & May match company) and his brother were Quakers and played a leading role in the development of Plymouth, making starch, soap and refining sugar, along with their famous Swan Vestas matches. James bought considerable amounts of land in Manaton from the Courtenay Estate in the 1840s, including Heathercombe, Heatree and Hedge Barton, with Ford being let to several families.

He sold the estates and farms to John and Robert Kitson in 1863.

THE KITSONS

William Kitson, 'the maker of Torquay', was born in 1800. He was steward of the property of the Palk family, and also a lawyer and banker.

He had two sons, John a lawyer, and Robert a banker; having bought the estates in 1863, John bought his brother's half share in 1885. It seems that William had already built Heatree House, because he was entertaining friends there in the 1860s.

John Kitson died in 1911, and left the estate to his godson and first cousin, John Archibald Kitson, Clerk in Holy Orders, who died in 1947.

TENANTS AT FORD

Willcocks Family:
In the 1900s, Joseph and Bessie Willcocks (see also section on Torhill) were renting Ford. They had three sons Herbie, Richard and John, and a daughter Nellie. After school, it was John's job to rush

Above: *A watercolour of Ford by S. de Vere Welchman, painted in 1908.*

Right: *Ford Farmhouse today, the home of Jane and Christopher Beeson.*

The ash house at Ford.

home and get the pony, Lil, ride her to Moorlands in Long Lane and bring in the cows for milking.

They left when the Rev. John re-organised the estate after the First World War.

The Webber Family:
Gideon Webber was employed by the Rev. Kitson as foreman of the Heatree Estate in 1923–24; this included two Hookner Farms, Kendon, Ford, Vogwell and Torhill. He and his wife Evelyn had previously been at Gidleigh and Heathercombe. When they arrived they already had eight children, seven girls and a boy, and their ninth and last child, Joyce, was born at the farm in 1925.

Joyce Cross and her sister Phyllis Bickham and brother Gideon recall that they led a wonderful life, with many children of a similar age living in nearby farms, including Cyril and Eric Skerrett, two families of Hills, and Ted Osborne from Heathercombe, Claude Perryman, Muriel Coll, Jack Grimsby, Ron, Norman, Hazel, and Frances

Gideon and Evelyn Webber c.1930.

Gideon, Joyce and Phyllis Webber, early 1930s.

Perryman, Ivy Wreford and Johnny Pearce from Torhill; they all met up at Heatree Cross to walk to school.

It was not such fun for the older sisters who went into service at the Kitson household when they left school. Many of this little group passed the exam for Grammar School, including Joyce and Phyllis, but the families could not afford the transport. Nevertheless they recollect that they

The five Webber girls. Clockwise from right: Florence, Joyce, Phyllis, Nora, Winifred c.1935.

were given an excellent education by Mrs Prowse, even though they left school at fourteen years.

Mrs Webber worked terribly hard, making all the butter and cream and doing the poultry and geese for the big house. Although they had a separator for the milk and cream, all the butter was made by turning it by hand and, if it was a hot day, Evelyn took it to the leat and turned the cream with the tub submerged in the water. The milk was from South Devon cows, the sheep were Exmoors, and Large White pigs were kept to provide the Kitsons with pork and bacon.

Mrs Webber (née Garrett) was a remarkable lady. She had come to the westcountry from Marlow, Bucks, as a nanny to the de Havilands who lived in Gidleigh Rectory;

Not only did she have to learn the ins-and-outs of farming and dairy work, but as well as her family she had to board a cow man, George Hill ('Gidge'), and a rabbit trapper, Bill Marks. There was no bathroom.

Rabbits were collected, with poles threaded through their feet, by Lester Crump, who took them to Moretonhampstead station, where they were sent off to London in wicker hampers.

'Gidge' took small animals to market in a horse and trap, but cattle lorries run by Albert Hill and Stan Norrish took the larger stock. Sheep were driven on foot to spring grass in Bickington. Other workers were Jack and Leonard Skerrett, Sid Perryman, Joe Osborne and Fred Webber.

Left: *Ford Farm in snow. As with other nearby farms, Ford has a close connection with the legend of Kitty Jay and it was here, in a barn, she was said to have ended her life.*

Below: *Bee boles at Ford. The straw bee skips were placed here out of the weather.*

There was a very modern innovation at Ford, this was a little railway which carried a tip wagon; it originally came from the quarry at Hay Tor, and ran from the stables to the muck heap just before the ford. Apart from the children having fun riding on it, it made the cleaning out of stables much easier. The children also used to sit on top of the ash house and watch their father breaking in moorland ponies on a long rein. 'Gidge' was a strong and determined man, who would rather die than admit defeat. Having broken in a Dartmoor pony with some difficulty, he would ride it around the estate.

When Leonard Skerrett's wife was expecting her second child at Cripdon, 'Gidge' rode over to Leonard, who was ploughing at Natsworthy Gate. 'Gidge' took over the ploughing and told Leonard to ride the pony back to Cripdon: 'But be careful, he's a slippery little heller,' was the advice he gave.

When the Kitsons changed from farming to forestry, the Webbers had to leave and went to Linscott in Moreton.

Dartington Hall 1934-39:

The farm was then let to the Dartington Trust, with a Mr Hudson as manager. The Trust brought new ideas which were not appropriate for this type of farm. Cyril Skerrett's father, Leonard, was shepherd to Blackface sheep which escaped from the fields, and much time and effort was spent in retrieving them. But at least the Trust bought him his first pair of Wellingtons. Also working then, were Jack Skerrett and Fred Webber.

Jack Bowden:

Mr and Mrs Bowden then rented the farm, and eventually bought it from John Kitson's son in 1948. They had no children, and built the bungalow opposite, named 'Wayside', retiring to it in 1959.

Jane and Christopher Beeson:

Christopher and Jane Beeson then bought Ford. Christopher had previously farmed at Gratnor in North Bovey, before marrying and going to Canada. Originally they employed up to six people, and grew barley, kale and turnips, as well as running a flock of Scotch Blackface, Closewools and Border Leicester. They have always run a suckler herd, which started with Angus Friesian cross Hereford, went to South Devon and eventually Charolais cross South Devon in the late 1960s.

Jane is a well known writer. Their sons and daughter were married from Ford, and although Christopher is over 70, they are still enjoying farming.

CRIPDON

The name Cripdon, earlier known as *Criperdon* or *Creporden*, comes from Old English *crype*, meaning 'narrow passage'. It is an ancient farm, which was once separate to Ford. It is approached through the lane to Ford and is now in ruins. It was unique in having an outside granite staircase.

Again we have to go back to the Nosworthys to find John of Creporden, born 1640, who left it to his son, John, born 1677. He married Elizabeth, daughter of Thomas Nosworthy of Cann (Canna).

We then have Oliver Nosworthy of Crippodon and Torhill, born 1718, who married Margaret Nosworthy of Leighon, followed by Oliver's son, John, born 1768, and his wife Joanna, who died at Ford. Their son, John, born 1799 married Ann Pethybridge.

From 1780–1830 Oliver and John were paying £1.11s.3d land tax. John died in 1871 and, of six children, he left Margaret and Oliver of Cripdon. Cripdon Farm then became part of the Kitson estate, and from this time on it was occupied by farm labourers.

An 'Encroachment' is recorded in the 1830s. Thomas Nosworthy of Torhill complained that:

the owners of Cripdon have erected a cottage within the last 20 yrs. The labourer employed by the owner (John Nosworthy Junior), stocks the down (to which he has no right) with pigs. Funeral 6 weeks since from cottage, Mr French told the person living there that he should deny them crossing Hayne Down, and sent a man for that purpose, they however proceeded with the corpse from the cottage along the path.

Mr and Mrs Perryman and family:

William ('Nailer') and Miriam Perryman lived at Cripdon at the beginning of the century. William worked for the council on the roads with Arthur Brown. William and his son Frank laid the first piece of tarmac to be seen in the Newton Abbot area. It was between Jay's grave and Hedge Barton, and was put in a rural area as an experiment to see if it was any good. They had a large family, of whom George was killed in the First World War. Fred was gassed in the war but survived, lived in Manaton, and died at the family' s home in Mellowmead.

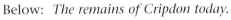

Right: *A drawing of Cripdon, as it was before it fell into ruin.*

Below: *The remains of Cripdon today.*

Of the hundreds of photographs that parishioners provided for use in this book, this has to be among the most extraordinary! It shows Charles Perryman pole vaulting on Manaton Sports Day c.1920. Note the trilby hat!

Frank was born in 1902, left school aged twelve, and was put 'into service' at Wingstone, where he was paid five shillings a week. His first job was to clean John Galsworthy's shoes! This only lasted two or three weeks because he found a better job working horses for seven shillings and sixpence a week. Frank married Freda Willcocks and became a farmer, first at Bowden in North Bovey, where he continued to mend roads, hiring his horse and cart to the council, and then in 1946 at Southbrook Farm, Buckland. They had a daughter, Marion, and a son, David, who has done wonderful work raising money, as chairman of the Ashburton branch of friends of Rowcroft Hospice. He owns the Round House and Craft Centre at Buckland.

Charles was born at Holwell and, when he was three weeks old, there was a bad fire and the family moved to Cripdon in 1899. He was in the army in the First World War and later lived at Barracott, where he worked for Mr Willcocks at Torhill as horseman. He married Annie Rose Leaman from Foxworthy Mill and their wedding car was driven by Cecil Hunt. They can be seen in the photograph on page 36.

They lived at Barracott, next to the Brown family, and then rented Horsham and Water farms. They had four children, Ronald, Norman, Hazel and Frank (see photograph page 63). Charles was on the sports committee and belonged to the Rifle Club. Charles and William Brown built the granite wall around the church. His son Norman remembers pumping the organ.

Jack was a sergeant and lost a leg in the Great War. The 'pension' provided to war invalids by the government was to train them in a skill. In Jack Perryman's case he trained as a shoemaker with Mr Harris in Bovey Tracey. He lived at Blissmoor with his wife Emerita from the early 1920s where his son, Pat, was born.

He had a collection point for shoes in the village. Mrs Hugo remembers him making a special pair of shoes for her mother, who had four toes; in fact he was well known for making special shoes, such as those for a club foot, and size 12 boots for the butcher's boy.

Later he moved to Fordgate where their daughter Betty was born and then 1 Mellowmead, where a small workshop was built, the Perrymans being the first occupants. Business was barely subsistance level, and he also sold cigarettes: Woodbines at 2d for five. In 1939 Jack rented some fields from Beckhams and kept poultry, but had to till the land for potatoes when the war started.

Bill was the elder son, and worked as a dairyman at Ford, and later for the Mortimores at Great Hound Tor. He finally lived with Sid at Mill Farm and was a great supporter of the Church.

Lewis Hern working with a horse-drawn mower at Cross Park (opposite Town Barton), c.1930.

Sydney worked for many people in the village, including the Kitsons at Hedge Barton (where Lewis Hern – see photograph above – also worked), Miss Needham at Southcott, and Penny Keogh at Deal from 1969 onwards. He lived with the family at Mellowmead and then Mill Farm. He was an excellent gardener, working for Miss Everard and Freda Wilkinson. At some point he worked on the Fernworthy reservoir.

Lucy had a son, Claude, who was brilliant at school, and Miss Prowse said he would go far. He worked for Robert Hern at Becky before joining the Royal Marines and becoming top in his section. He was lost with HMS *Cornwall* in the Second World War, his name appearing on the war memorial.

The Skerrett family:
Leonard and Mabel Skerrett lived at Cripdon with their two sons, Cyril and Eric, between 1930–32. Cyril and his father have written an account of this in their reminiscences. Living there after that were Ned Brown and another family of Webbers. This Mrs Webber caused a stir because she rode a motorbike! In 1934 Cripdon became infested with rats and the house was vacated; materials from the roof were taken for use on the Heatree estate.

Left: *Mrs Skerrett with her son.*

Right: *The Skerrett family c. 1920.*

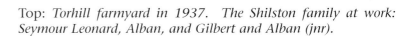

Top: *Torhill farmyard in 1937. The Shilston family at work: Seymour Leonard, Alban, and Gilbert and Alban (jnr).*

Above: *Mr Willcocks, who rented Torhill from about 1921, holds the head of the horse pulling the wagon with Penny Keogh and members of the Ripman family on baord.*

Left: *A family nurse holds the reins of ponies with Nick and Peter Ripman in the saddle. This photograph was taken on Manaton Green c.1920 when the Half Moon inn was being rethatched.*

TORHILL FARM

Torhill is a sixteenth-century farm that was probably a long house. It now occupies an area of about 180 acres. As this was another Nosworthy farm, with family members in adjoining Ford, Canna, Cripdon and Heathercombe, it is difficult to know who exactly owned which fields.

We start with John and Mary of Torhill, then their son John (1575–1645) and his wife Susanna who died in 1615. They and their son, Oliver, are buried inside Manaton church. The farm then went to Oliver's brother Thomas (1615–1680), passing to his son John (1650–1687), who married Julia Bownd in Manaton church in 1673.

Their son, George, had a son, William, who died aged two years and this Torhill line died out, passing to a cousin, John, who had two wives named Mary, the second of which had two daughters, also named Mary. The second daughter Mary survived and married the widowed Oliver of Cripdon, who thus was also of Torhill.

Their son John (1799–1871), married Anna Pethybridge in 1823 and they are both buried in Manaton churchyard. John and Anna had six children, of which John, Stephen, Anna and William are of Torhill. William was born in 1839, and a William of Torhill died in 1863. After this the farm must have passed into the Bryant and then Kitson estates.

The Pethybridges were there at the beginning of the century and Charlie Perryman worked for them.

Willcocks family:
Herbert Willcocks was born at Bonehill, before which his parents had rented Holwell. He rented Torhill from about 1921. Herbert did not marry, and was looked after by a widow, Mrs Jane Pearce, who had a son named Johnny, nicknamed 'Doctor'. Mr Willcocks let the farm during the summer, and the Ripman family used to take it, starting in 1922. He went to Town Barton, Ilsington, in 1937.

The Shilston family:
Mr Seymour Leonard Shilston and his wife Florrie bought the farm from the Kitsons in 1937. Mr Shilston had previously had a milk round in Chudleigh. They had one daughter, Ethel, who married Gilbert Freemantle of Doddiscombsleigh, and they had two sons, Gilbert and Alban. The farm was run as a hillfarm with a Galloway cross

Torhill farm and vegetable garden, c.1930.

Hereford suckler herd, and Exmoor and Scotch Blackface sheep. The dairy side was South Devons.

Gilbert married Emily Creber, and Alban married Betty Roberts in 1951 and moved to Neadon, where they rented about fifty acres from Miss Haines. They ran a dairy herd, South Devons and then Friesians; the sheep were Closewools and Suffolk cross. They lived there for 34 years and Betty remembers helping with jumble sales and teas, and dressing up for the Church Fair on the Green, organised by the Welchmans. They had two sons, Michael and Norman, who did not go into farming. Alban died in 1996 and Betty lives in Chudleigh.

Gilbert and Emily and their two sons, Stewart and David, continued to farm Torhill with Leonard, and a Friesian dairy herd was started in the early 1950s for a few years.

Florrie died in 1965, aged 76, and Seymour Leonard in 1975, aged 87. They are both buried in the churchyard.

Gilbert and Emily have retired, and their sons farm different sections of the land.

Left: *Lilly Dunning feeding the fowls at Deal c.1930.*

Below: *Jim Dunning driving the binder at Deal in the 1930s.*

Left: *Jim Dunning at Deal.*

Above: *Deal farmhouse in 1935, possibly with Mrs Dunning at the gate.*

Left: *Major Pat and Penny Keogh.*

DEAL FARM

Deal farm has a granite farm house built in the 1600s, and numerous stables and outbuildings. Its name is supposedly derived from the shape of the road, which extended up to Hayne Cross, along to the Green, down the main road and back up to the farm in the shape of a 'D', thus D-Hill. The earliest recorded owner of Deal was John Pethybridge in 1780. He seems to have been the owner of several farms in Manaton, and in 1800 was paying taxes on Water, Manaton Lea and Hills, Vogwell and Heathercombe. He also rented North and South-Middle Challacombe. His last recorded tax was £1.10s.4^1/$_2$d in 1830.

At some point it was owned by the Earl of Devon, because he sold 5000 acres to the Rt Hon. W.H. Smith in 1890, and Deal became part of the Hambleden Estate. Tenants prior to this were John Potter, Sam Potter and James Horrell. Hambleden estate buildings are easily distinguished by red bricks around the windows of granite outbuildings. In 1929 the acreage of Deal was 136 acres.

Mr and Mrs Dunning:
George and Lilly Dunning became tenants in 1911, having previously been farming at Heatree. They had two sons, Reg and Jim, and it appears they bought the farm in 1929, when the Hambleden Estate was sold by Rendell & Sawdye. Jim Dunning was married to Lily, and they took over from his father, and sold up in 1941.

Tom Heath worked on the farm, and also Bill Howe in the 1930s. Bill had a difficult time when he arrived on his first day: he was asked to take the South Devon cows and the bull up to the field from the yard. The cows went up straight away, but the bull just stood by the muck heap. After several allempts to move him, he went to ask Jim Dunning for help. He was told that the bull stood by the muck heap so that you could get on him and ride him! Bill discovered that he also had to ride him home.

In those days cattle to be sold were driven by the Dunnings down the road to Teigngrace, on Mondays. They rested there in a friend's field until Wednesday, when the drovers came from Newton market to collect them. Pigs and sheep were taken in a trailer pulled by an old Austin 6, which had to be hand-cranked. Invariably the starting handle was left in, and found to be missing when they returned from market. Jim and Bill would call in at the Smalls' caravan site in Newton Road, where the Small boys had a secondhand and car spares shop, to buy a new handle. They were often asked to stay for lunch by Granny Small. The first time, she said to Bill:

'What do you think you been eating boy?'
'Don't know' says Bill.'
'Tis Hedgepig' [hedgehog] *answered Granny Small.*

George Dunning built the bungalow 'Rockside' for his sister, and he and Jim ran the petrol pumps where the shop used to be. The customer rang a bell at the pumps, and when it rang at Deal someone came running. George Dunning sold the land for 'Oak Tree' and 'Moor House'.

Jerry and Glen Maslem:
Jerry and Glen bought Deal in 1942, and ran the pumps with their son Graham. Glen and Graham went to The Rock Inn, Hay Tor Vale, in 1951.

Mr P. L. Harris:
Mr Harris had been living in Deal Cottage, and he and his brother and sister moved into Deal in the 1950s. The Kinsey family came down from the North of England with the Harris' and then ran the garage. Brian Evans was the farm bailiff and lived in Deal Cottage with his mother.

Judy Miller:
Judy bought Deal in 1959 and had a racing stable there. She was a very fine horsewoman, and had gallops on Swine Down before it was fenced in. She sold because it was too far from the main race courses, so she and her trainer Ted Fisher moved to Chewton Mendip near Bath.

Major Pat and Mrs Penny Keogh:
They bought Deal in 1969. Earlier they had been farming at Willingstone in Moretonhampstead. They ran Hereford cross store cattle, Landrace cross Large White pigs, and contract-reared young calves. While Penny Keogh looked after these animals Major Keogh bred horses, which he also broke in and trained; some of his horses did very well. Pat Keogh died in 1974, and Penny continued farming with a Hereford cross suckler herd and subsequently sheep.

Penny Keogh has recently retired from farming, and, together with some fields she bought from Mr Freddy Pearce, the land is let.

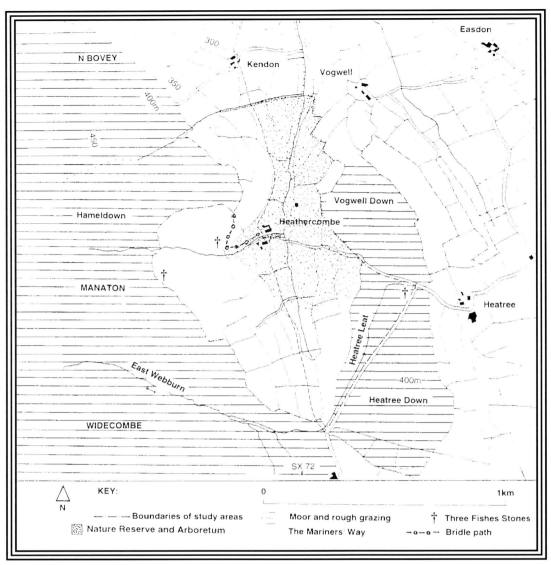

Top: *A map of the Heathercombe Valley showing the location of adjoining farms and properties, and the area of the arboretum.* (From *Heathercombe* by Claude Pike)   Above: *North Heathercombe longhouse.* (Photo courtesy Stephen Woods)

HEATHERCOMBE

Heathercombe is a small valley which lies in the Western part of the parish up against Hameldown. It separates two parts of Manaton parish: to the west the open moor of Hameldown and the isolated settlements of Challacombe and Soussons beyond it; to the East the farms centred on Manaton village. Being on the margin of the cultivatable land in the parish, Heathercombe has seen farming activity wax and wane over the centuries.

That farming has always been a struggle at Heathercombe is only too evident from the observations in the early eighteenth century survey of the estate of the Earl of Devon. Commenting about the tenements in the 'West Lands' of the parish from Soussons in the west to Torhill in the east, it states:

This part is very poor, cold and hungry grounds, full of rocks, and naturally heathy but by the extraordinary pains and costs of its owners, produces good rye, some wheat, but more oats and barley. Here are some meadows between the hills, not sufficient to maintain their cattle in Winter were it not for the help of clover grass. Their Commons in this part are Heathy Downs... Hamble [Hamel] Downe is in common to all his Gracis tenements in this part as well as Tutebarro where the said tenements cut turf for their present supply.

Heathercombe had been inhabited during the late Bronze Age, when the hut circles on Heatree and Vogwell Downs were occupied and the associated Heathercombe reave built, but the settlement was almost certainly abandoned when the climate subsequently deteriorated, and habitation was probably not resumed until after the arrival of the Saxons in the seventh century. From then onwards the area of the valley under cultivation was progressively extended from the more easily cultivated lower slopes up on to the adjacent 'heathy' land.

Heathercombe was from an early date divided between two farming tenements called South and North Heathercombe. Both tenements were included in the list of rates levied in 1613 for the repair of Manaton Church, and it would appear that these tenements – like those in the rest of the parish – were relatively stable until the nineteenth century. The Rate levied on each of the Heathercombe tenements at only ls.6d was next to the lowest in the parish – and compared with 6s.3d for Hound Tor, 3s.3d for Langstone and 2s.4d for fforde – indicating that these were some of the poorest tenements in the parish.

However in the fifteenth and sixteenth centuries the sale in the Chagford Stannary of tin ingots derived from tin streaming activity in the Heathercombe Burn – of which much evidence remains in the form of mounds of stones near to the Burn – had probably made a significant contribution to the income of the inhabitants, and it was during this time that they built North and South Heathercombe, longhouses typical of the fringes of Dartmoor.

Both were built into the side of the hill so that the higher part, the hall, could be occupied by the farmer and his family and the lower part, the shippon, by his animals. Each longhouse had a cross passage giving common access to both hall and shippon.

It is evident from the smoke-blackened timbers in the roof of Heathercombe North that at first there was an open fire in the centre of the hall, that there was no upper floor, and that the smoke escaped through a hole in the roof

The late sixteenth and late seventeenth centuries – the Elizabethan and Restoration periods – were relatively prosperous times for farmers in the South West, and like others in the area the Heathercombe longhouses were substantially upgraded, although they still retained their typical longhouse layout. Chimneys were constructed with fine dressed granite fireplaces, having ashlar'd fire backs which formed walls of the cross passages. Stone staircases were inserted in the hall walls to allow access to an upper floor over the hall, and the roofs were raised, in several stages, to give adequate headroom upstairs.

Then, or later, the existing outbuildings were built, including, at Heathercombe North, piggeries with fine granite troughs; a bank barn and a stone-roofed ash house. Bee boles were built into the garden walls to house the skeps which were used before the advent of bee hives.

Apart from the longhouses there was also at this time a corn (or 'grist') mill in Heathercombe powered by water from the Burn - which may earlier have served as a tin blowing-mill, and which probably served other tenements in the West Land of the parish.

The early eighteenth century survey of the estate of the Earl of Devon shows that the Heathercombe tenements, along with nineteen other tenements in the West Land of Manaton parish, then lay within the Manor of Little Manaton and formed part of the 'Kenton Manor' estate of the Courtenay Earls of Devon. The Survey recorded that, apart from tenements at Challacombe and Soussons, the rents paid by the copy- and lease-holders of the Heathercombe tenements, at 5s.6d and 5s. respectively, were at the lowest level of Manaton's West Land tenements.

Nevertheless, during this period, farming in the valley sustained the two farms, and the large fields which had been formed as the cultivated area extending up the sides of the valley were subdivided, indicating rather intensive use of the land. Indeed the high point in the expansion of the farms into the 'heathy' land was reached at the end of the eighteenth century when the impressive wall enclosing the large Newtake was constructed. This was however followed by the steady decline of farming in the valley.

By the time of the Tithe Apportionment in 1842, both farms were in common ownership, namely that of John Pethybridge, and several of the fields had been incorporated into the adjoining Vogwell Farm, which was then farmed by another member of the Pethybridge family. Heathercombe's corn mill was by now in ruins.

During the next quarter century ownership of the Heathercombe farmhouses and adjacent fields passed to James Bryant of Plymouth, as mentioned elsewhere in this book. However in 1868 Mr Bryant, who had moved into Hedge Barton, sold his Heathercombe property to John and Robert Kitson, sons of William Kitson who had developed a substantial part of Torquay and founded the Torquay law firm of W. & C. Kitson (now known simply as Kitsons).

The Kitsons brought great change to the part of the parish around Heathercombe, evidently with a view to establishing a splendid estate. Besides Heathercombe, they bought up a number of other farms nearby, including Heatree, Vogwell, Kendon, Ford, Canna and Easdon, and at Heatree they built a mansion, Heatree House, where they resided.

Activity on the farms which the Kitsons bought was rationalised and based primarily at Heatree, Vogwell and Ford. At Heathercombe a cottage, Burn Cottage, was built to house a farm labourer for the estate farms. However the struggle to farm the upper slopes and other poor-yielding areas of the Heathercombe valley was abandoned during the 1880s and 90s. The change to a new – and no doubt less unproductive – use was accomplished by the establishment of extensive plantations of mixed conifer and broadleaf trees in all but the most fertile parts of the valley. The so-called Jubilee Wood was planted in the year of Queen Victoria's Jubilee – 1887.

Clearly, however, the Kitsons – and particularly John Kitson, as Robert died in 1885 – also wanted to create an attractive amenity estate. At Heatree the stream below Heatree House was dammed to create four large lakes. Similarly, over the hill in Heathercombe, not only was the Burn dammed to create several lakes and ponds with attractive waterfalls, but also paths and bridges were built to make walks through the woodlands and beside the streams, and relatively-newly introduced

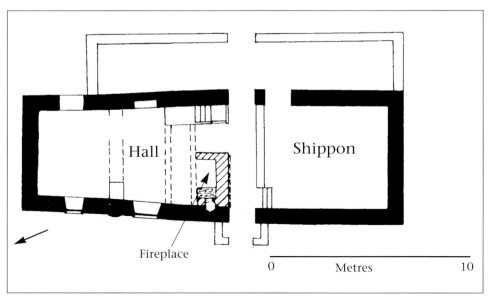

South Heathercombe longhouse showing the mid fifteenth century walls (dark coloured) and the 17 century fireplace (hatched). The drawing is based on a plan in the excellent publication Some Widecombe Longhouses, *by Jenny Sanders and Elizabeth Gawne*

specimen trees such as Western Red Cedar and Douglas Fir were planted, together with shrubs such as Rhododendron and cherry laurel.

With farming continuing only in a diminished state Heathercombe in this period of high Victorian prosperity took on a new role as part of a woodland and amenity estate. However on the death of John Kitson in 1911, his estate passed to his cousin and godson the Reverend John Archibald Kitson, Clerk in Holy Orders.

Evidently the new occupant of Heatree House – who was Rector of Manaton from c.1927–31, had either fewer means or less interest in the amenity of the Estate than his predecessor, as it became neglected.

Burn Cottage was occupied in the 1920s by Mr Hill who was employed as ploughman on the estate. His daughter, Mrs Tuckwell, well remembers the long daily walk from Heathercombe to Manaton school, and subsequently to Wingstone where she worked as a domestic servant.

During the 1920s a bungalow, Heathercombe Brake, was built high up on the western slope of the valley and was let to Messrs Whitehead and Tindale who started a silver fox farm there, catering for the fashion popular at that time. Their customers included Princess Marina, Duchess of Kent.

North and South Heathercombe ceased to function as farms. Heathercombe North was let during the 1920s and early 30s as a holiday home to a publisher, Christopher Sandford, who published some sixteen books under the imprint 'At the Sign of the Boar's Head in Heathercombe.' Jeremy Sandford, his son, later achieved fame as the author of the television play *Cathy Come Home*.

In the late 1930s Heathercombe North was let to a Commander Gibbons and his wife, the former Miss Ellery Hull (whose brother Field Marshal Sir Richard Hull KG, GCB, DSO, was later to become commander of NATO forces in Europe). After the couple divorced, Mrs Ellery Gibbons married Alec Kitson, son of the Reverend John Kitson, and they moved into South Heathercombe. During and immediately after the Second World War, Captain Evans, who commanded HMS *Repulse*, rented first Burn Cottage and then Heathercombe North for his wife and three sons to live in whilst he was at sea.

In 1947 the Reverend John Archibald Kitson died and the Heatree Estate was broken up. Heathercombe North was bequeathed to Alec Kitson who moved into the house with his wife, Ellery. South Heathercombe farmhouse and Burn Cottage were bought by Ellery Kitson herself, and

Heathercombe Brake, where fox farming had stopped during the war, was bought by two ladies who wanted to run a nursing home there.

Most of the woodland and farmland was bought by the Devon & Courtenay Clay Company of Newton Abbot as a source of timber for its underground ball clay mines in the Bovey Basin. During the war some of the plantations of the 1880s and 90s had been felled, and following its purchase the clay company felled most of what remained – including many fine Douglas Fir trees. However the permission for the felling given by the Forestry Commission stipulated that all the company's land be dedicated to forestry. A 25-year programme of re-planting was begun in 1952, initially mainly with Japanese Larch whose timber would best meet the company's expected need for pit props.

Nursing home and other plans for Heathercombe Brake having come to nothing, the property was bought in 1956 by Miss Quantick, a member of the Plymouth Brethren. She proceeded to establish the Heathercombe Brake Trust, an educational charity to provide accommodation for deprived children sent to her mainly by inner city local authorities. Under Miss Quantick's dynamic leadership the charity expanded very considerably, acquiring a number of substantial properties in Manaton parish including, in particular, Heatree House which became the headquarters of the Trust – as well as premises in Teignmouth. Many who spent several months or years of their childhood at Heathercombe return to see it with their families.

Ray Hugo, while at Langstone, recalls some of these children who were accommodated at Clapperway:

I would watch them walking up the hill to Langstone on their long trek to Heatree each day. Thin and blue with cold in winter, and hardly looking as though they would survive the walk. In a few weeks, however, they were transformed into strapping youngsters, with colour in their cheeks, striding out up Langstone Hill.

During the 1950s and early 1960s Mrs Kitson let Burn Cottage to members of the Hearn [Hern] family. Sam Hern, together with Arthur Raymont who lived at Vogwell Cottage, were employed on the woodland estate. Mrs Kitson also let South Heathercombe until it was sold in 1960 to Mr and Mrs Turner, who in turn sold it on in 1962 to Fountain Forestry who rented it to Mr Rushton, one of their forestry managers.

Claude and Margaret Pike at Heathercombe.

In 1964 The Devon & Courtenay Clay Company merged with Watts, Blake, Bearne & Co. Because of the long-term liability inherent in the re-planting obligation, the Heathercombe property was put up for sale and was purchased at Jacksons, Stops and Staffs valuation by Claude Pike, the then Chairman and Managing Director of Watts, Blake, Bearne. This marked the beginning of a new era for Heathercombe which, to a great extent, involved a reversion to the aims of John Kitson at the end of the nineteenth century in developing the valley as a woodland and amenity estate.

In 1965 Claude Pike bought Burn Cottage from Mrs Kitson. It was then in very poor condition. He rebuilt it in a mountain chalet style and thereafter spent practically all his weekends at Heathercombe with his wife Margaret. He worked to restore the ponds and paths which had become completely lost in a jungle of over-grown vegetation, and, having a great interest in trees for many years, he established an arboretum and planted many interesting species of both trees and shrubs around the estate. The story of this work is included in his book *Heathercombe – The History of a Dartmoor Valley*, published in 1993.

South Heathercombe was bought by Mr and Mrs Chapman in 1966. In the same year Alec Kitson died. Mrs Kitson's son, Christopher, having emigrated to Australia, she decided in the following year to sell Heathercombe North to Claude Pike. More recently the house has become the home of John and Svetlana Pike and their children. In 1979 Mr Chapman died and his widow sold South Heathercombe to Miss Diana Blount, one of whose forebears was created Earl of Devon in 1603.

Following his purchase of the woodlands in 1964, Claude Pike engaged Fountain Forestry to manage the woodlands. A number of local people were employed over the years to complete the forestry replanting programme with a variety of coniferous species including Douglas Fir, Sitka Spruce and Western Hemlock, to construct new forest rides and fences and to progressively thin the plantations.

Now, at the beginning of the new millennium, whilst a few of the trees planted at the end of the nineteenth century still survive as fine specimen trees, the forest planting of the 1950s is approaching maturity and a new cycle of felling and re-planting is beginning.

TOWN BARTON

Barton, meaning barley enclosure, is a common Devon farm name. Town Barton, meaning the farm in the village or settlement, is also common and there are Town Bartons at Sandford and Ilsington as well as Manaton. Hoskins says that the name usually indicates a farm with a long and interesting history. Manaton's Town Barton is right in the top part of the village, by the Green and the church.

Recent history reflects late twentieth century changes in the farming scene on Dartmoor. In 1979 the farm was sold at auction in lots, and so the integrity of the old farm disappeared. Robert and Kathleen Perkins bought the farmhouse, half the buildings and some land, and brought up their two children Adam and Katie here.

Susan Smith of Cross Park retained the use of half the buildings and some of the land, and has continued to run a South Devon herd. The remaining land was purchased by various individuals.

Robert Perkins, a retired Lt-Colonel of the Royal Marines, purchased more land as it came up around the parish, and farms a suckler herd and a flock of white-faced Dartmoor ewes. A famous anecdote tells of a passerby overhearing the Colonel herding his cattle down the road: 'Come along, come along,' halting them as a car approached, and continuing with the command 'As you were!'

The buildings are substantial Hambleden buildings and include a fine roundhouse on the north side of the main barn where a horse drove a threshing machine in the barn.

Working backwards, the previous owner was George Hart who bought it about 1949 and farmed it until his death in 1979. He had a milking herd of Ayrshires and ran sheep on the moor. He was a Scotsman and was employed at the prison farm at Princetown. He kept unusual pets: two monkeys which he used to take out on ropes. Ray Hugo remembers them running up and down trees, and that one of them used to coil the rope up as it ran down the tree. Philip and Brian Warne remember one of the monkeys throwing slates down off the roof at them as they waited for the school bus at the bus shelter!

Charlie Crout used to work for George Hart and remembers taking in a piece out of the home field to make into a vegetable garden. The little stream

Town Barton, thought to be a photograph taken c. 1900. If so the family in residence were the Cumings who can be seen posing for this picture; a man at the gate, three women and a child in the garden.

from the crossroads was piped under the garden and flowed through the vegetable patch. Charlie used to shovel out all the silt on to the garden. Kathleen Perkins still does that – no wonder it is such a free-draining and fertile vegetable patch. She still digs up broken bits of clay pipe nearly every week.

Miss Wilkes and Miss Harrison lived at Town Barton in the 1930s and 40s – they must have rented it as it was still owned by Jim Harvey. Charlie Crout remembers milk churns being taken down to the Kestor on the running boards of their bull-nosed Morris.

It has been reported that Town Barton was run as a guesthouse – a visitor asked to see round it in the 1980s and said he remembered coming to stay with his aunts, the Misses Harvey, when they ran it as a guest-house – but no-one else remembers it use in this way.

In 1929 it was sold out of the Hambleden estate along with a lot of other Manaton properties, and was bought by Jim Harvey for £1800. This was the same local entrepreneur who had run the Half Moon, built the Kestor and took visitors out on trips in his horse-drawn carriages. At the time it was tenanted by E. L. Cuming on a yearly Michaelmas tenancy. Jim Harvey put his workers

Unknown man with a fine horse called 'Banker' at Town Barton c. 1910.

in the two cottages and they worked Town Barton and Mill Farm for him.

It is believed that the old Town Barton farmhouse was the building used as the milking parlour in the 1970s, and now used by Moor Print. The house was burned out and the opportunity was taken to build a new house, and use the shell of the old house as a farm building. The buildings were subsequently much improved by Lord Hambleden, probably in 1896, as there is a stone with this date on it in the yard wall next to the Rifle Club. Two buildings are let as light industrial units to Mel Goddard of Moor Print, and to the Wright brothers of Manaton Joinery.

The new house was probably built around 1830 and it appears on the tithe map of 1842. The house still has a cast iron cooking range with 'Harvey Manaton' on it (see the section on blacksmiths on page 153).

Two photographs of Mrs Cuming, feeding fowl and geese at Town Barton c.1910. A sale notice from 1887 mentions Mr E. Cuming, who was presumably the father of the E. L. Cuming, the 1929 tenant. We know that Edward Cuming died in 1910, aged 76, and that his wife, Mary Aggett, died in 1909 aged 70.

Unknown dairymen at Town Barton at the time it was part of the Hambleden estate. No doubt these workers typified the modern approach that Lord Hambleden wished to apply to all his farms.

Unknown family at Town Barton c.1900.

An interesting panorama of Cross Park, Town Barton, the School and the Church c.1900. The barns appear to be newly roofed and this would have been part of the work undertaken by the Hambleden estate around that time. A small building, now disappeared, appears in the field in front of Cross Park, while the road up to the cross roads is glimpsed through a farm gateway (left, centre) of the photograph, close to where Heemstede (now Mill House) was built.

CROSS PARK

Little is known of the origins of this fine thatched house standing on the crossroads opposite Town Barton. From its front gate it receives one of the finest views in Manaton, across the green and up towards the church and Half Moon. It has been the home of Susan Smith and her family for many years. Susan's father was a retired Brigadier and early photographs show the family in residence.

As mentioned earlier, Susan retained the use of part of Town Barton's barns and several acres of land following the death of George Hart. She, and Francis Germon, better known to all as 'Bump' Germon, bred a fine herd of South Devon cattle here and one of life's more pastoral scenes for those passing by was to see these superb beasts being herded alongside the Green from one pasture to another.

A great supporter of village activities, Susan is to be found at most of the local events and is also a keen and able horsewoman. She once provided cream teas from Cross Park.

Above: *Cross Park c.1910, a figure in uniform standing on the veranda.*

Left: *Francis Germon repairing the wall on the left of the lane at Cross Park running toward Mill Farm.*

Above: *Southcott farmhouse from a postcard photograph c.1914.* Below left: *Members of the Wills family who farmed at Southcott in the late 1930s.* Below right: *Miss Needham haymaking with Sid Perryman and Frank Beer, in the 1940s.* Below: *Drilling seed at Southcott in the 1940s.*

Feeding the puppies - Southcott c.1945

SOUTHCOTT

Southcott, or Southcote, is a thatched granite farmhouse with traditional stone buildings and about 79 acres of pasture and rights on Hayne Down. The house has been listed as being of special architectural and historic interest. It was probably remodelled in the late seventeenth or early eighteenth century.

The Southcotts were Lords of the Manor of Manaton and Hound Tor in the sixteenth and seventeenth centuries. In *Families of Devon* the Southcotts or Southcotes were shown to be living here in the reign of Edward III (1327–1377).

Their line of descent is through Michael Southcotte to William of Southcott to Nicholas Southcote to John Southcot of Indio, who was clerk of the peace in 1556. Indio, which was once a priory in Bovey Tracey, was the ancient seat of the Southcotes, Knights after the Supression, they possessed it in the reign of Charles I.

John Southcott (1561) had Phillip Southcott of Southcott who married Dorothy Robinson 1617.

'A close of land called Leighon Parke' was granted in a lease to the Stokey family by Thomas Southcote in 1590. Whether the messuage Southcott in Manaton belonged to this family, or was named after this family, or merely because of its position, is not known. In 1599 Thomas Southcott gave Ivy Cottage, Manaton, for use of the church (it was re-built in 1818).

Nosworthys seem to have owned Southcott for a period and in the eighteenth century the Southcotts disposed of all their property in the Parish.

In 1653 Southcott is referred to in the will of William Nosworthy of Staverton, in which he leaves it to his daughter Jane Nosworthy who married Thomas Pope.

In 1663 Southcott is mentioned in a rate made for the poor. It does not mention the occupants, but probably it was the Pope family, because they are mentioned on the same document.

In 1691 Southcott is referred to in a document in which Dorothy Bowden conveyed one-eighth part of it, and other properties, to Nicholas Nosworthy. In 1726 Alexander Nosworthy conveyed it to William Lambshead of Ilsington.

Between 1780–1800 Southcott was owned by Alice French and let to Thomas French, and between 1810–1820 it was owned by John French and let to George Ley.

In 1812 the French family of Wingstone have a lease for 99 years, including South Hayne and Southcott (Pence-Hole); consideration 440 pounds, and a moidore of gold.

In 1830 it is owned by William French, and let to William Pethybridge. Between 1780–1830 the tax was £1.8s.1d. It has been said that at one time Exeter Cathedral owned it and used the farm as a retreat for clergy.

There is a post card of Southcott in 1914, on the reverse is written: 'Mrs S. Love lets lodgings 10 shillings a room'.

In the 1920s the Misses Collett lived there and ran a taxi service in an 'old tourer', one of them lived in Half Moon for a while. (In 1907 a Phyllis Collett worked at Foxworthy – see photograph on page 68).

Captain Thompson bought it in 1927; he then built Laneside and moved in. Mr and Mrs Arthur Skerrett (his wife Mary was James Howe's daughter from Cross Park) and their children Roy, Jack and Margaret lived behind Laneside and Arthur worked for Captain Thompson in 1933–35. They then went to East Ogwell.

The Wills family:
The Wills family came from Heathergate, Dawlish. In 1935 there was an annexe at the back of Laneside where the Wills family stayed for a while, until other tenants left the farm. The Wills were employed by Captain Thompson to work the farm and did so until 1941. They had three girls and a boy. One of the daughters, Evelyn Clark recalls:

There were very few houses in Manaton at that time, only farmers and their workers. I remember Bill and Lilian Lentern at Hayne, the Andrews, Annie Dunning, the Winsors, the Wrefords, Crouts and Perrymans. During the early part of the war my parents had to clear all the furniture from two large bedrooms for troops, I think they were on exercise. It was for a short time. My mother had guests in the house – full board two and a half guineas a week.

Capt Thompson sold Southcott in 1945, having previously gone to live in a cottage near the Church. The Ripman family bought Laneside in 1938. The Wills bought Webland Farm in Avonwick and moved there in 1941. Mr and Mrs Old were tenants after the Wills.

Miss Needham 1945-56:

Miss Sylvia Needham bought the farm in 1945. She kept a herd of horned South Devons whose line she could trace back for a hundred years and gave 40 per cent butterfat. She worked the farm with horses. During the 'Great Snow' of 1947 she saw no wheeled vehicle for six weeks.

She employed Sid Perryman, who was also her trusted friend. 'A dear chap called Sid came to work and with his older brother we got the place into shape, once they had finished there wasn't a weed to be seen.'

Only one water spring supplied Southcott, Laneside and Springfield (that latter now renamed Where the Woozle Wasn't). Miss Needham was short of water, and jokingly recalls that when all the Ripmans bathed there wasn't any water for the stock! The Agricultural Board gave her a £500 grant to put in concrete drinkers and a new spring.

Miss Needham moved to Broadaford and then Widecombe. She was a founder member of the White-faced Dartmoor sheep association and finally retired, aged 85, when she sold her last White-face ram at Ashburton in September 1999; it won first prize in the best coated ram category.

Mr and Mrs Gordon Warne 1956-1992:

Gordon and Isabel Warne came from Blackawton with their three sons, Brian, Norman and Philip.

Gordon's parents had farmed locally at Hookner and Whiddon Down. They started with 20 Closewool ewes and a South Devon suckler herd. The boys went to North Bovey School, later Phil trained as a mechanic and Brian and Norman worked on the farm.

Life was very hard at first, and the work was done with a horse. Later Brian bought an old Austin truck. He also had a logging business round the village.

Norman married and left the farm, and Brian married Linda who is a trained nurse. She worked at Hawkmoor until they started a family, Sarah, Ruth, Ben and Tim. Since then she has been working for the Moretonhampstead Health Centre and is a well known District Nurse.

Brian and Linda Warne:

Gordon died in 1992, and Brian was able to buy the farm. He has always contributed to village life and since 1960 has held various offices including chairmanship of the Parish Council, the Show and Fair Commitee and the Parish Hall Commitee. He is now back on the Parish Council as Vice-Chairman. He and Linda support the Church, Linda singing in the choir and Brian, as a bell-ringer, is Captain of the Tower. He has a busy contracting business, and also runs a suckler herd and sheep.

Left and below: *Sylvia Needham working at Southcott in the 1940s.*

Left: *Sid Perryman on the wain and Frank Beer making the rick for Miss Needham at Southcott c.1940.*

Below: *Gordon and Isabel Warne and family at Southcott in the mid 1950s.*

Below: *The Austin pickup which was used on the farm, and for delivering logs by Brian Warne.*

Right: *Gordon and Isabel Warne at Southcott with Norman, Brian and Philip c.1956.*

The Leaman family outside Horsham c. 1915. Henry and Alberta Georgina Leaman rented the house from Robert Earle, later moving to Foxworthy. Their children were Annie Rose, Adolphus (Dolph), Dicky and Blanche. The house has remained remarkably unchanged over the years apart from the roof which was burned in 1946 and replaced with cedar tiles, then slated in 1997.

Left: *Charles Perryman working at Horsham Farm in the 1930s.*

HORSHAM AND BECKHAMS

Horsham and Beckhams have shared boundaries and land has passed between one farm and another – not unusual for Manaton farms. Horsham farmhouse is a very old Devon longhouse dating back to medieval times in parts and to the early sixteenth century. It retains its cobbled cross-passage, typical of Dartmoor longhouses. It was originally one storey only, open to the thatch. In Elizabethan times it was changed to two storeys. A lovely oak panelled wall was put in to divide the dairy from the large kitchen–living room with a huge open hearth, the shippon being made into a farm parlour.

It has changed very little since then, except for the roof which burned in 1946 and was replaced with cedar tiles and then, in 1997, with Welsh slate. For some time the house was rendered and painted white, but this has since been taken back to the original granite. The old cobbled farmyard contains a large granite water trough, fed by a leated stream. Granite farm buildings include a dog kennel.

The Manaton Church Rate for Horsham in 1613 was two shillings.

John Nosworthy (1575–1648), of Horsham and Kendon, was an early owner and William, son of John of Horsham, became the first headmaster of Exeter Free School in 1633.

John of Horsham had a brother, James of Torhill. His son was also well known, because he became the Rev. John Nosworthy.

The other property associated with Horsham is Wester Bickham (Beckhams). In 1642 the Southcotes are known to have had a 'Bargain and Sale' between them and John Tapper and Mathias Nosworthy of Moreton: 'for appurtenances at Horsham and a close called Wester Bickham, 15 acres in Manaton.' It was sold to George Merdon and James Nosworthy in 1648.

There is mention of a John Nosworthy of Horsham (b.1720), marrying Elizabeth who gave birth to a daughter, Katherine, in 1749.

The next owner was William Holman (c.1780–1820) who left it to his son, John, who in 1830 was paying land tax of 18 shillings. At Horsham the 1841 census records: John and Mary Holman aged 40, Steven Crout aged 20, Sarah Crout aged 15, Deborah Crout aged 7, Sarah Quick aged 15, Joseph Bray aged 15. The 1851 census: John Holman (registered blind) and his wife, Deborah Crout and Richard Bray aged 11. In 1851 the acreage was 33.

The 1861 census records John Holman and his wife, Joseph and Agnes Winson. The 1871 census, John Holman and wife, John and Jane Winson. The 1881 census, records Richard Bishop and his family.

A strange story was told to Peter and Hazel Manners-Chapman who now live in Horsham. An historian arrived to see the house having discovered that a boy from Horsham had gone to the Peninsular War and had returned in about 1810 with a Spanish wife and her mother. The father refused to have them in the house and they lived in a little cave, which still exists with black smoke marks on the roof, in the woods south of the Horsham–Ridge Road track. The husband was then injured or killed by a 'bolt' that came down the chimney, and the Spanish mother and daughter were seen selling 'simples' and bunches of herbs in the village.

Wester Bickham, became Beckhams, West Beckhams and East Beckhams and was still owned by the Nosworthys, being left in his will by William Nosworthy of Ford to his daughter Jane, when he died in 1820. Between 1780–1830 William and then John were paying 17s.3d land tax. The ruins of the old longhouse are on the North side of the Becka Brook.

Robert Earle:
Towards the end of nineteenth century Horsham and Neadon both belonged to Robert Earle, an estate agent from Torquay. He came to the property at weekends and holidays for shooting and fishing. He and his family came by train to Lustleigh station and walked over the Cleave.

One Friday in the winter, Mrs Earle started walking with Maud as a toddler, from Lustleigh station and half way over the Cleave, a tremendous snow storm started which wiped out visibility. They took shelter under an overhanging rock and huddled together in a sort of little cave. By tremendous luck Robert Earle decided to get the last train to Lustleigh instead of waiting until the following morning. He was struggling through the snow when his gun dogs started whining and barking and they led him to his wife and child. He was able to get them back to Chez Nous.

Both Neadon and Horsham were let to tenant farmers. It was in 1890 that Mr Earle converted a cow shed east of Horsham into a cottage called Chez Nous. In those days telegrams had to be delivered the same day if the address was within a couple of miles of the Telegraph Office. Horsham was too far from Bovey, but not Lustleigh, and the poor Posty had to walk over the Cleave whatever the weather!

Robert died in 1904 and his widow in 1911, and the property was left to his daughters, Miss Maude and Miss Dorothy Earle. Neadon was sold and Horsham remained in the family. Maude married the Rev. Cyril Donne in 1913 and although not living permanently in Manaton retained Chez Nous for holidays.

Miss Dorothy Earle:

Miss Earle farmed Horsham herself with a worker, John in the 1920s. She bought four fields known as Glebe fields, which adjoined Horsham. About 1930 she built Ty Clyd (now called Hunters Wood) at the end of Ridge Road and lived there until the beginning of the war. She had already built a small extension to the north end of the farmhouse and this, together with three rooms from the main part, formed Horsham Corner, where she lived during and after the war. Later she bought Chez Nous from her sister.

At that time the telephone exchange was run by Mrs Frost at the shop at the top of the green. Miss Donne, Miss Earle's niece, telephoned her aunt one day and a voice interrupted: 'Baint no good you'm phoning your Aunt Miss Esther, at this moment she'm crossing the Green.'

During the war Esther's car was licensed for private hire and as well as being ready to drive day and night, especially to take members of the armed forces to or from trains at any hour (her war-work). She was retained to drive members of the Home Guard to secret locations on the moor, in the event of invasion and she continued a taxi service after the war. She was a firm task master and one man in the village remembers her setting an alarm clock for his period of work.

Miss Earle was a supporter of the Church and did a great deal for the Parish. She was in at the beginning of the Manaton WI in 1930, being its second President, she was also District Captain for the 1st Manaton Girl Guides, 1941–46, helped run Manaton Show and was a 'good Parish Councillor who stuck to her guns,' ending up as Chairman.

The Manaton Girl Guides seemed only to exist during the Second World War. They collected rubber and tins in a little barrow for the war effort. The President was Mrs Gordon Baillie, the District Commissioner Mrs Kitson and the District Captain Miss Earle. The only surviving guide discovered is Mrs Jean Harris (née Frost), who lives in Bovey Tracey.

Miss Earle improved the old bridle path from Water to Horsham by permission of landowner, Major Woodhouse, in the late 1920s. The wonderfully named Slinkers Lane (so called, it is said, as it was used by those 'slinking' up the back way to Half Moon from the village, avoiding the vicar's admonition!) was used by horse and cart, and occasionally car, up to 1930s. In 1973 she built the road over the fields from the end of Ridge Road, following an old cart track.

On Miss Earle's death in 1975 Horsham and Chez Nous came to her nieces, the Misses Donne.

The Pilkingtons at Horsham c. 1955. Gerry and Val's connection to Manaton remained long after they left in 1957. Their daughter Barbara married Dave Amery who played cricket for, and captained, Manaton Cricket Club in the 1980s. The cricket club held annual barn dances at Ullacombe Farm which Gerry, and later their son, Mark, farmed. Val made cricket teas for many years.

TENANTS

Mr and Mrs Sanders:
Tenants from 1932–1936, Mr and Mrs Sanders and their sons came from Ashill, East Devon. They kept South Devons. Mrs Sanders sold cream and eggs in the village, and the boys walked up Slinkers Lane to school. They moved to Bickington, and Mike still farms in Higher Lemonford.

Charles and Rose Perryman:
Rented Horsham 1937–1942 (see Cripdon) and then farmed Mill Leat at Holne. They had three sons: Ronald was in the Signals during the Second World War and then became a policeman. Norman helped farm Mill Leat until he married and went to West Stoke and now lives in East Ogwell. Frank farmed Mill Leat and now lives in Buckfastleigh (see photograph on page 62 of the boys on top of hay at Horsham). Their daughter Hazel married Mr Merchant and lives at Woodland.

An evacuee Sydney Sykes, got married and came back to Manaton and took Horsham, he hired cows, but it did not work out.

Mr and Mrs Gerry Pilkington:
Gerry and Val rented Horsham in 1955. They ran a dairy herd, having only a horse for transport, the churns were pushed right up to the main road to the milk churn stand at Deal Cross in the baby's pram. There was no phone and no bath-room; Slades from Bovey delivered groceries. They left in 1957 and bought Mill Farm. Their son, Mark, was born at Horsham and now farms at Ullacombe, Hay Tor, where he and his wife have, among other things, a successful free range egg business.

The Hill family:
The Hills, with son Roger and daughter Susan, farmed with horses, and kept a dairy herd of Shorthorns and South Devons.

Mr and Mrs Brian Woolley:
Milked 6-8 Ayrshires. Brian played for Manaton Cricket Club until it disbanded in the early 1960s. They were here for short while only and after this the farmhouse and land were let separately. John Coaker rented all the land for some time.

Hazel and Peter Manners-Chapman:
In 1968 Peter and Hazel Manners-Chapman took the farmhouse with their two boys James and Hugh. Hazel nursed at Hawkmoor for fifteen years and Peter helped Paulie James with the milk round. Later he distributed the papers and to the great luck of the village still does!

Bill Howe recalled being taken by his father in the 1920s, to see the first steam Traction Engine in Manaton. It went down the lane by Horsham and got alders out near the river. Alder was to make clogs and was taken away by wagons pulled by horses.

Above: *Hugh and James Manners-Chapman outside Horsham in the late 1970s.*

Right: *Hazel Manners-Chapman at Manaton Show and Fair c.1985. She presided over the auction each year, raising funds for the parish.*

Left: *Great Hound Tor Farm and the medieval house (now a camping barn), as it was in the late 1940s when it was owned by Thomas and Elizabeth French.*

Below: *Elizabeth French in the yard at Great Hound Tor c.1940.*

Below: *Mrs French and Brenda Beer (née Coniam) in the garden at Great Hound Tor.*

Above: *'Nannie' (centre) who helped at Great Hound Tor, having been evacuated from London during the Second World War with her daughter Anne (left), and Barbara Beer c.1940.*

Left: *Thomas French c.1940.*

GREAT HOUND TOR FARM

The present farmhouse built in the early 1600s is a well-preserved longhouse with unique cobble designs in the cross-passage, said to have been laid by French Prisoners of War. If so, this is by no means unique to Hound Tor and a number of other farms in the area have similar cobbled floors, although the patterns at Hound Tor are unusual.

Opposite the farmhouse is a much older building that was once a medieval dwelling. It has a chimney in the upper end wall with a handsome timber lintel and the remains of a stone staircase. It was built as a 'Barton' farm whose owner lived elsewhere, eventually reverting to use as a barn when the new house was built, and is now a beautifully restored camping barn.

There has been some discussion as to whether the medieval house is the original *Hundertora* mentioned in Domesday. The supposed boundary of the Manor of Hound Tor includes Halwill (Holwell), Hedge Barton, Swine and Hayne Down, Leighon, Greator, the medieval village and Great Hound Tor Farm. According to Elizabeth Gawne:

It seems unlikely that the Domesday settlement would have been on the site of Great Hound Tor Farmstead, which is only two fields away from the Manor boundary and does not include Hayne Down above. Also Dartmoor Manorial Settlements were established on high ground above valleys filled with woodland and were cleared downhill. Great Hound Tor would have been surrounded by thick woodland.

Miss Gawne considers that House no.3 at the medieval village was the manor.

Hooker in his *Synopsis* records: 'Hugh de Hountor Knight was in King Richard I thyme (1189-1199) seized of the whole tything of Hountor,' and that a later Lord of the manor 'Sold the same unto Walter Dymock, a Lincolnshire man employed in the tin works of Devon. It is now Thomas Southcot's.'

The Manaton Church Rate was 6s.8d in 1613, the highest in the 'East Land'. Considering that the rate for 'Leane' (Leighon) was only 1s.6d, Great Hound Tor was the major farm.

To the East of Great Hound Tor Farm there is a small field known as 'Heales', and this and 'Leane' are grouped together in the Land Tax. Leighon

was a 'parcel of Hound Tor Manor' in a document of 1649.

Robert Nosworthy (1626–1699) of Leighon, Yeoman of Hound Tor, married Mary Archer (d.1671) of Ilsington, 1657. They had 8 children, one being Steven of Foxworthy.

In 1664 Robert leases a 20 acre field named Barn Park, part of the Barton of Hound Tor, with Robert Nosworthy of Listleigh (Lustleigh) to Richard Hayward of Manaton, a bond for £20.

Hound Tor seems to become linked to Leighon through the Nosworthys and then owned by the French family of Wingstone.

Apart from the field called Pipholes it comprised 162.880 acres; Hound Tor Common 197.692 acres. Land Tax Assessments record the following owners and occupiers:

Hound Tor part of:

Date	Owner	Occupier
1780	Thom. Lane	Thom. Heyward
1790	Alice French	Will. French
1800	Will. French	ditto
1810-30	ditto	ditto

Hound Tor part of:

Date	Owner	Occupier
1780	Thom. Nosworthy	ditto
1790	Alice French	Alice French
1800	ditto	ditto
1810	John French	Will. French
1830	Will. French	ditto

Hound Tor part of:

Date	Owner	Occupier
1780	John Davy	Stephen Nosworthy
1790	Sam. Jackson	ditto
1800	Robt Nosworthy	ditto
1810	Robt Nosworthy	ditto
1830	ditto	Gilbert Frost

Pepholes (Pipholes) 44.177 acres:

Date	Owner	Occupier
1780	John Nosworthy	George Ley
1790	Will. Nosworthy	ditto
1820	Mary Nosworthy	Will. Nosworthy
1830	Robt Nosworthy	ditto

William Nosworthy (1826–1888), was owner of Great and Little Hound Tor. The Frenches then let Great Hound Tor to several tenants, including the

Mortimores from the turn of the century. Harold Mortimore was born at Great Hound Tor in 1904. His father was killed by a fall in the yard during a pony round up. His wife continued as a tenant on her own and then with her son. Thomas Mortimore was a tenant in the 1930s and went to Ashburton in 1938.

Thomas and Elizabeth French had already bought the farm from the Wingstone Frenches in 1936. They moved down from London and Mrs French's mother, Mrs Horsefall, was brought from Suffolk during the Munich Crisis.

The Frenches grew some cereal, had a Galloway herd on the moor, some Closewool sheep and kept South Devons for dairy. Lewis Hern worked for Mrs French as did Frank Beer who lived in Homer Heales (built by Mrs French) between 1959–1966. Frank and Florrie Beer had previously lived in a cottage at Leighon from 1940 where Frank planted the rhododendrons with Frank Coniam the keeper. Before that they were at Neadon Cottage where their daughter Brenda was born.

Miss Anne (Andy) Baxter started to help Mrs French with the milking and farm work in 1960, and lived in when Mrs French broke her shoulder, eventually living in half the house. Andy married

Mick Moreton in 1970 and they had two daughters 'Catty' and Rose. The Moretons farm Exmoor sheep and have a suckler herd. Mick has been a stalwart of Manaton Cricket Club since its refounding in 1976, first as a player and continuing as treasurer.

• • •

One morning, in the early days of the Second World War, Jack Howe was cycling down the hill to deliver the post and had to take evasive action to avoid hitting Mrs French's car. He skidded into the wall and was taken to Hound Tor and mopped up by Mrs French and her friend Miss Courtenay. When the blood and grit was being sponged off Miss Courtenay let out a gasp: 'Good heavens man you've lost your eye!' He replied 'Don't worry Miss, I lost that years ago.'

Another friend, Miss Laura Maud Hill, returned from a walk in the village and said to Mrs French. 'You seem to have a lot of one-eyed people in this village, I've met three, the postman, the verger and the blacksmith.' Not realising that they were all the same man – Jack Howe. He was known to state that he saw more with one eye than most people did with two.

Above: *Mrs French and Frank Beer with 'Gunner' and 'Nobby'.*

Right: *Andy Moreton stands at the doorway to the cross-passage at Great Hound Tor Farm in front of the cobbled floor, said to have been made by Napoleonic prisoners of war. It is certainly known that officers (held originally at Princetown prison) were paroled in villages around the moor – there is a parole stone on the road near Natsworthy delineating the limits beyond which prisoners could not proceed.*

LEIGHON AND GREATOR FARM

The name Leighon comes possibly from a weak plural of the Old English Leah (Lea) and Leighon is 'Leyne' in *Parochia Mannedonne* 1291. The original ancient Leighon was a house by Leighon Tor; the ruins still exist.

In 1613 the Church Rate was Leane 1s.6d, Leanie Park 4d.

The Nosworthy family:

There are records of the Nosworthy family living and farming in Manaton from the early 1500s. Manaton Registers commence in 1654, but Bishop's transcripts and extracts from wills have survived from an earlier date.

Many ancient farmsteads sheltered the Nosworthy family of Manaton down the ages, a number of which are included in this book: Neadon, Leighon, Canna, Torhill, Cripdon, Ford, Greator, Holwell, Heathercombe, Barracott, the Challacombes, Easdon, Vogwell, Horsham, Beckhams, Foxworthy, Little Silver and more.

Of these Leighon is remarkable for its unbroken run of occupation by the Nosworthys, from 1597 until the end of the nineteenth century. There are records of two other families living at Leighon before, Richard and Barbara Bounde in 1570 (there is a quitclaim dated 1571 whereby Alexander Northaway and Robert Jefferye of Ilsenton [Ilsington] quit the title to Aslehene or Leane to Richard Bounde), and also the Stokey or Stookey family 'before 1608'.

Before this Leighon was tied up with the Manor of Hound Tor and was within the Manor boundary. In those days Leighon was a longhouse, and Thomas (c.1535–1604), who is buried in the floor of Manaton church, seems to have been the first Nosworthy to own it. His son, Robert(1577–1629) inherited, and thus it went to his son, Steven (1604–1647), of Leighon also of Foxworthy, who married Jone Grey of Lisleigh (Lustleigh) in 1624. It then went to their son Robert (1629–1699), of Leighon and Yeoman of Houndtor, who married Mary Archer of Ilsington. Robert was a constable of Manaton and his son Stephen (b.1658) married Margaret Preston in 1682. Their son Robert (1685–1752) of Leighon married Mary Hamlyn of Widecombe in 1721. Their son Stephen (1734–1791) of Leighon married Joan Ley of Manaton in 1763, and he left it to his son Robert (1765–1849) of Leighon and Foxworthy. He married Sarah Wills of Rudge, Lustleigh, dying at the age of 84, and his son Robert of Leighon (b.1804) inherited. Robert died in 1885, aged 81, and is buried with his wife Eliza and his seven-month-old daughter in Manaton churchyard.

This was the end of the Nosworthys at Leighon, and, previous to Robert's death, it was bought by Prebendiary Wolfe in about 1855.

The Rev. R.R. Wolfe:

The estate was 1500 acres and included Beckaford when Wolfe bought it. He altered the original longhouse by building the front hall, porch and sitting room, and raising the roof. The house became two storeys of 4 bedrooms, dressing room, bathroom, and four servants' bedrooms up a separate staircase. There were a drawing room, dining room, study and extensive servants' and butler's quarters; he also put in the trout ponds. Prebendiary Wolfe and his wife feature in the history of the school. He was the treasurer, and gave talks to the school, introduced games and, from 1893, supplied prizes. He died in 1902.

Washington Singer:

The Singers bought in 1902 from the executors of the Rev. Wolfe; in the deed of sale it is put thus:

'...formerly described as a farm commonly called 'Hayne' otherwise 'Leighon,, otherwise 'Lean' otherwise 'Leyne' and land known by the name of 'Greator' otherwise 'Grator' otherwise 'Gravetor.'

Washington Singer – as Master of the South Devon Hunt c. 1900.

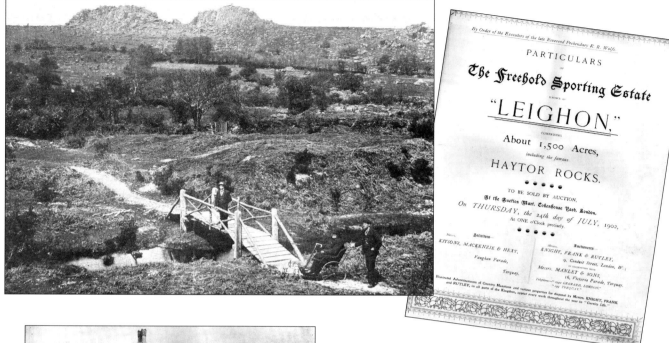

Above Left: *The Reverend Wolfe who bought Leighon estate c.1885. He can be seen in this photograph in his wheelchair overlooking the bridge he had built upstream on the Becka Brook. It is interesting to note how much of the river valley appears to have been turned over by tinners.*

Above: *Title page of the sale document when the estate was sold in 1902.*

Left: *Leighon House c. 1900.*

They bought about 1500 acres, including Leighon House, Leighon Farm, Greator Farm, Common rights and the freehold of Haytor Down, for £9500.

Washington Singer's second marriage was to Ellen Mary Longsdon, who then lived there with their joint family, Cyril and Nancy Longsdon. Their son, Grant Singer, who was born in 1914, was killed in the Second World War. In 1914 a licence to take water from Haytor Quarry for 1000 years was arranged between Washington Singer and the Rural District Council.

Washington died in 1934 and left the estate to his wife who rented it to Captain and Mrs Wheeler between 1938–1941. Captain Wheeler was American. Their daughter Susan Brewer has many memories of this time, including army trucks camping on Leighon Drive, and a huge field-gun in the field below which made craters on Hound Tor and Hay Tor. They once had to duck as bullets flew across the top of the reservoir when they were out walking.

Captain Wheeler was in the Manaton Home Guard, and Susan remembers an amusing stirrup pump demonstration at Water. Mrs Jean Harris (née Frost) of Bovey Tracey had to bath Susan for her Girl Guide Badge!

Major and Mrs John Crocker Bulteel then bought it. They had two daughters; he was clerk of the course at Ascot. Sir John founded the Leighon Stud of pure-bred Dartmoor Ponies in 1944. He bred them for ten years and in that time produced some first class ponies, and descendants of Plymouth Rock and Meadow Sweet are winning today. He died in 1956 and his daughter sold Leighon back to Cyril Longsdon who lived

Above: *The Wheeler Family at Leighon, c.1940.*

Above Right: *Mrs Wheeler, Susan and Stewart at the fishing hut, Leighon ponds.*

Right (back row l-r): *Mrs Ellis, with Mary Chandler holding Ian Clements, (front) Shirley Ellis, with Susan Wheeler and her cousin.*

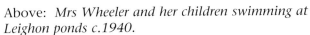

Above: *Mrs Wheeler and her children swimming at Leighon ponds c.1940.*

Right: *Captain Wheeler, riding at Leighon c.1940.*

The only known photograph of Greator Farm which is now just a ruin. This picture appeared in the sale particulars of Leighon estate in 1902.

there with his third wife. The farm was then 154 acres of land, excluding Haytor Down.

The Leighon estate was put up for sale in July 1975 by R.C. Longsdon. Beckaford Farm was bought by the tenant Brian Rice and the major part of Haytor Down (in parish of Ilsington) was bought by the Devon County Council. In June 1977 the remainder of the estate was bought by Mr and Mrs A.R. Cullen.

Mr and Mrs A.R. Cullen:
They bought Leighon House with stables and groom flat, Leighon and Greator Farms, Leighon Lodge and Cottages, plantations, part of Haytor Down, a moiety of Houndtor Down and the Lordship of the Manors of Ilsington and Bagtor – in all 750 acres. They have six children and keep a Murray Grey suckler herd and Cheviot sheep.

GREATOR FARM

A quarter of a mile from Leighon are the remains of this farm. It was an old farm but not a long-house, described in the sale particulars as 'a small house containing 6 rooms, suitable farm buildings comprising Barn, Stable, Sheds etc.' The acreage was 111. The church rate in 1613 was 2s.4d.

In 1696 it was owned by John Nosworthy of Lustleigh, in his will of that year he left it to his wife Jane. It also states that Greator was occupied by Thomas Nosworthy. In 1840 Robert Nosworthy of Greator Farm was paying a tithe on Swallerton, which thus implies that it had ceased being an inn.

When Singer bought the estate in 1902, it was let to John Smerdon who was sitting tenant; he had inherited the lease from his father Thomas Smerdon. They also rented Leighon Farm. The annual rent for Greator and Leighon in 1902 was £125, a yearly tenancy with 12 months' notice; the tenant to do repairs and pay rates and taxes.

The farm was burnt down in the 1920s and the Smerdons moved to Leighon farm. There are said to be two ghosts.

LEIGHON FARM or THE HOME FARM

This was built by the Rev. Wolfe and the Smerdons were there until the late 1920s. The farm was 'a neatly built house' and had four bed-rooms, two sitting rooms and domestic offices and outbuildings. It comprised about 94 acres. It also had the use of the Leighon farm buildings, barn, stable, cow stalls and pig sties etc.

The Brown Family:
Moving to the farm in the 1920s, they came from Hookner North Bovey, and before that Blackaton. William Brown was married to Annie Rose Leaman from Foxworthy. Their son Arthur

Left: *Leighon Home Farm c.1960.*

Below: *PC Perryman and his family who became 'father' to Dickie Perryman.*

married Miss Piper whose parents lived at Leighon Lodge. William Piper, her father, was the Singers' gamekeeper and is buried in the churchyard. Her mother retired to the bungalow at Beckaford.

Arthur Brown was farming Leighon when the point-to-point was held on Black Hill in March. It snowed for three seasons running and was eventually moved to Forches Cross.

The family moved to Holne in 1933. They had two sons, Henry born at Leighon and Michael at Holne. William Brown's brother, Kenneth, built Springfield between the wars, now named Where The Woozle Wasn't – next to Southcott.

The Perryman family:
In 1934 the farm was leased to Richard James A. Perryman (Dicky) and his father and brother; they came from Lakeland Farm, North Bovey. The land was 178 acres and included Greator. The rent was £80 per annum increasing to £100 after 6 years. It is interesting to note that the lease is signed by Ellen Mary Singer and Franklin Morse Singer of Monte Carlo, Monaco.

Dicky and his first wife, Ivy (née Harvey) had three daughters, Ivy and Joan, twins, and Jean. When Ivy died Dicky married Betty Breeze whom he had originally employed as housekeeper in 1949. Mrs Breeze had a son, Brian, and a daughter, Marion. Dicky and Betty then had a daughter Liz and a son Richard.

Betty Perryman (née Jenkins) worked very hard but was used to a busy life, having been one of

fourteen children. Cooking was done on a big open fire with crucks and kettles for hot water. There was a four-legged stand with a big pot for boiling washing. There was no bathroom until the 1960s and the W.C. was outside. Tilly lights and candles were used for lighting and the beds were warmed with hot coals in warming pans. Groceries came from the travelling shop run by Jimmy Churchward every Thursday, the weekly order being posted until the Longsdons put in a phone.

Their own pork was salted down. Betty and the girls hand-milked 14 cows, South Devons and one Jersey. There was a hand separator and the pan with cream was kept over simmering water. In the 1950s butter was sold at 5 shillings per lb. and the cream was sold in pound and half pound jam jars.

Mrs Perryman also worked at Leighon doing the fires for the Bulteels and Longsdons and was paid 5 shillings an hour.

Dickie farmed Leighon for fifty years. Along with the cows he ran Greyface sheep, then Closewools and finally Scotch Blackface. He was encouraged by George Hart of Town Barton in running Blackface, because George had run them as farm manager at the prison in Princetown.

Dickie delivered the cream locally, first on a pony, then a bike and finally an old Ford that doubled as a sheep carrier. He also grew vegetables and several acres of potatoes.

At first he only had two cart horses and Betty, used to help with ploughing and harrowing.

Later came a 'Fergie' then an International. When the tractor first arrived he was going too fast through a gate and shouted at it to 'Whoa'.

When Jim Crout of Mellowmead was aged eleven, in the 1950s, he helped Dickie spread 'slag' by hand in buckets. It came by train to Newton Abbot station and was delivered in bags at £2 per ton. Slag was waste material from steel mills rich in potash. It was slow acting and was known as 'the old farmer's standby' and was spread at half a ton per acre. Around 1959-60 Jim also helped till potatoes with the old Fergie. It took two days to do two acres of potatoes!

Dickie was a popular village character and was actually born in the Kestor; he was well known in the local hostelries (to which he would sometimes be delivering produce), often giving people lifts via local inns. Although not very tall, he has been described by a friend as a 'big man' who could take anything. He had an aversion to modern inventions and had some old fashioned beliefs; he could never accept that tractors had taken over from horses.

Dickie died in 1984 and the land was taken in hand by the landlord. His wife Betty still lives in the village and their son, Richard, farms locally, having married Sally Harries (daughter of Jim and Jenny who lived for many years at Manaton Gate), a DNP ranger. They have two children.

LEIGHON LODGE AND THE COTTAGES

There are quite a number of Manaton families and names who are associated with Leighon – and a few of them recorded here:

Bill Howe's sister Hettie (Harriet Emily) was cook at Leighon. She married Jim Peters and lived in one of the cottages. Kenneth Dixon lived in the Lodge; his grandfather was the gamekeeper, Mr Piper. Trevor and Mrs Doreen Yates also lived here. Doreen was also a cook at Leighon.

Frank and Alice Coniam were gamekeeper and cook in 1930s–40s. They moved to Woolleigh in Bovey Tracey then to 'Green Loaning' in Chapel Lane. Lena Harvey was Alice Coniam's sister.

Leighon Cottage No.1 was rented by Wing Commander and Mrs French of Great Hound Tor in and after the Second World War, for £13 per annum, for Frank and Florrie Beer. The Beer's daughter, Brenda, was born in her grandparent's house, Neadon Cottage, before they moved to Becky Falls. After Leighon they worked for Betty French and lived at Homer Heales, then at 3 Mellowmead.

Major Walker lived at cottage No.2 c.1964.

Viv Weaving and her children, Peter and Natalie now own one of the cottages. The other is a holiday let.

STORM AND FLOOD 1938

Frank Coniam was gamekeeper and he kept all the pheasant pens and hutches beside the brook. A tremendous storm came on 4–5 August; the whole area was flooded and all the pheasants, their eggs and pens were washed away. The flood then rushed down the valley and hit Becky Falls, completely altering its shape; it used to be much steeper but the top stones toppled off and fell to the bottom.

Left: *Dickie Perryman with his son Richard who now lives at Fordgate.*
Above: *Dickie Perryman.*

BECKAFORD

The house was constructed in the late 1700s, although in the sale particulars of 1899, it states that the house is of comparatively recent construction! It is stone built and slated as are the farm buildings. In the Land Tax Assessments 1780–1830, it is named Beckafords. In 1780 it was owned and occupied by John Christopher; between 1790–1810 it was owned by Ann Christopher and occupied successively by Joseph Winsor and William Holman. Between 1820 and 1830 John Wills owned and occupied the property. It is interesting to note that a William Winsor was renting 'Nedecleave' from Viscount Courtenay between 1780-1800.

In July 1899 it was sold to the Rev. Fox for £2100. Thomas Winsor was in occupation at the time of sale. For many years before, the Winsor family had farmed it as tenants for three generations, starting in the mid 1800s. Eventually it passed from Tommy Winsor to his daughter Lucy Winsor who married Fred Dymond.

Beckaford and, above right, Blue Haze.

His other daughter, Nancy, married Alan Cleave and they farmed at Sigford. By strange coincidence, their son now farms Mill Leat, where Charles Perryman went in 1942.

In 1899 the annual rental was £65 per annum; in 1956 £75, and the same in 1964. In September 1912 it was sold to the Singer Estate by William Russell Fox. The Dymonds farmed until Fred was killed, in 1970, when his tractor overturned in a steep field. They had a daughter, Mildred, who is in New Zealand, and a son, David, who lives in Bovey Tracey.

In 1970 Brian and Jean Rice then took the lease and had a dairy herd of Friesian cows. In 1975 they bought the farm from Leighon Estate.

In 1985 it was bought by Tim Lewis who sold most of the fields on the other side of the road, bar one, to Mr Cullen of Leighon. In 1986 it was bought by the Andersons from Haytor who ran a South Devon suckler herd.

In 1989 Stewart and Tessa Lake purchased it. Stewart is a veterinary surgeon and he and Tessa run a hill farm, including grazing on Black Hill.

BECKAFORD BUNGALOW (Now Blue Haze)

This building is much older than it looks, having originally been built of wood and asbestos by Rev. Fox around a hundred years ago. It is shown on a map of 1912

The history of its occupation (where known) is as follows: 1923 – a family named Braunton; 1926–27 – Colonel and Mrs Francis; 1934 – sold to the Singers; 1937 – empty for 2 years; 1939 – Mrs Piper. In 1944–45 it rented by Mr and Mrs G.W.A. Rowland, in 1956 for £107.2s.0d pa.; in 1964 for £112 pa.

In 1964 it was bought by the Rowlands who had four children. Their daughters Mrs Gaywood and Mrs Walker now live in Moretonhampstead. Their son Michael was shot in Rhodesia; Brian lives in Blackpool.

It was bought in 1974 by Rosalind Barnett and two years later by her son Jimmy. He married Carol in 1977 and had four daughters Sophie, Paula, Louise and Rachel.

Mr and Mrs Barnett improved the house and made it a more solid consruction. Originally the property was supplied by an old ram-pump that kept jamming, and the Barnetts put a new pump in the roof.

When the house was being improved, a room was discovered that had been consecrated and was found to have been a chapel, likely used by Rev. Fox for services.

Mr and Dr Munk bought the house in 1988 and re-named it Blue Haze.

View towards Wingstone from Hayne Down, with the church and Lustleigh Cleave in the background.

Wingstone farmhouse today: home of Peter and Maggie Kapff.

Wingstone farmhouse at the time of the Endacott family occupation in the 1920s.

WINGSTONE

Also known as Winkson, Wyngeston, Wingestone and Winkesdon, it became a farm comprising 104 acres of pasture and arable, and 250 acres of common land, until 1983, when it was divided in half.

The granite farmhouse was originally sixteenth century, but carved granite arches and a pillar have been found which suggest an earlier building. The old kitchen, with dual fireplaces and bedroom above, survived a fire in about 1810, when the rest of the house facing south-east was rebuilt in the Regency style. A sixteenth century fireplace in the main sitting room was also left standing.

The house is in a beautiful situation, with views to the sea at Teignmouth. There are several listed granite outbuildings, including a barn with barn owl holes at each end. Hayne Down is owned by the farm, where Bowerman's Nose has looked down on the comings and goings for thousands of years. Moyles Gate at the south end of Hayne Down is named after a man called Moyle who once lived at the nearby cottage. Swallerton is a corruption of 'Swine-a-down' and it was once a cider-house named 'The Houndtor Inn'.

The earliest surviving lease for Wingstone is dated 1569:

Lease for two lives
1. William French, yeoman Slapton
2. John Frenche the younger, husbandman, Manaton.

Consideration: 100 marks
Premises: messuage, land and tenement called Wyngeston, parish of Manaton, with common of pasture on Hayne Downe.
Rent: 40s quarterly.

Some early leases exist between the Courtenays and the Frenches (1764 and 1812). Others refer to land leased from the Nosworthys (1679) and to the 'Winkson and farmland' (1819).

In 1873 Nathan Stone is renting the farm but not the house and garden, as is the same in 1878 for Elizabeth (widow) and John Hannaford. Nevertheless the records show that a member of the French or Ffrench family lived at and or rented Wingstone from the sixteenth century until the late 1800s. An interesting lease is to Walter Campion, a blacksmith from Ilsington in 1735. It is a consideration of 5 pounds for the Smith's shop, newly erected near Crosspark Close belonging to Wingstone.

The roundhouse at Wingstone. These buildings were to be found on many farms and contained horse-works, or whims, which enabled horse power to drive various pieces of farm equipment. This pen and wash drawing, which hangs at Wingstone, was made by John Galsworthy's nephew, R.H. Sauter, a refugee in the Great War who stayed with the Galsworthys c.1914. Sauter was a significant figure in the Belgian Impressionist movement.

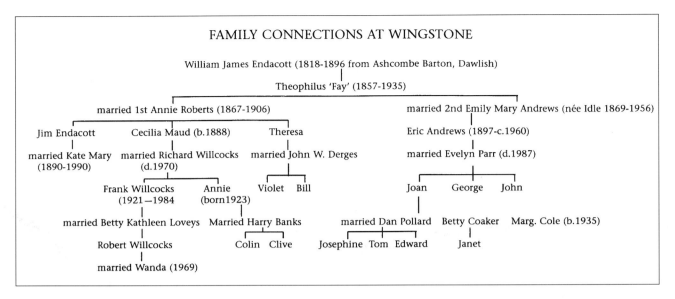

FAMILY CONNECTIONS AT WINGSTONE

William James Endacott (1818-1896 from Ashcombe Barton, Dawlish)

Theophilus 'Fay' (1857-1935)

married 1st Annie Roberts (1867-1906)   married 2nd Emily Mary Andrews (née Idle 1869-1956)

Jim Endacott   Cecilia Maud (b.1888)   Theresa   Eric Andrews (1897-c.1960)

married Kate Mary   married Richard Willcocks   married John W. Derges   married Evelyn Parr (d.1987)
(1890-1990)   (d.1970)

Frank Willcocks   Annie   Violet   Bill   Joan   George   John
(1921—1984   (born1923)

married Betty Kathleen Loveys   Married Harry Banks   married Dan Pollard   Betty Coaker   Marg. Cole (b.1935)

Robert Willcocks   Colin   Clive   Josephine   Tom   Edward   Janet

married Wanda (1969)

Land Tax Assessments show that in 1780 Alice French was paying £2.18s.2½d, as were John and Thomas French through to 1830, and at that time they actually owned the farm. Thomas French was leasing land in 1873, and was buried in the churchyard in 1891.

It is also known that Theophilus Endacott rented Wingstone from a French at the end of the nineteenth century and his father, William James Endacott died at Wingstone in 1896, aged 88. Theophilus died in 1935, when the farm was taken over by Eric Andrews, the son of his second wife , Emily Mary. The Andrews succeeded in buying the farm in 1945 from Colonel William Percy French.

Theo (whose nickname was Fay) had two daughters by his first marriage; Maud married Richard Willcocks, whose brother Herbert farmed Torhill, and their son Frank worked on the farm when he was young. Theresa married John Derges. Before Theo's first wife, Annie, died, she went up to London on the Galsworthys' behalf, to testify that they were living together as man and wife, this was to help in obtaining Ada's divorce from John Galsworthy's cousin. There was also a sister living with him, named Thurza (1854–1927), dying at Wingstone.

Theo was from a family of seven sisters and seven brothers a number of whom died young. Theo was also looking after nephews Jim and Clifford Endacott.

Frank Willcocks married Betty Katherine Loveys and they farmed Oxenham Farm, Sigford, where their son Robert was born in 1947. Maud lived in a bungalow nearby. Frank had a sister, Cecilia Anne, who married Harry Bateson Banks; they have a son Colin Clive.

Theophilus and his second wife looked after John and Ada Galsworthy, from 1906 to 1924. The horses were stabled on the farm and Mrs Endacott cooked for the Galsworthys and their guests on a big open fire in the kitchen and later a range; the meals were carried through to the front of the house on trays. This meant that Mr and Mrs Endacott, Eric, Thurza their aunt, other children, dependants and farm hands all lived and ate in the kitchen. Nevertheless the Galsworthys were very generous when they left

Cecilia Maude Endacott wife of Richard Willcocks.

Left: *Theophilus Endacott with his flock at Wingstone c.1920.*

Below: *Theophilus with his family, from left: Theresa, Jim, Cecilia and Emily (née Andrews).*

Below left: *Theresa Endacott*

Above: *Richard Willcocks.*

Above Left: *Frank Willcocks, son of Cecilia and Richard.*

Left: *The Dairy School certificate given to Mrs Willcocks in 1908. Devon County Council ran dairy schools throughout the county at this time, teaching modern hygienic methods of dairying.*

Joseph Willcocks with his grandson Frank, at Wingstone

and Mrs Endacott was given most of the household furniture, effects and paintings.

Eric Andrews enlisted in 1914 – Galsworthy noted that he was a first rate rider and shot. He joined the Devon Yeomanry and was sent to the Dardanelles where he lost an arm, and was later fitted with an artificial limb, despite which he was still a proficient rabbit shooter. Margaret Andrews still has the arm!

John Mortimore, born Neadon 1892, looked after Galsworthy's horses when they were at Wingstone.

At Hayne there were two very ancient farms, North and South Hayne, long since gone. In the land tax records they were owned by the Frenches. Hemery in *High Dartmoor* states that:

> under the E.N.E. shoulder of Hayne Down is the ancient border farm, from which Down and Brook took their name. In 1637 a daughter of the Northcote family of Hayne married an Elford of Longstone.

In those days Hayne Cottage belonged to Wingstone, and Theophilus' nephew, Jim Endacott, and his wife, Kate Mary, lived there and worked on the farm until Eric took over. They

Left: *The marriage of Eric Andrews and Evelyn Parr.*

Below: *Three generations at Wingstone: Mr and Mrs Eric Andrews, Mrs Endacott, Joan, George and John Andrews.*

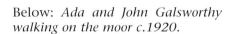

Left: *Emily Endacott (née Andrews) was housekeeper to the Galsworthys from 1906-1924. The story of the Galsworthys at Wingstone would warrant a book in its own right and the current owner, Maggie Kapff, along with her husband Peter, has gathered a great deal of information and many photographs relating to the Galsworthys time there. Many of the greatest literary and political figures of the day came to stay at Wingstone and it was clearly influential in many of John Galsworthy's writings.*

Below: *Working at Wingstone in the 1920s.*

Below: *Ada and John Galsworthy walking on the moor c.1920.*

Below right: *John Galsworthy on 'Peggy' at Wingstone 1918.*

then went to Ifforford Farm, Widecombe, and retired to Water Cottages, Manaton. Kate died in 1990 aged 100.

The next occupants of Hayne, 1935-1941, were Bill and Lilian Lentern. Bill was employed as a farm labourer at Wingstone and Lilian is remembered for presenting the Lilian Lentern Cup, which is given each year at the Show and Fair.

There was a round house at Wingstone, which was blown down in the forties, containing a horse-work or 'whim', the drive of which went through the barn wall, and was used for threshing and chaff cutting etc. Most farms in Manaton either had a horse-work or water-wheel. Round houses still survive at Town Barton and Deal.

Wingstone was a mixed farm, with sheep, South Devon cows for milk and meat, corn, root vegetables, and pigs. Mrs Endacott made butter and clotted cream. The Galsworthys noted that nearly all their food was grown on the spot, with heather honey on the comb, homemade cider, and junkets laced with homemade sloe gin. The well-stocked orchard provided apples, plums, and pears.

Farm workers during 1920s and 30s were, among others, John Mortimore, Wilfred Creber, Pat Perryman, and the Lenterns who lived at Hayne. There were also work horses to look after: 'Lion', 'Prince' and 'Grey', until the first Ferguson tractors appeared in the late 1930s. There was open house amongst the young, and Charles Crout, Cyril Skerrett and Norman Perryman still remember happy times playing on the farm and a generous welcome in the kitchen.

Derrick Cowling, the nephew of Phyllis Clements, recalls:

Happy memories include many visits to Wingstone, my sister Pat and I had huge teas in the kitchen. My favourite was bread golden syrup and a thick layer of clotted cream. On the farm John Andrews tried to teach me hand milking, this usually developed into a milk fight. When we were supposed to be picking up potatoes, these proved excellent ammunition to hurl at each other!

Times were hard farming in the 1930s and wool was kept back and saved until the next year to no avail, the hard fact being that farming makes more money in times of war. During the war the front of the house was rented to two single ladies, one of whom, Miss Affleck, died at Wingstone and is buried in the churchyard.

Mrs and Mrs G. Harris:
The Andrews left in 1947–8, and the farm was bought by Mr and Mrs Harris who had come from Bovey Tracey. They were mainly interested in horses, and Mrs Harris rode side-saddle, among her horses being 'Mac' and 'Wings'.

Mr and Mrs Cyril Daw:
In Bovey Tracey, Cyril Daw had worked for the Harrises, and he came up with them, and lived in the end of Mill Farm (East Corn Mill) for a year while Mrs Harris built another bedroom and a new kitchen at Hayne Cottage. The Daws had previously worked for the Rev. Kitson at Heatree, and their son Peter was born at a cottage in Heathercombe.

They lived at Hayne from 1949–1960, and in 1951 Mrs Harris leased the farm to them, keeping a few fields for her horses. She also sold them the existing live and deadstock for £2091, at prices which are fascinating to compare with today.

Cyril and Olive had five children, Peter, Michael, Wendy, Cicely and Margaret. In 1960 they all moved to Landulph in East Cornwall using cattle lorries, Cyril driving the tractor and baler. Brian Warne from Southcott helped them move and stayed on to settle them in. The girls have all married and had families. Peter farmed for a while and then went to gardening, and Michael is still farming at Whitchurch.

Mr Lee and then Mr Wadsworth bought Wingstone and Hayne in 1960 and early 1961, two very short ownerships.

Mr and Mrs Eric Biggs:
In 1961 it was bought by Pearl and Eric Biggs, who farmed it until 1970. Their two daughters Sue and Sally worked on the farm.

There is a vivid account of the winter 1962–1963 told by their daughter Susan Haughton:

The snow started 28 December 1962 with a terrific blizzard that filled the drive with snow, it snowed the next day with bitter winds and freezing conditions and again on 3 January. The snow came halfway up the french windows on the verandah. There was no water, and we got it from the stream and the well, drinking water came in a churn from the Kestor Inn. Water came back mid January. We had 180 sheep in the yard; a narrow path was cleared down to the Mill and up the road to the Green and down the drive. The sheep were walked along this to give them exercise as they were in lamb. More heavy

Inventory & Valuation

of

LIVE & DEAD FARMING STOCK at WINGSTONE FARM, MANATON.

Property of Mrs E.S.HARRIS taken over at March 25th.

1951 by Mr Cyril Daw.

F. Inspected March 27th. 1951. VB/33/CHH.

Valuation.

		£.	s	d
BULLOCKS. (South Devons)				
"Heather" Heifer in milk.		50		
" Mary Petre" Cow in milk & calf.		48		
" Sibyl" Heifer calved Feby 19th.		52		
" Sarah" Cow in milk calved Feby 14th.		50		
" Buttercup" Cow in milk & calf.		45		
" Furzy Top" Heifer in milk & calf.		58		
3 Steers 18 mos to 2 yrs old.		100		
1 Heifer.	@ 26/-/-	45		
2 Heifers.	@ 21/-/-	52		
2 Steers.	@ 18/-/-	42		
3 Heifers.		54		
1 Steer.	@ 11/-/-	14		
4 Steer Calves.	@ 14/-/-	44		
3 Heifer Calves.	@ 6/-/-	42		
3 Steer Calves.		18		
		714		
PIGS.				
9 Suckers.	@ 50/-	22	10	
Cross bred Sow(3 litters)		12		
SHEEP.				
12 Closewood Ewes 6 th and full mouth.				
20 Ewes 2ths.				
& 32 lambs.				
(2 Barren Ewes and 2 Ewes not lambed	6/10/-	208		
are included in the Ewes above)		99		
22 Ewe Hoggs.	@ 90/-	9		
2 Wethers.	@ 90/-	6	6	
1 Closewool Ram.				
HORSE.				
" Blossom" Grey Mare 6 yrs. abt 15.2hh.		52	10	
Set nearly new Cart Breeching.		12		
POULTRY.etc.				
12 Buff Rock Hens.	@ 15/-	9		
G. I Hen Coop.		3		
6ft X 4ft. Timber Poultry House.		6		
150 yds of 6ft Netting and posts		7	5	
comprising run.		5		
2 rolls Sheep netting.		6	15	
150 yards of Rabbit netting	@ 45/-	6		
Poultry Ark.				
	c/fwd.	1178	6	

Above: *Inventory and valuation of live and dead-stock at Wingstone at the time of its sale to Cyril Daw in 1951.*

Above right: *Olive and Cyril Daw at work in the harvest field, Hayne 1956.*

Centre: *Margaret Daw at Hayne, 1956.*

Right: *Cyril Daw ploughing 1st field in front of Hayne, Easter 1957.*

blizzards came on 2, 4, 5 February, and the road to Bovey was cut off. There was still snow hanging about in the second week in March.

Most people needed cattle and sheep fodder, but the blizzards meant that helicopters could not be used. A huge 4 wheel-drive army lorry came to us and it got stuck in the yard, and was winched up the drive on the beech trees, one tree at a time. The sheep in the yard used to be against the door, and they fell in when you tried to open it. More than once my father, who was a slight man, was carried along on the backs of the sheep, with buckets flying everywhere at feeding time.

When it finally thawed, a local farmer and his son took the muck out of the yard and it was two feet thick.

At the worst of the freeze, I found a cow, not ours, on the road absolutely frozen stiff, it was still breathing and couldn't move, even though it was standing up. The owner came with bales of straw, and rubbed her all over until he could move her.

It was actually a very beautiful time, and once the blizzards stopped the sun came out. Until the roads were cleared, anyone who had a Land Rover would shop for everyone else. People who didn't normally go to the pub, all walked there, and it brought the village together.

People who lived up at the Laneside and Southcott area, would walk to the village on top of the hedges.

We milked 18 Jerseys, and kept big flat pans of milk in the larder and skimmed the lovely yellow cream off, and sometimes had it on our cornflakes. The milk was taken up to the top of the drive in churns. We had to sell the dairy cows when we had more beef cattle, as we were not allowed the beef subsidy if we were milking.

The cattle were mainly Galloways with an Angus bull, but sometimes we hired a Hereford bull from the Shilstons at Torhill farm. We had Scotch Blackface sheep when we started, but spent all our time looking for them, so then we went to Devon Closewool, and a few Dorset Horns.

Sue taught the Sunday School with May Towning. One of the pupils, Jenifer Greenaway, remembers that when Miss Towning's house, Cherry Trees, was being built, the pupils helped dig the foundations, and put a time capsule under one of the corners; it was a tin containing coins, *Parish News* and the names of the children who helped.

When Sue and Sally got married, the farm was

too much for the Biggs. Eric loved his animals and was always very considerate to them, they were always sold in top condition. The Biggs moved to a smaller farm in North Devon.

Mrs and Mrs Tom Corkery:
Tom Corkery bought the farm in 1970, and as he was still running his garage at Peamore, his son-in-law D.F. Gaze and daughter Wendy ran the farm. This inscription was found under wall paper in June 1990:

> *D.F. Gaze, farm worker Nov. 1970, at time of alteration July 1973.*
> *60 single suckler beef cows, (Galloway and Hereford cross)*
> *120 sheep Exmoor half bred.*
> *6 sows.*
> *10 acres sheep keep 1 year.*
> *10 acres oats 1 year.*
> *Buy in all hay.*
> *Wife Wendy (née Corkery)*
> *Children, Christopher 4yrs, Joanne l8 months.*

The Corkerys had a second daughter, Joan, who was married from Wingstone, and the Gazes emigrated to New Zealand.

Tom ran the farm with a suckler herd and was well known in the South Devon Hunt, sporting a top hat. On becoming slightly lame, he had a new house built on farm land for a manager, and divided the farm in half in 1983, moving into the new house, and running a mixed suckler herd. He died in 1993 and this house and farm was eventually sold to the Rich family.

For eighteen months from 1983, the Baverstocks ran the old farm, but it was difficult to sustain a dairy herd on 60 acres of in-by and Hayne Down, and they sold in 1985.

Dr and Mrs P.E. Kapff:
Peter and Maggie bought Wingstone in October 1985, and run a mixed suckler herd, now mainly Galloway and Scotch Blackface and Cheviot cross sheep, and also a small flock of Black Welsh mountain. These hardy hill breeds have been chosen so that they can out-winter on Hayne Down, which is still part of the farm. The only real disaster apart from the 1990s beef crisis and lamb dropping to half price, has been the gales in 1990, when several beech trees blew down, blocked the drive and main road, and there was no telephone or electricity for two weeks. Since then a generator has been bought.

BLISSMOOR

The history of Blissmoor is controversial. It may have been built to house the manager of the tin mine, the remains of which lie in the little valley below. Behind it are ruins of old granite buildings which may have been part of Cripdon.

The whole area is covered with remains of earlier occupiers, from Bronze Age field systems and reaves, to spoil heaps left by miners. In the first records available, it is let by the Kitsons to Jack Perryman and his wife Emerita; he was a shoemaker (see section on Cripdon) in the early 1920s. Then Jack and Ena Harvey had it; it is thought they bought it from the Kitsons. He was a warrener and mole catcher, also running a smallholding and keeping pigs.

At some point a Russian couple named Sevitsky lived here. Serge was a Cossack cavalry colonel and is said to have earned money riding bareback in the circus. His wife was a ballerina and it is said they came over to escape the Russian Revolution.

In 1963-1964 a Mr Bluck bought Blissmoor for £1000. He was a crime reporter for the *News of the World*. He also owned the Highwayman's Haunt Inn near Chudleigh and had four children.

From 1964 onwards Blissmoor has been the home of Clem and Margaret Otho Briggs who bought it for £3750. They have added a bathroom and made many improvements. Clem has taken a number of the recent photos used in this book.

NOBODY ASKS FOR THE KEY OF "BLISSMOOR"

Woman of the Sad Face Lived There

This is "Blissmoor" and its garden as they appear to-day.

"SUNDAY EMPIRE NEWS" REPORTER
Manaton, Devon, Saturday.

AN empty cottage stands on the edge of Dartmoor not far from here. There is a housing shortage in the neighbourhood and the local council would requisition the cottage if anybody wanted to live there. But nobody does.

They call the cottage "Blissmoor." Behind its staring windows lies the story of Serge Sevitsky and his beautiful Russian wife—a story that began many years ago in the pomp and glitter that was the Imperial Russian Court.

Serge was then a dashing cavalry colonel, his wife a dainty ballerina in the Imperial ballet. They fell in love, married, and were happy until the revolution brought their world toppling around them.

Humble haven

Serge brought his bride to...

Part of a somewhat sensational newspaper cutting from the Sunday Empire News *reporting the mystery of the cossack who lived a Blissmoor.*

Top left: *Florence (Ruby),
Arthur and Doris Brown
in deep snow c.1940.*

Top right: *Arthur Brown
ploughing at Heatree c.
1935.*

Centre: *Barracott today.*

Right: *Ruby (left) and
Doris Brown 1999.*

BARRACOTT AND BOODOWN

Barracott has also been known as Barrow Cott or Boda's Cot, the latter from a personal name. Barracott is a longhouse and a Grade 2 listed building which remained with its shippon at one end until the late 1880s. The shippon was converted to a second cottage in the early 1900s.

It was another Nosworthy property, eventually to pass into the Kitson estate. In the wills there is mention of Higher and Lower Barracott, but this could refer to the field names.

In 1764 Lower Barracott was 28 acres and farmed by Jane, John and Andy Whedon. Upper Barracott was 36 acres and farmed by John Langdon.

The story of Kitty Jay has also been connected with this farm by some people, and two separate persons have seen the ghost of a young girl upstairs in the old part of the farm.

The will of John Nosworthy of Coombe, North Bovey, who died in June 1832, records: 'To my wife Ann, one-fifth part of Higher Barracott, Lower Barracott, Cann etc.' His eldest son, also John Nosworthy, married Mary Pethybridge of Barracott. John and Mary had three sons and three daughters. John died in 1842, leaving his estate to his wife and children. It eventually passed into the Kitson estate and was lived in by Mr and Mrs Mortimore, whose daughter, Florence, was born at Barracott in 1885. She married Robert Hitchens at Manaton Church in 1906 (see pages 37-38).

Mr and Mrs William Brown moved there with four children at the turn of the century. They had come from Cleave Cottage on The Manor House estate in North Bovey. During the renovations when Barracott was eventually made into two cottages, the family moved to Cripdon Cottage before the Perrymans lived there. They moved back to the end nearest the road for one shilling a week rent. They had six more children Arthur, Doris, Ruby, Rose, Mabel and Lilian. Mr Brown ('Whackam') worked on the roads and blasted rocks with Alexander 'Zander' Crout, and trapped rabbits. Arthur later worked on the Heatree estate.

In the early 1900s, occupants of the east end of the house were Mr and Mrs Williams from Hatherleigh. Then came the Churchwards, Mr and Mrs Marsh, Mr and Mrs Charles Perryman and Mr and Mrs Ash.

Barracott was sold to the Shilstons with Torhill in 1937. They kept the land and the house was rented to the Browns and Ashes. These two families lived there until 1948. Barracott was then sold and the Browns went to Ivy Collage on Manaton Green and the Ashes to Fordgate. Doris and Ruby Brown still live in Ivy Cottage and have wonderful memories, many of which they have shared for use in this book. Both sisters served in the WAAF during the Second World War, Ruby being Mentioned in Dispatches.

Barracott has had many owners since 1968. They include Mr and Mrs Wood, Mr and Mrs James, and Jim and Val Lee (1986-1996). Jim became treasurer to the P.C.C. and he and Val later moved to Bovey Tracey.

BOWERMAN'S COTTAGE

Bowerman's Cottage was a barn converted by Gilbert and Alban Shilston for their parents, but they never moved in. It was rented by the Lenterns after they left Hayne. Miss Betty Bindloss who then lived in Highweek, bought it in 1964 for a weekend cottage. She also let other family members and the Girl Guides use it. Before her death in September 1999, Miss Bindloss had been a stalwart of the village, being a member and at one time chairman pf the PC. She was also a JP and had a lifetime involvement with the Girl Guides, culminating as County Commissioner.

In 1969 she sold the cottage to the Girl Guide Association for a small sum, and bought Easdon Cottage from her friends the Lees. She later moved to Ridge Road, and then to Bovey Tracey.

BOODOWN

Boodown is a farm above Barracott built by the Shilstons, David, Pam, Kevin and Tina. David Shilston rears cattle and sheep. Pam works at the Moretonhampstead Health Centre.

The aptly named farmer Farmer (fourth from right), his family and workers, proudly displaying the certificates awarded to them for dairying skills c.1900.

Highly Desirable Freehold
STOCK-RAISING and DAIRY FARM
KNOWN AS
"LANGSTONE"

Situated mid-way between the Villages of North Bovey and Manaton, being about 1½ miles from each, about 12 miles from Newton Abbot, with Weekly Market, 15 miles from Exeter, with Weekly Market, 3 miles from Moretonhampstead, 6 miles from Bovey Tracey (with Station, G.W.R.), 7 miles from Chagford and 10 miles from Ashburton. The Property is within easy reach of some of the best known of Devon's Beauty Spots—Haytor Rocks about 2 miles, Becky Falls about 2½ miles and Lustleigh Cleave about 3½ miles.

The Attractive Ivy-covered Farm House

is substantially built of stone, stuccoed on the exterior, with slated roof, is approached by way of a 13th Century arched gateway, along a path lined by Box Hedges to the Front Porch with 13th Century Arch. The Property stands well back from the road and contains :—

13th Century Entrance Porch with seats,

Tiled ENTRANCE HALL with built-in cupboard,

LOUNGE, measuring about 15 ft. 6 in. by 12 ft. 8 in., with fitted bookcase with cupboard under, and fitted cupboard, fitted fireplace with white marble mantelpiece and surround,

DINING ROOM, measuring about 16 ft. by 13 ft. 9 ins., with fitted red tiled fireplace, window seats and three built-in cupboards,

KITCHEN, measuring about 15 ft. by 10 ft., with fitted aluminium sink and draining boards in green enamel ; Ideal " Cookanheat " No. 20 range, two built-in cupboards and fitted window seat and with beamed ceiling and tiled floor ;

BACK ENTRANCE LOBBY leading to large CONSERVATORY,

DAIRY with tiled floor and fitted shelves,

STORE with fitted shelves,

BATHROOM with bath (hot and cold), sink (hot and cold), and draining boards ; built-in cupboard ;

Outside W.C.

Left: *Sale document from 1953 when the Hugos purchased Langstone.*

Above: *Ray Hugo at Langstone.*

LANGSTONE

Langstone (*Langatone*) has been occupied since the Bronze Age and the remnants of a hut circle are still to be seen there. The manor of *Langestan*, as it was known, was one of four properties in Manaton Parish recorded in the Domesday Book (Neadon, Manaton and Hound Tor being the others). Owned then by Baldwin, Sheriff of Devonshire, it was tenanted by one, Hugh, and comprised 4 ferdings and 2 ploughs, mostly managed by free-men (a ferding was a measure used in the Domesday Book but the size is not known. It is thought to comprise a few acres only). At the time of record, the manor supported 4 villeins (free-men), 4 boarders, 1 serf, 2 beasts, 3 swine, 11 goats and 13 sheep. In all, there were 11 acres of meadow and 12 acres of pasture, the lot worth 10 shillings a year.

The buildings recorded in Domesday have long since been replaced but the main building is thought to have been on the site of the present Great Barn.

Subsequent records are silent until the year 1580, when Andrew Heyward, yeoman and scion of the modern Heyward family, was born at Langstone. It is not known how long the Heyward family had already owned Langstone, but they were to keep it until 1915. The Heyward name is well-known throughout the district with family members having farmed in the parishes of Manaton, North Bovey, Moreton, Lustleigh and Chagford on the moor, and in Highweek, West Ogwell and Wolborough, all near Newton Abbot. A comprehensive history of the family has been published.

The farmhouse is of longhouse pattern, with the barn behind it thought to contain remains of the old manor. The present porch has a thirteenth century arch. The church rate in 1613 was 3s.8d.

All of the following are buried in Manaton Churchyard: Andrew Heyward born Langstone (1580–1655); Richard Heyward (1610–1667) of Langstone and Upper Langstone, married Thomasine French of Manaton; Andrew Heyward (1640–1719), married Susan; Richard Heyward (1689–1771), married Mary Smerdon of Buckland-in-the-Moor; William Heyward (1722–1803) married Margery; William Heyward (1764–1847), married Mary Nosworthy of Neadon. Thomas Heywood (1793–1874), married Elizabeth Heyward of Sanduck and their son Thomas lost three fingers in the Boer War, emigrating to British Columbia; daughter Ellen (1828–1900) married John Eveleigh, farmer 1869; John Thomas Heyward Farmer (b.1870) married Emily Jane Merchant, 1894; their daughters Dorothy Mary (b.1895) and Gladys Mary (b.1911).

John Thomas Heyward and his wife, Emily, farmed Langstone until 1918, when they sold the farm and moved to Moretonhampstead. Billy Peake then bought it; he employed a farm girl called Beattie Squires. Then four unknown families farmed it until it was eventually put up for sale and purchased by Ray and Mary Hugo. The farm was then 114 acres, 1 rood and 36 poles and became 130 acres.

Ray Hugo recalls that up to the 1950s the farm relied on hand labour and horses. Prior to 1939 the farm was self-sufficient in feedstuffs and the water-wheel and thresher were in place. Subsidies started in 1937, involving the returns of details of livestock, crops etc.

At the outbreak of war, committees came into being to oversee what crops should be grown. Much permanent pasture was ploughed up to enable cereals to be grown, this continued until the early 1950s. By this time mechanisation was becoming widely used, including milking machines, and tractors. This period marked the end of the old ways.

By this time many more subsidies were available for things such as calf rearing, lime and slag. There were also guaranteed prices for cereals. The Milk Marketing Board fixed the price of milk on a monthly basis, higher in winter than summer.

Most of the farms produced milk, this being collected daily in 10 gallon churns and taken to Daws Creameries in Totnes. A milk stand survives outside Langstone Cottage.

When Ray first started farming he had an attested herd of Ayrshires which he bought for £80 each. He had 50 Devon Closewools and a Dorset Down ram in the 1950s. In 1960 wool was 4s.1d per lb. There were subsidies on ploughing, lime, slag, and heifer calves, make-up on lambs and a marginal land grant. Clarks from North Bovey were his contractors.

The Hugos, with their two daughters, Alison and Jane, now also ran a B&B business.

Mains electricity came in 1950. There was a ram pump for water in the yard, mains water came in 1976 from Fernworthy. When bulk milk collection started at about the same time. Ray gave up milking and ran a suckler herd of Hereford cross Friesian cows with a Hereford bull and later a Charolais. Jim Crout worked on the farm for some time in the 1960s.

Ray and Mary are great supporters of village life. Ray was on the Parish Council for 24 years and was three times the Chairman. He was Chairman of the British Legion and the Show and Fair. He is on the PCC and for 16 years he has been a churchwarden.

Ray always calls a spade a spade, a straight forward man with a wonderful sense of humour. Mary is well known for her work for charity, the Christmas Fair, and lately the Children's Hospice and Moreton Hospital have benefited from her hard work.

The farm was bought by Mr and Mrs Michael Hurd in 1986. Mr Hurd died in 1995 and Margot still lives there and lets the land. Ray and Mary Hugo enjoy their retirement at their home in Ridge Road.

Above: *Langstone cottage c.1910. This beautiful thatched cottage has remained pretty much unchanged since this picture was taken. It has been the home of Mrs Rickard for many years.*

Left: *Two young ladies having fun in tin baths at the garden of Langstone Cottage c.1900.*

MILL FARM (EAST CORN MILL) AND MILL COTTAGE

In the seventeenth century Mill Farm was originally The East Corn Mill in Manaton, the West Mill being at Heathercombe. The actual wheel was against the west wall of the house, fed by the mill pond and a leat which came across the fields of Wingstone from Hayne Brook. The Mill is now a Grade II listed restored thatched house, still with a mill pond and about 4 acres of ground. In early days there was a little house on the Hayne Brook, north of the Mill called Mill Cottage.

Land Tax Assessments identify the following owners and occupiers:

Date	Owner	Occupier
1780	William Moore	Grace Moore
1790	ditto	William Moore
1800	Peter Tarr	Peter Tarr
1830	John Tarr	John Lewes

Peter Tarr was also the owner of West Mill between 1810–1830.

Records reveal a few of the people associated with this property: in 1820 a bargain and sale is recorded between Peter Tarr, Miller, Manaton, William Tarr shoemaker Manaton, and Joseph Gribble of Ashburton, for 'Part of land belonging to the Mills £7.' In 1872 there existed an account of succession in real property of George Tarr on death of Sybella Tarr widow, deceased, and another in 1882 from George Tarr to Thomas French concerning debts.

A map of 1906 shows East Corn Mill (disused), so presumably it became a private dwelling at the turn of the century.

At this time it seems to have been owned by the Frenches, and was let in two parts to various tenants. Later on it was rented by Jim Harvey and used to house farm workers at Town Barton.

Mr and Mrs Lewis and Gwen Hern Senr lived there in 1920s–40s, in the Mill end. Mr and Mrs Heath and their sons, Francis and Tom, lived there in the 1930s and then went to Doccombe. They worked for Jim Harvey and Jim Dunning. Jim Harvey's son, Sid, also lived there.

In 1956 the farm was bought by Val and Gerry Pilkington from Mrs Bentley-Taylor (née French) for £800; they rented an extra 25 acres and ran a small farm.

Will and Sid Perryman were in the east end as sitting tenants up to Sid's death in the early 1980s. In 1960 it was sold to the Thurlows who stayed for

Charlie Crout at Mill Cottage.

eight years and then in 1968 sold to the Murrays who kept pigs. In 1969 it was bought by Mr Millard a probation officer. In the 1970s Mr and Mrs Norman Corkery owned it, then 1986–7 Mr and Mrs Douglas Geikie. Circa 1991 Mr and Mrs David Faber (he came from the Faber publishing family and later became an MP) made extensive alterations, and added a new wing. In 1994 David and Joyce McEwan Mason with two daughters and one son purchased the property and live there at the time of writing.

MILL COTTAGE

In the early 1900s this cottage was rented by Mr and Mrs Alexander ('Zander') Crout. Charles Crout, father of James (Jim), was born there. The Crouts then bought Freelands Cottages in the 1920s, living in one and renting the other to Mr Snell, a cobbler.

From 1923–4 and up to 1933 Mr and Mrs Arthur Skerrett lived here with their two sons, and their daughter Margaret was born there. Margaret's grandfather was James Howe, the postman, who lived in Cross Park. They moved to the flat behind Laneside before it was rebuilt. Margaret still lives in Moretonhampstead.

Miss Wadland then kept a little shop here from which she sold sweets, tobacco and a few groceries all kept in boxes in a little shed at the back. This was later moved to the old school house.

Miss Wadland was the last to live at Mill Cottage and it was pulled down about 1960.

Above, clockwise from top left: Mill Farm porch and Mill farmyard in the mid 1950s; the back of the mill showing its position nestling into the hillside; 'Zander' Crout gardening at Freelands in the 1920s.

GLEBE FARM AND GLEBE TERRIERS

This was the farm surrounding the Rectory, traditionally owned by the incumbent Rector. In 1679 this was the Rev. Richard Eastchurch and the holding was considerable. Besides the 'Old Parsonage House' there was a house and cottage behind. The dwelling house had:

1 hall, 1 parlour, 1 kitchen, 1 buttery, 4 chambers and a study. The floor of the kitchen and buttery are paved with stones, the hall is boarded and the parlour earth. There is l barn, 1 stable, 1 shippon and 1 bakehouse in which there is one chamber. The walls of the house are stone.

It is unclear if this refers to the Parsonage or the house, but it is probably the former because of the gardens. There are two gardens called Higher and Lower Garden containing half an acre lying behind the dwelling house. There are then fields divided into 33 acres between the road, churchyard, school and Horsham.

Returns are the same until 1727 when '1 cellar, hall partly wainscotted and stables etc.' are added.

From 1780 to 1830 the owner was William Carwithen and the occupier Robert Nosworthy. From 1880 the Revd Carwithen occupied the property.

Dorothy Earle bought four Glebe fields in the 1920s, the rest are either built on or divided up between Half Moon, Town Barton, Cross Park, Ebworthy and others. The field names include: Blondwells, Crosshills, Gullaston, Wester Park, Horsham Hill, Langapark, a moor called Broadlands, Shrublands, Tor Park, Crofthills, Dall(?) Park, George Park, Santerre, Shoole Park and Fforeherne.

LATCHEL

The origin of the name of this property is obscure. On the Tithe map of 1842 it is referred to as Letchole and appears to have been assessed as part and parcel of Water. The house was built around 1890 and was originally called Park Villa, but it is appropriate to include it among the farms for it has long been Manaton's dairy, run by Paulie James. She latterly gave up dairying as more stringent regulations were brought in. Those who recall the trip along Chapel Lane to fetch a pint or two of deliciously creamy milk, leaving payment in a dish on the counter, or writing up in a book the amount of milk taken, bemoan the passing of those days.

Paulie James' father returned from Canada just prior to the First World War to join the army but because of a medical disability was unable to continue soldiering and took up farming instead.

The family then moved to Latchel in 1918. He began with one cow on one acre to supply his own family of six, but soon expanded to three cows as the locals began to appreciate the quality of the milk (and there was a lot of TB around in those days). The family began by making butter and selling off the scald or skimmed milk at about one old penny a pint. There were no bottles but small cans which continued to be the way until the late 1930s. By 1922 they were selling from the dairy the first full milk to villagers.

Milk was raw, virtually straight from the cow. It was unpasteurised but in those days regulations were lax if not non-existent. The business extended to cream and then ice cream, the latter being wheeled round the village in a push chair!

During the period between the wars there was no wholesale collection of milk so local farmers would make butter and cream and take it to sell at the local markets, while the skimmed milk was fed to pigs or calves. The delivery of bottled milk locally started in 1936 with deliveries to about a dozen village houses. The war brought rationing and the milk round was extended using a bicycle with a crate.

Bulk collections were started with churns picked up from stands at Town Barton and on the roadside at Deal Cross. Increasing restrictions on the processing of milk during and after the war caused many producers to give up but the James's continued with a larger delivery round of bottled milk. Paulie ran the round during the 1950s using an old Standard Nine and then a new Austin Eight bought for just over £300. 'Ginger' Clements, who began the paper round after the war took over the round for several years. In the mid 1970s Peter Manners-Chapman took over both the paper and milk rounds and his two sons would bottle the milk before leaving for school. Daily deliveries were reduced to four and then three days a week. Helen Moss took over the milk delivery for a while until Paulie decided to sell milk only from the dairy in the mid 1980s.

Sadly the era of the Latchel Dairy ended in May 1999 when Paulie sold her last pint of milk, the victim of increasing regulation and inspection costs. As well as her regular customers, Paulie had supplied milk to Manaton Cricket Club for their teas, and many a visiting team commented on the richness of 'real' Devon milk. Paulie's family and her small herd of Guernsey cows had served the people of Manaton for over 80 years.

The milk must get through! Milk deliveries by horse and sledge from Manaton Dairy at Latchel to Ridge Road c.1945.

Farming scenes in Manaton from Paulie James' photo album show how fast things have changed in a few decades. All work here involved horse-power and hard physical labour. Even going to school was by horse power - Paulie is off to her tutor in the picture above right. Note also that the observatory tower in the photo (top left) has its glass dome intact. All these pictures were taken in the 1920s, except for the portrait of Paulie which was snapped at Manaton Show in August 1999.

THE HAMBLEDEN ESTATE

In 1890 the Rt Hon. W.H. Smith (of newsagent fame) bought a large holding from the Earl of Devon whose family had owned it for 500 years.

The estate included 5000 acres around Moretonhampstead, North Bovey and Manaton. In 1891 W.H. Smith died and Queen Victoria gave his widow a Viscountcy, which later passed to his son, Frederick, who became Lord Hambleden. He made a great contribution to the life of the area until his death in 1928.

He repaired and improved farmhouses and farm buildings, built sturdy farm cottages, and used simple iron fencing around his land, still seen in several places – around Becky Falls for instance. In Manaton, examples of Hambleden farms are Deal and Town Barton, where the granite farm buildings with slate roofs and red-brick surrounds of windows and doors are characteristic of his improvements. The Town Barton Cottages, now Rose Cottage and Two Oaks Cottage, are also typical Hambleden buildings, substantially built with the red brick detailing, and with solid outbuildings. The great number of holly trees are also a legacy from these days as Viscount Hambleden did not allow any to be cut down on his estate.

The Manaton part of the estate, including Becky Falls, was auctioned on 2 August 1929, and one outcome of great future benefit to inhabitants of Manaton was the purchase of the Green for the parish by the Reverend Kitson. Lot 6, Town Barton, tenanted then by Mr E.C. Cuming, was sold with the two cottages to Mr J.S. Harvey for £1800. Lot 12, the stone and thatched dwelling at Top of the Green, used as a Post Office, was 'sold privately'.

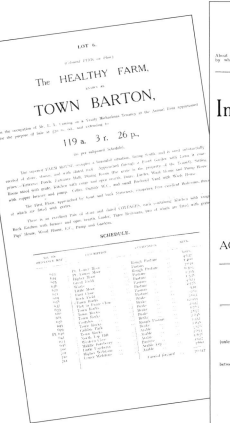

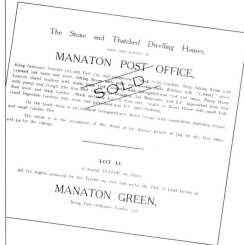

Particulars of sale relating to the Hambleden Estate when it was sold in 1929. The sale included Town Barton farm, the two cottages (now Rose Cottage and its partner), the Green and the Post Office, along with Deal Farm, Becky Farm and Becky Falls. As related elsewhere, the Post Office was sold prior to auction.

An aerial view c.1960 clearly showing the areas of the village known as Freelands and Water. Separated from the church and green by a good half mile, they are recorded as distinct settlements in earlier times.

Paulie James and her father at work in the fields c.1930. In the background is the familiar shape of Latchel Plantation topped by the observatory tower.

8 - Freelands and Water

Manaton, in the hundred of Teignbridge and in the deanery of Moreton, lies about four miles from Moreton Hampstead, and about eight from Ashburton. Freeland and Water are villages in this parish. The manor belonged, at an early period, to the family of Dennis of Blagdon, and having passed by successive marriages to Horton and Thorn, was sold by the latter to Dymock. From Dymock it passed through the family of Britricheston to Wivell, of whom it was purchased by Southcote. The manor of Great Manaton belongs now to the Rev. R. Lane of Coffleet. Lord Courtenay claims manerial jurisdiction over Little Manaton.

Rev. Daniel and Samuel Lysons in their *Magna Britannia*, published in 1822, thus recognise the separate nature of both Water and Freelands as 'villages' within Manaton. With so much new development around them these two places are merged, but there is no doubt that the oldest surviving houses in the village area, excluding the Green, are the cottages at these two places. Quite how Freelands came to be sited here is not so clear, although the siting of Water, by its very name, seems obvious. Its present mill building possibly replaces an earlier one on this site, whilst the leat running alongside Chapel Lane provides a constant supply even in the hottest summer.

FREELANDS

The origin of the name Freelands, is not known. It is called variously 'Wreyland' and 'Relland' in early documents, but the tithe map in 1842 refers to the area by its modern name. The original dwellings comprised the two facing the road, and one behind, with the house known as Freelands standing slightly apart. Rockend, today the home of Betty and Eric Wilson is of later date. It is possible that the lane alongside the cottages continued as a trackway across to Horsham and into the Cleave. A communal water pump once stood at the foot of this lane, evidenced by the remaining granite trough. The house called 'Freelands' has undergone many architectural changes in the last few decades.

Freelands, a photograph taken in the 1960s before the stone barn on the right was incorporated into the house.

Originally these older dwellings housed many more families than they do today; Francis Germon grew up at 3 Freelands, and there are tales of ten or more children sleeping in one room at other cottages. The Crout family, Tom Pollard, Martin Relland (not connected with the original name), George and Joan Tebbs, Peg Lloyd, Sonja Oxland and family, and the Butlers are some of the people who have lived here. No 3, now the home of Britt Merrison, was used in the film *Run Wild Run Free*, the story of a Dartmoor pony, produced in the 1960s.

No 3 Freelands, a photograph taken in 1977 before major rebuilding. It contains a Grade 2 listed spiral granite staircase.

Freelands house has been redeveloped on a rather more grand scale then the others. In the late 1960s early 70s it was the home of the Griffins, and then Mrs Calverly. Latterly it was the home of Captain and Mrs Bearne.

The granite bus shelter was built c.1976, under the eye of Horace Rose, then Chairman of the Parish Council. Before that the land had been a parking area for Freelands and an earlier building here had been, so local lore has it, part of the smithy and even a school room.

WATER

Water or Watter was known earlier as Oditor. The old dwellings surrounding the little green are known today as Water Cottages. Water House is a thatched stone and cob house with a tiled and gabled addition. It is a listed building and parts of it are reputed to be 500 years old. It has pasture of 7.5 acres.

In earlier times it is considered that there were two or more farms in this estate, or possibly the house was divided in two. In the Manaton Church Rate of 1613 it mentions Easte Watter and West Watter, both rated at 3 shillings.

In 1575 a close called the Wester Bickham, 24 acres, was let in tenure to Joan Nosworthy, widow (see section on Horsham). In 1670 there is a document between Sir Popham Southcote and his son and E. Hall and John Nosworthy for a debt; the tenant is Mrs Hooper.

Throughout the eighteenth and nineteenth centuries names of owners and occupiers of Water, Water Park and various parts of Oditor included: Nosworthy, Pethybridge, Scutt, Long-Oxenham, Wills, Harvey, Potter, Aggett, Winsor, Ellis, Caunter and Oliver.

Between c.1880–1905 Mr Barnham owned Water House and added the new wing. He sold one and a half acres of land for building Latchel (originally Park Villa) to Silas Harvey.

Colonel Samuel Woodhouse then lived at Water and, between 1919–1940, his son, the Rev. Major James Woodhouse. Having returned from the First World War, James started and funded the Armistice Dinner. He regularly played for Manaton CC. He took Holy Orders and lived in the Rectory between 1930–37 but still owned Water estate. Of his two sons Samuel, who was born at Water in 1912, eventually became the Ven. Woodhouse, Archdeacon of London and Canon Residentiary of St Pauls; he died in 1995. Hugh married a daughter of Sir Samuel Harvey.

The house was then rented by Miss Furze and companion, and then Mr and Mrs Waterfield who were hunting people.

John Lee was Farm Manager for Colonel Woodhouse; he had been his coachman, and was highly respected by both church and farm. Mr Rule was farm manager and lived in Water cottages. Charles Perryman rented part of Water with Horsham in 1937, and Robert James rented the farm land during the Second World War.

Water House. A photograph taken at the time of its sale in 1972.

Residents at Water in the Nineteenth Century
(taken from the Baptismal Registers)

Date of Baptism	Name	Resident at	Father's Occupation
1804 March	Elizabeth Holmer	Water	Labourer
1815 June	Sussana Harvey	Water	Quality carpenter
1815 February	Richard Harvey	Oditor	Taylor
1817 July	Richard Harvey	Water	Labourer
1818 February	Ann Harvey	Oditor	Carpenter
1818 November	Lydia Langworthy	Water	a base child
1818 November	Sarah Gifford	Water	Labourer
1823 November	Mary Bray	Water	Labourer
1823 April	Ginny Harvey	Oditor	Carpenter
1824 February	Eliz. Ann Charter	Poor House	Base child
1824 February	Charlotte Pethybridge	Poor house	Base child
1829 February	Frances Scutt	Water	Yeoman
1830 November	Henry Bak or Bate	Water	Smith
1831 July	Mary Ann Germon	Water	Labourer
1837 January	Samuel Derges	Water	Labourer
1838 April	Louise Gifford	Water	Labourer
1838 June	Thomas Harvey	Water	Labourer
1838 November	John Germon	Water	Labourer
1838 December	Silas Harvey	Water	Carpenter
1839 July	William White	Water	Yeoman
1844 March	Sarah Hall	Water	Labourer
1845 January	John Gifford	Water	Labourer
1846 November	Thomas Gifford	Water	Labourer
1848 August	Elizabeth Jervis	Water	Labourer
1848 March	Mary Ann Tatershall	Water	Labourer
1851 December	Margaret Babyjohn	Water Aged 12	Labourer
1852 December	Susan Ann Stevens	Water	Labourer
1876 June	Mary Ann Wrayford	Water	Mason
1876 July	Alice Wreford	Water	Labourer
1876 February	Mary Ann Northcote	Water	Labourer
1882 March	Harry Northcote	Water	Labourer
1882 December	Edith Mary London	Water	Labourer
1884 February	William Wreford	Water	Labourer
1884 February	Bessie Northcote	Water	Labourer
1884 July	William London	Water	Labourer
1891 October	Ellen Stevens	Water	Labourer
1891 November	Helena Wasford	Water	Labourer
1894 August	Ernest Wasford	Water	Labourer
1895 March	Ellen & William Crout	Water (twins)	Labourer
1895 September	Bessie Stevens	Water	Labourer
1897 September	Dorothy Harvey	Water	Carpenter
1898 June	Edith Ann Wreford	Water	Labourer

Note: Base children were those born out of wedlock and the Poor House is thought to have been in Newton Abbot and the workhouse in Okehampton. Most of the above names also occur in the burials records of the nineteenth century.

Top left: *The lane through Water Farm c.1930.*

Above: *Aunt Liz Creber at Water with May and John Hutchings and George Creber c.1935.*

Left: *Bill Howe on his first leave from the Navy, with his parents Jack and Emily. He was later sunk in HMS Gloucester evacuating Crete in 1941, and was held as a POW in Austria for four years.*

Below l and r: *Two views near Water in the 1930s. They both show the old tower complete with its glass dome.*

Far left: *Mark Germon with Bill Howe at Water, 1924.*

Left: *Harriet Emily John (Aunt Hettie), the future Mrs Jack Howe.*

Below: *Mark and Anna Germon.* *He was the blacksmith in Manaton*

Shortly before this a man called Mr Bryant rented Water for two years and bred exotic birds; they were held in cages in the meadow and one day a tremendous gale came and blew the cages away; neighbours spent ages trying to rescue parrots from nearby woods!

Between 1940–1945 Captain Langbourne lived here. He was CO of the Home Guard from 1941. Between 1948-1971 Mrs Tatham bought the house and garden from the Woodhouses, the fields having been gradually sold off earlier. Mr and Mrs Rogers rented from Tathams.

Mr and Mrs Asher bought the house in 1972. In 1975 a terrible fire swept the roof and it was re-thatched. Mrs Asher still lives at Water.

WATER COTTAGES AND MOUNT PLEASANT

Dorothy Harvey lived at Water Cottages in the 1930s. She was the daughter of Silas Harvey, who was not only a carpenter and builder but also the undertaker. He built Latchel (Park Villa) as a Guest House and helped build the rifle clubhouse and ran the sports before the First World War. He was much valued and respected in Manaton. The family later moved to Mount Pleasant.

These cottages are in the style of the mid nineteenth century and were originally thatched.

Following occupation by the Harveys, residents have included Mabel Crout, Roger Liggins, the Oliver family and currently Mel and Jan Goddard and three sons, Joe, Charlie and Jim.

Occupants of Water Cottages in the twentieth century include Emma Neck, Richard Henry and Elizabeth Ann Creber (Aunt Liz) and their sons Wilfred and Lewis. Lewis was horseman at Water. He married Ethel Beatrice King who died in childbirth in 1931. Their son was Wilfred George. Later Lewis married Olive Hill. George was a delicate child, but recovered to do much for Manaton especially with the Rifle Club, and worked at Wingstone, Torhill, and Beckaford.

Other residents included: John Wreford; Susan Stevens (née Neck) who married Jimmy Stevens; Jack and Deborah Germon and their sons Fred, Francis and George; Jack and Emily Howe and their daughter Hettie and son Bill (Jack was the local blacksmith, the verger and a bell ringer); Mr and Mrs Jim Endacott; Mr and Mrs John Lee, farm manager at Water; Mr Rule farm manager at Water; Bill Hutchings (postman) his wife Violet and their son John and daughter Mary; Mr and Mrs Gordon Raymont (c.1950–1972) who kept a fruit shop in Bovey Tracey. Mrs Raymont was organist at North Bovey, and Gordon is remembered as a great rabbiter.

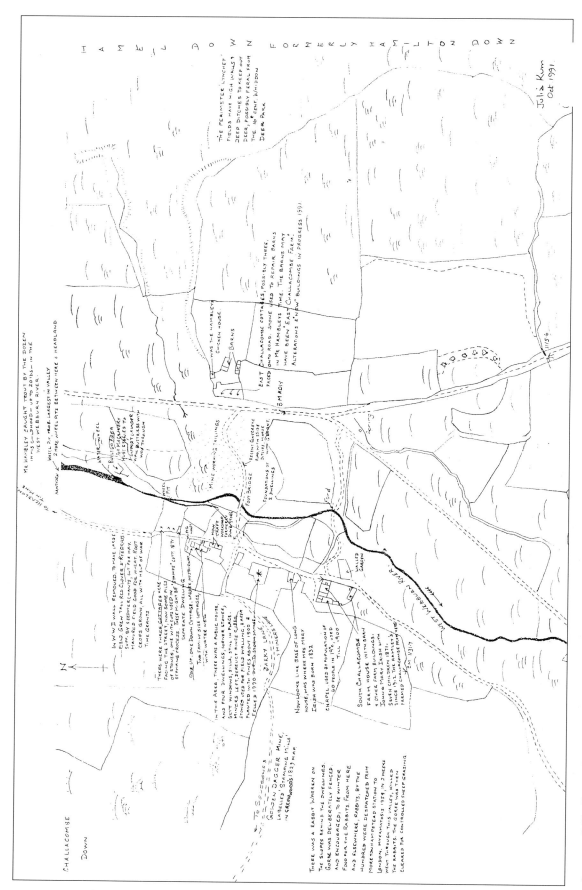

A map of Challacombe as the settlement was laid out during the nineteenth century heyday of mining in the Manaton area. It was based on observations made by W.G. Hambley of Moretonhampstead who had farmed at Challacombe, together with his father, from 1912 to 1970. His grandfather, William Hambley, was a copper miner from Cornwall. The landscape he recalled must have been much as it was at the time of the 1871 and 1881 Manaton census when at least sixty people lived at Challacombe and Headland. (Used with the kind permission of its compilers, Alison Simpkins and Julia Kumik)

9 - Lost Houses of Manaton

In today's world of high property prices, particularly in the National Park, it is difficult to believe that at one time houses were simply allowed to disappear. Indeed, whole villages were swept away as we know from the demise of the medieval settlement at Hound Tor. The truth is that people were more at risk to disease and poor climate. To lose one's job could mean starvation. Thus dwellings were often temporary shelters, built to house the family while work was at hand; left to the elements when it was not.

At Challacombe, a whole village once existed where miners and their families lived while working at the nearby Golden Dagger mine. In 1991, Mr W.G. Hambley of Moretonhampstead who had formerly farmed Challacombe, together with his father, Norman, from 1912 until 1970, walked through the Challacombe settlement with two local historians – see map opposite.

In A.R. Hunt's journal of Foxworthy he describes the position of a 'lost' dwelling on the Horsham side of the Cleave. The remains of another can be seen (rapidly deteriorating) on the bridle path to Peck Farm in Lustleigh. Perhaps the best known in that area, however, is Little Silver Cottage which once stood on the Manaton bank of the Bovey opposite Foxworthy. This pretty cottage survived into the twentieth century but was demolished and the stone used in the barns at Foxworthy.

As already described, the ruins of similar dwellings can be found at Cripdon and at Mill Farm, while only a single photograph remains of what was once a large farm at Greator.

In gathering material for this book, three photographs were provided which show an unidentified dwelling that at first was thought to be at Horsham. Its identity remains a mystery.

Long demolished, Little Silver Cottage once stood near the clapper bridge at Foxworthy.

Right: *Another view of Little Silver Cottage.*

Below: *Parke House lies beside the bridle path between Foxworthy and Peck. This photograph was taken around 1900 and the building was ruinous even then. A few years ago it was possible still to identify the fireplace here, but time has eroded the ruin to a pile of stones.*

In his book Small Talk at Wreyland, *Cecil Torr remarks:*

At the inn at Manaton I once heard a group of old inhabitants talking over various buildings that had fallen down, and quarrelling as to which of them had made the greatest noise in falling.

Right and above: *Three views of an unidentified cottage. In the picture on the right it is possible to see that the right hand end of the building is roofless - is it being rebuilt?*

10 - Inns and Public Houses

In common with most rural areas the inn was a focal point of the community, not least as a hostelry for travellers. In many cases these were simply a house with a barrel of ale or cider on hand, and these 'pot houses' largely went unrecorded. Some were 'church houses' - effectively small breweries housed in a building owned by the church and it is likely that one existed at Church Cottage in Manaton. We do know, however, that The Houndtor Inn existed at Swallerton, now the home of Bryan and Jane Harper, although this appears to have ceased trading by the mid 1800s. This inn would have been used by those travelling to and from Ashburton and beyond, it being a well-used trackway at that time.

HALF MOON INN

Early photographs of the green clearly show the pub on the right and the Post Office on the left. It later became a private house, initially let out by Mrs Frost.

Doris Brown recalls looking after the children of Dr and Mrs Webb who rented Half Moon for the summer c.1927. She subsequently accompanied them to Australia, in 1928, where she remained for two years.

For forty years Jeanne Du Maurier, sister of the famous author, Daphne, lived at Half Moon. Her cousin, Noel Welch, still lives there and has gifted it, together with its formal garden and woodland, to the National Trust.

In the late nineteenth century the inn was kept by the Winsors, but on the marriage of their daughter Emmalina to James Stanbury Harvey, their new son-in-law took over as landlord. The Harvey family has been traced back to the early eighteenth century to Humphrey Harvey and Elisabeth Stonebury of Chagford. They were the parents of James Harvey who was born in 1871. Another son, Cyril, died in France in the First World War and is commemorated on the Manaton War memorial; his brother Sydney died in 1959.

James, a tall imposing man, was poorly educated but succeeded by hard work and a business instinct which made him a rich man amongst his peers in the parish. The village population at the turn of the century was about 300. He used horse and carriage to transport wealthy visitors on guided tours of Dartmoor, impressing people with his folk stories and knowledge of the local area.

James later went on to build tea rooms where the Kestor Inn now stands.

Once The Hound Tor Inn, it is not difficult to picture Swallerton as a wayside inn, as it has changed so little over the years. Thor Heyerdhal, of Kon Tiki fame, stayed here while writing the book about his epic voyage.

The South Devon Hunt meet outside Half Moon on Manaton Green c.1900.

James S. Harvey standing at the door of Half Moon.

Silas Harvey, whose family had been in Manaton for over 150 years, married James' sister Edith in 1895 and lived at Mount Pleasant. He was known for his ability as a carpenter and was the village undertaker. He is credited as having built the Rifle Club in 1909. Silas was wise and skilled at estimating size and weight; it was said that he could build a house without plans or drafting instruments. His ability to estimate the weight of a pig with a few rudimentary measurements with a piece of string was widely used by local farmers.

The village smithy was owned by Philip Braund and, with his assistant George Howe, he made anything from horseshoes to ploughshares to spades and rabbit traps. Philip was by all accounts a man of humility and compassion, loved by his neighbours and respected for his skills. He would entertain in the Half Moon on his concertina but he was given to sudden bouts of aggression, laying down his instrument and accusing the company of saying that he was drunk. Flailing his arms at all and sundry, one of the company would rescue the concertina whilst the others would restrain Philip and lead him home. Next day all would be forgotten.

Beer and cider were used as an encouragement to the reapers to keep working to bring in the harvest and, in 1911, the nephew of James Harvey (William Brown) was asked to carry a gallon stone jar to where the reapers worked with their scythes in the local fields. The footpath was rough and once over the stile and descending a slope the young lad decided to roll the heavy jar to relieve his tired arms. The jar struck a rock, cracked, and the precious beer soon disappeared into the soil.

Returning to the inn to face his uncle and collect another jar he was accompanied the second time by one of the domestic servants.

A song or rhyme was recited in farm, field and factory relating to this practice:

The Kestor Hotel (it later became an Inn) c.1920 shortly after it was built by James Harvey as his home. Among those standing on the balcony is Em Brown, Francis Germon's auntie.

James Harvey and his customers at the Kestor Inn celebrate Jubilee Day, 6 May 1935.

KESTOR INN

Work boys and be contented,
As long as you've enough to buy some beer;
We'll let the bottle pass,
and we'll have another glass,
If you'll only put your shoulder to the wheel.

William Brown returned to London after a one month stay with his uncle at Half Moon. He was escorted by a Royal Marine Corporal, Jack Cousins, who had been brought up as an orphan by the Hutchings family of Manaton.

The Kestor Inn was built by James Harvey in the early 1900s, first as a private residence and then as a hotel. Photographs show it as an imposing building, complete with wrought iron railing and veranda.

Nearby were the tea rooms which served the growing numbers of visitors brought to Manaton by the attractions of the moors and Becky Falls. Having taken the train to Moretonhampstead, Bovey or Lustleigh, day trippers would continue

Above: *James Harvey in the tea room which he built at the Kestor.*

Left: *An earlier facade of the Kestor Inn c.1975*

Below: *Roger and Chris Hughes celebrate with Joyce Rowley (formerly Snell) at a fancy dress party.*

Above: *Nigel Ford, Kestor landlord until 1996.*

their journey by coach and horses, later by motor charabanc, stopping off for tea in the afternoon.

After the war the Kestor became more of a typical village pub, with lounge and public bar. Indeed, it remained with this layout, through a succession of landlords, up until the late 1970s.

Publicans in the period included Roger Liggins, who later had the 'Greator' holiday flats designed and built. There followed Roger and Chris Hughes who continued the tradition of supporting and encouraging local activities, including the hosting of Christmas parties for the village children. Dick and Jean Taylor followed, and whilst Jean worked during the week in London, Dick ran the pub, bringing some much needed batting skills to the Cricket Club! At about this time the pub sign proudly began to proclaim itself Headquarters of the MCC!

The customer is (nearly) always right! Mike Baker in reflective mood.

Around 1985, the pub was bought by Peter Brackenbury who had previously been landlord of the Ring O' Bells in North Bovey. He carried out extensive renovations to the interior of the Kestor, removing the public bar and opening a dining area where the veranda had once been. This was in response to the declining trade in village pubs, brought on not least by the tightening of drink driving laws. Pubs now had to be places to eat as well as drink.

Shortly following the renovations the Kestor suffered two fires, the first relatively minor, but the second completely destroying the interior. Again extensive redesign was incorporated into the rebuilding undertaken by Peter Brackenbury.

On completion Peter then sold the pub to Nigel and Alison Ford who greatly increased the promotion of the Kestor as a restaurant. They too supported all the local activities, with Nigel playing in the cricket, darts, and pool teams. As Nigel occasionally worked at Torbay Hospital as a nurse, it was not unknown for an injured Manaton resident to call in to the Kestor to get some immediate First Aid over the bar!

In 1996 the Kestor was purchased by the present landlord and ladlady Martin and Brenda Aspinall. They have entered into the spirit of life in our small community and have given generous and enthusiastic backing to the children's play area project. They retained most of the staff who had worked with the previous owners, including Ellie, who works behind the bar, while their Thai chef has brought the delights of oriental cuisine to the wilds of Dartmoor.

The important role played by the village inn, taken for granted by so many people, is at least assured, in Manaton, of continuing happily into the twenty-first century.

Right: *The Glen at Becky Falls c.1950. This was the tea room and gift shop.*

Opposite: *passengers disembark from two charabancs stuck in the lane near Becky Falls c. 1920. Some things don't change!*

Below: *The falls as they were sixty years ago c.1940.*

There was a pleasant old house at Becky Fall, burnt down on 18 April 1875, and rebuilt as one sees it now; and I have a full-length portrait of my great-great-great-grandfather, John Langworthy, sitting in the porch there. He has been described as 'reading his bible, and looking as if he didn't believe a word of it,' but it really is a law-book. The painter was Thomas Rennell. There are many pictures of his in Devonshire, mostly labelled Reynolds by mistake for Rennell. Sir Joshua and he were fellow-pupils in Hudson's studio in London, but had not much in common afterwards.
Becky was a lonesome place till the new Manaton road was made, but now lies open to excursionists, and has lost something of its charm. While the old house remained, I coveted it more than this. It passed from John Langworthy to his daughter Honor, the wife of Nelson Beveridge Gribble, and then to their eldest son John Gribble, and to his eldest surviving son John Beveridge Gribble, who very soon got rid of it.

Cecil Torr: *Small Talk at Wreyland*, 1916.

Left: *The Old Manaton Road was the main easterly route out of the village until the Terrace road was built in the 1900s. Remnants of this unmetalled track remain and can be walked today via Beckhams, down to the lovely packhorse bridge over the Becka Brook, exiting on to the modern road above Reddaford.*

11 - Becky Falls

Mention Manaton to many people outside the area and the name conjures up Becky Falls, a well-known beauty spot just south of the village.

The Becky or Becka Brook is a tributary of the Bovey, and the Falls are where the brook plunges 70 feet over huge granite boulders, in a beautiful steep wooded valley. For centuries visitors have come to see the Falls and enjoy the woodland walks. By Victorian times, people were coming to visit Becky Falls by train to Bovey Tracey, and then by carriage. The new county road had by this time been cut through the open moorland, and was known as the lower terrace, the upper terrace running along the contour from Haytor to Beckaford and down the steep Beckaford Hill. Crossing describes Becky Falls as 'beloved of all visitors to this part of the moor'.

Thomas Eales of Pillars, by the Green, a keen family researcher and former churchwarden, has discovered a family connection with Becky Falls in the eighteenth century. John Langworthy (1711-1786) of Becky Falls was the father of Honor who married Nelson Beveridge Gribble at Manaton on 5 March 1764. One of their daughters became the grandmother of Emily Fulford Eales who was the wife of the Rev. William Thomas Eales, vicar of Yealmpton from 1857 to 1887. Their daughter, Elizabeth, compiled a large book of pictures and history entitled *Some Records of the Eales Family* which provided Mr Eales with this information and two paintings.

There is a plaque in St Winifred's in memory of Honor Gribble who died on 7 October 1799. Mr Eales discovered from Cecil Torr's book *Small Talk at Wreyland* that she was actually interred in the chancel, presumably in the Langworthy vault. Unfortunately during one of the restorations, the floor plate of the Langworthys was removed when a new chancel floor was laid.

When Honor's daughter-in-law Josepha Gribble died at Ashburton she was brought to Manaton to be interred near her mother-in-law, by special request. Mr Eales comments on this unusually close relationship between mother-in-law and daughter-in-law! He also points out that his own daughter-in-law was Sue Gribble of Bovey Tracey, and his daughter was Honor Eales, now Honor Wright.

Becky Falls formed part of the Hambleden Estate between 1891 and 1929, when it was sold for £4250 to Mr Crossman. At the time the farm was tenanted by Robert Hern and George Dunning. Pat Perryman's cousin worked at Becky Falls, possibly for Granny Hern, and milked the cows which were kept in a barn which subsequently became the house now called Treetops and home of Derek and June Morris. Granny Hern made clotted cream from the milk to serve with cream teas at Becky Falls.

Among visitors who stayed at Beckwood Cottage at the Falls while it was tenanted around the beginning of the twentieth century was the poet Rupert Brooke. He found the peace and beauty made it easy for him to gather his thoughts. Sir Arthur Quiller-Couch's poem 'Manaton' which he wrote in 1896, also mentions the 'stones of Becky Waterfall'.

The property has changed hands several times since the 1950s, and its attraction for tourists has been developed with footpaths, nature trails, a big car park, tea-rooms and shop. Owners and occupiers have included Arthur Weston, Cyril and Liz Giles, Jack Palmer, Christianna and Martyn Morgan and currently (1999) John Harding. It features in many of the tourist publications for Dartmoor and provides welcome employment for many local people, especially students, during the summer months.

Right: *No.1 Mellowmead, home of Jack Perryman in the 1930s. He was the first occupant of this house after it was built. His workshop for making and repairing boots can be seen in the background.*

Below: *Mellowmead in snow.*

Below: *Ebworthy as it was in the 1920s. It was later used by Miss Quantick of Heatree as part of her Trust providing for inner city children and was renamed Heatherway. Today it retains its original name and is the home of the Boughey family.*

Above: *The Misses Emery at Moorcrest in the 1930s. They were responsible for a great deal of charitable work locally and internationally. Visitors to the house included Lord Hambleden, the Du Mauriers and Agatha Christie. It is now the home of Captain Brian and Joan Newton.*

Right: *Neadon Cottage, now Little Neadon, as it was in the 1930s. It was the home of Colonel G.A and Dorothea Wadham and their daughter, Anne (later Vallings) during the Second World War. Subsequent owners included Pete Downey. It is now the home of Anna and Simon Butler.*

12 - Mellowmead and Other Homes

At the end of the First World War the need for new housing in the parish became a major concern. This was in part due to major social changes wrought by the 'war to end all wars'; returning servicemen had glimpsed the possibilities of a different world which turned upside down the old social order. Women, who had tasted independence through war work, were about to be able to vote for the first time.

In rural areas such as Manaton life continued much as before, although the Depression in agriculture placed severe strains on the relationship betwen farmer and worker. The problems of tied farm cottages became more acute, while at the same time it became possible for men to seek work further afield. Public transport, bicycles and motorbikes provided ordinary men and women with cheap means of transport. They also needed somewhere to live and public housing was on the agenda in rural areas.

In Manaton there had been various manoeuverings in order to secure a suitable site for new houses. The Newton Abbot Rural District Council favoured a site below the Kestor at 'Freelands Plantation' while the locals wanted to live in the land behind the school. James Harvey had a vested interest in the latter site and suggested selling it for £150, almost twice the price the NARDC had in mind!

Eventually the Council got its way and the houses were built. In November 1929 the name Mellowmead for these houses was officially adopted. For many years, until the sell off of council houses in the 1980s and 90s, these houses, and the bungalows built later, provided excellent housing for the people of Manaton. Their existence meant that Manaton families could continue to live in the parish, whilst new blood kept alive the prospect of youth.

Today these houses represent an interesting mix of owner-occupied and council owned housing, although the problems of securing affordable property for locals within rural areas has by no means gone away.

• • •

This book for obvious reasons concentrates on the older houses and farms in the parish for that is where the history lies. Even so, as the years pass it is interesting to note others types of building that have arrived in the twentieth century. This is not to forget very recent building – a new house behind the Kestor is even now (1999) nearing completion, certainly the last to be built in this millennium.

Despite increasing regulations on planning within the National Park a considerable amount of private housing has been built in the area of Freelands and Water, and more along Ridge Road. Newer 'agricultural dwellings' are to be found scattered throughout the parish.

In the Edwardian period and running up through the 1940s there continued a vogue for second homes in the country, and for isolated dwellings built for people to retire to. These are often blessed with magnificent views and have become as much part of the moorland landscape as the ancient farmhouses. Whatever their size and location all these houses, for most people in the parish, are simply 'home'.

Few Manaton families in the 1920s could afford a car let alone servants or chauffeur. This is Cunningham, chauffeur to the Emery family at Moorcrest. He wore a dark green uniform and before the car he drove a horse and pair for the family.

The village blacksmith, Jack Howe, outside the forge c.1920.

13 - The Working Life

Apart from those directly engaged in agriculture, there are very few people today whose employment is contained within the parish. This is in direct contrast to the years before the Second World War when very few would have travelled far to work. In the late nineteenth and early twentieth centuries work was often hard and relentless, and usually for six days a week. There was no time off, few holidays, and no State sickness benefit or pension.

Aspects of the life of an ordinary family are painted in the reminiscences of Cyril Skerrett:

My grandmother had been born at Drewsteignton in 1859. I am not sure what the family background was but almost certainly she came from a working-class home. I have been told that she left school at nine years of age yet, despite this, she had a keen and active mind into old age, was well spoken, wrote well and commanded respect of those she came into contact with.

I have also been told that she went into service when she was quite young, probably into a farmer's house, for I recall hearing how she was sent out into the fields pulling turnips in the winter, crying bitterly because of the cold. Life 'in service' could be hard, even cruel, in Victorian times. It would seem that she continued in this form of employment for, in the 1880s, she was working for the Mallock family at Cockington Court near Torquay. It was there that she met my grandfather, George Henry Skerrett, who was employed as a carter on the estate. They were married there in 1882.

I am not sure how long they continued to live there but at some stage they moved to work for the same family at Huccaby, near Dartmeet, a very different location from the warm and sheltered area around Torquay. No doubt it was a hard life for them and yet not without enjoyable times for my father recalls my grandmother speaking of going to parties in the homes of, presumably, other working class folk in the neighbourhood. She must have had a number of children by then – she was to have ten in all and all raised to healthy adulthood. That in itself must have been rather unusual in those times.

It seems that, in addition to her other work, she looked after the building which served as a church on Sundays and a schoolroom during the week.

Why the family left Huccaby is unknown. Why they moved to the North Bovey area is also a mystery. The only thing I am sure of is that in the early years of the century they were living at Vogwell Cottage and that my grandfather was working for the Kitson family at Heatree as a carter. It was at Vogwell Cottage that my father was born in 1905, the tenth and last child. It must still have been a hard life for there were probably four dependent children at home and my grandfather's wage was 12 shillings per week. It is difficult to estimate what a comparable wage would be in the 1990s but certainly it was little more than a bare subsistence income for a family in those days. Around that time my grandfather's wage rose to 13 shillings per week and he suggested to my grandmother that perhaps they could save some. This proposal was flatly rejected – my grandmother had scrimped for so long that she was determined to have a little more money with which to meet the family's needs. It is an indication of her determined spirit that she had her way.

BLACKSMITHS

Jack Howe is the blacksmith seen in the only surviving photograph of the Manaton forge from the 1920s. This building is now a private house but is still known as Forge. The blacksmith in the 1850s was John Harvey, and Town Barton still has an old cast-iron cooking range marked 'Harvey Manaton'. Jack Howe was also the sexton and was responsible for lighting the street oil-lamp outside the church. He had a gadget on a long pole which he used to turn up the oil so that church-goers could see. Pat Perryman remembers that nimble lads could and did shin up the lamp-post and turn it down again, then hide until Mr Howe appeared, cursed in a non-sexton-like manner, and turned it up again.

Philip Braund was the blacksmith at the turn of the century. He and his assistant, George Howe, would make horseshoes, ploughshares, iron gates,

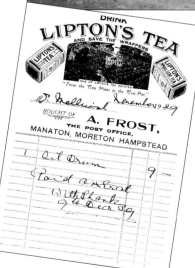

Top: *The village postmen c.1915. They are, from l-r: Jim Howe, Frank Hutchings and Harry Pike. Note the sign advertising the nearest recruiting office for Royal Marines and the Royal Navy.*

Inset: *John Frost, who at one time, in the late 1970s, ran the Post Office in the shop opposite the Kestor Inn. Alice Harriet Frost was his grandmother.*

Centre: *Outside the Post Office at Half Moon c.1930 l-r: Gladys Frost (?), Helen Hern (who married Francis Heath) and Mrs Alice Harriet Frost whose name appears on the sign. By this time there was also a telegraph office and public telephone here.*

Left: *A receipt for oil, used in oil stoves and for lighting, for Mr Melluish, dated November 1929.*

spades, wheel rims, rabbit traps, latches and hinges, anything in fact. His exploits at the Half Moon are described elsewhere in this book.

Mark Germon (in the photo of men outside the Kestor on page 145) was the blacksmith in the village for many years. Doris and Ruby Brown remember all the farm horses going down to be shod at the Forge.

POSTMEN

An early photo of the shop at Half Moon, probably taken around the First World War (see the recruiting notice for the Royal Navy and Royal Marines), shows three postmen. On the left is Jim Howe, who lived at Cross Park as the caretaker. He did the Heatree postal round and was a shoe-maker in his spare time, making his great-nephew Bill's first pair of boots. Doris Brown remembers Jim Howe giving her lifts home to Barracott from school - she sat on the front basket of the bike. In the middle is Frank Hutchings, who covered Water, Beckaford, Leighon, Becky Falls and Houndtor. Harry Pike, on the right, did the Neadon and Foxworthy area. Before Harry Pike, Mr Woodley used to bring the post by donkey. He had a shed at Hayne where he ran a tailoring business.

The post came to Moreton by train (before that by post chaise to Chudleigh), and the bags for Manaton were sorted into rounds in a little building behind Ivy Cottage. Harry Pike had a cabin along Ridge Road, near the big rock (Francis Germon remembers a Major Tolchard, an ex cavalry officer, who lived in a caravan here), where he was able to dry out and make tea before collecting the post from Manaton and riding back to Moreton with it.

At Christmas and other holidays, the post rounds were put out to tender to local people. Pat Perryman was a regular relief postman in this way. There used to be a bridge at Horsham which made the Horsham-Foxworthy route easier than it is now, but if the Bovey was in flood, the route would be impassable, and so the postman either threw the mail across the river or it had to wait until the river fell.

THE POST OFFICE, GARAGE AND SHOPS

Half Moon at the top of the Green was a pub and a post office before becoming a private house. The post office was run by the Frost family. The 'A. H. Frost' on the sign above the window was Alice Harriet Frost, grandmother of John Frost who still lives in the village. Her daughter Gladys took over and later the post office was moved to the former chapel in Chapel Lane in the early 1950s. It was run by Mrs Wreford and later taken over by Mrs Fisher.

An early photograph shows Gladys Frost, Helen Hern (who married Francis Heath), and Mrs Frost. Helen Hern operated the telephone exchange which was also at Half Moon. Doris Brown, who still lives at Ivy Cottage, remembers getting a penny every Monday, and going to spend it on sweets from Mrs Frost. She started school in 1914 and Mrs Frost was there then.

Cyril Skerrett remembers dried fish hanging up at the shop. His mother bought it for Good Friday and soaked it for ages to remove the taste of brine. He remembers it was called toe-rag.

Other shops were run at various times at different buildings. The Forge was run as the Post Office and shop by Johnny and Joan Johnson in the mid 1970s, Miss Wadland ran a shop at Mill Farm when she lived in the cottage there, and later, also in the 1970s, in the old school when she went to live there. Mary Reid sold cigarettes, chocolate and ice cream at Fordgate Cottages in 1959.

Travelling shops were very important in the days before most people had cars. Doris and Ruby Brown, who lived at Barracott as children, remember the excitement when a travelling shop arrived. Mr Harris came every Friday from Bovey Tracey with groceries; Mr Tapper came on his motorbike with a suitcase of clothes in his sidecar; Mr Staddon came from Bovey Tracey with pots and pans and crockery.

Pat Perryman remembers a baker called Doyle and a butcher called Soper delivering on demand from Moretonhampstead, and Mr Churchward delivered groceries from Ashburton.

Doris and Ruby also remember an open lorry with wooden forms which acted as the weekly bus to Newton Abbot. Their mother used it to go to the shops and to market. During the big snowfall of 1947 the only way to get to the shops was by horse. Communal shopping lists were drawn up and villagers took it in turn to ride to Moretonhampstead!

Meanwhile, on the corner opposite the Kestor, petrol pumps were installed by George Dunning from Deal. They were then run by Mr Richards who lived at Longfield on Ridge Road. Then the Harrises came to Deal and they brought the Kinseys to Manaton and built the bungalow next to the telephone kiosk for them. The Kinseys then set up a garage and shop as well as the petrol

Right: *Reg and Derek Kinsey and Frank Holly stand beside the petrol pumps at Manaton garage, opposite the Kestor Inn c.1939.*

Below: *Manaton Garage and Village Store as they appeared in the late 1970s. At this time it was in the ownership of Ken Boyce who worked in the garage, his wife in the shop. The benches outside were for the display of vegetables, mostly locally grown.*

Below: *Manaton Garage and shop in the 1960s. The shop was in the cabin adjacent to the garage forecourt. The Kinsey family lived in the bungalow on the right.*

Left and above: *Pat Perryman displays his father, Jack's, boot and shoemaking tools. As part of his pension from the Great War, in which he was wounded, Jack received training in a new trade. After many moves around the parish he lived finally at Mellowmead where he built a small workshop. Pat now lives in Bovey Tracey.*

Above: *The Clements on their paper round during the great blizzards of 1947.*

Left: *Peter Manners-Chapman delivering the papers to Town Barton.*

pumps and in due course the Post Office also moved here. A photograph from around this time shows the pumps with the Kestor Inn behind, and Reg and Derek Kinsey.

Pat Perryman remembers that there was no one manning the pumps full-time – you had to yank a rope which connected via a series of tall poles to Deal where someone would then ride down on a bike, pump the fuel up to ground level by hand from the underground tanks, and only then would the waiting vehicle get its petrol. Pat Perryman worked there in the late 30s as a boy

and remembers the prices – 1s.3$\frac{1}{2}$d per gallon of Essolene, for example. He also remembers a nocturnal prank which operated thus: two lads on bikes would pull up at the pumps and ring for service, positioning themselves a car's width apart. The attendant on the way down from Deal would perceive a car (the bicycle lights were exactly a car's width apart) but by the time he arrived at the pumps there was no car and no noise of one driving off. Hence the tales of phantom cars.

After the Kinseys came Ken and Jean Boyce and their two sons. They ran the garage from the

Left: *Shaun and Steve Wright in their joinery workshop.*

Right: *Mel Goddard of Moor Print.*

early 1970s until the main garage building was sold off for conversion into a bungalow. At the same time a two storey building was built where the old shop stood and this became the new Post Office and Village Stores

John Frost, after a spell in the army, ran the Post Office and stores in the late 1970s and early 80s. It was then sold to Nick Crout who ran it with his wife Glenda for about 10 years. Nick, an electrician, had earlier been in business with his brother Jim, trading as Crout Bros. He and Glenda had a son Kimberley and they participated in all the village activities, with Nick being an early member of the refounded cricket club in 1976.

Graham and Pat Everitt later took over the shop and Post Office and ran it until the mid 1990s when, sadly, Graham died. The building was then sold as a private house, leaving Manaton without a Post Office or shop.

PAPER ROUNDS

Mr and Mrs Clements used to live in Tanglewood in Ridge Road. They did a paper round for about ten years after the war. There is a photograph of their Austin 7 battling through the Great Snow of 1947. Mr and Mrs Baker of Crosshill did a paper round for many years after that.

Peter Manners-Chapman has brought the papers to Manaton for about 25 years. He has several drop-off points in the village and people collect their paper from the nearest box. A photograph shows him dropping off the papers in February 1999 at the box inside the Town Barton gate which serves the top end of the village.

OTHER CRAFTSMEN

Silas Harvey, born in Manaton in 1866, became the village carpenter and builder, and also acted as the undertaker (see also page 144).

Jack Perryman, Pat's father, trained as a bootmaker after being wounded in the First World War. He started his business at Blissmoor, but this was not ideal – if your boots needed repairing, you weren't going to walk out over Hayne Down in your bare feet. So they moved to Fordgate and thence to Mellowmead where they were the first occupants of number one. A small workshop was built next to number one Mellowmead for the boot business. Business was barely subsistence level so Mr Perryman also sold cigarettes; Woodbines were 2d for 5.

More recently two of the Town Barton buildings have been made into workshops. In 1986 Mel Goddard of Mount Pleasant turned the old milking parlour into a printing workshop, Moor Print, and has run it successfully ever since, with Darren Davey's help. The photocopier and fax machine are particularly useful to villagers these days. In 1988, Paul Merrison started a successful joinery business when he opened Moorland Joinery also at Town Barton. In 1995 he sold the business to Steve and Shaun Wright, brothers from Lustleigh.

14 - The Powers That Be

The backbone of any community is made up of the groups and organisations who work together for the common good. The efforts of those involved are often only appreciated long after the event, but this book reveals how important these people are, and have been, in making the parish what it is today. Not every organisation or body can be included but those following are representative of Manaton's community spirit.

THE PARISH COUNCIL

Despite a diligent search some years ago, the minutes of Manaton Parish Council before 1975 have unfortunately been lost and the record is therefore incomplete. However, it is interesting to see how many intractable problems recur with regularity, the lack of money being the perennial problem.

The muddy state of Slinkers' Lane, traffic hold-ups at Becky Falls, the narrows of Long Lane, the perceived danger at Langstone Cross, the speed of traffic through the village, pot-holes in the roads, parking of cars at Mellowmead, overhead electricity and telephone cables, lack of a police presence,

the potential and then actual loss of the shop, flooding due to blocked drainage and the lack of gritting in winter, are all matters constantly brought to the attention of the Parish Council.

Some ideas, though, put forward by parishioners, such as public lighting and lavatories, have been hotly decried by others. Their feasibilities have been explored, but always a majority of residents has been against them, or the cost has been too high.

In contrast, the achievements of the Parish Council have been many and various. Twenty years after the bus shelter on the Green had been handed over in 1953, it was decided that another was needed at the lower end of the village. Eventually, a piece of Freelands' garden was purchased and a stone wall was built around to protect the shelter from the weather.

The next acquisition was Mellowmead field and woodland. The land belonged to the Water Board and the Parish Council had long desired a small piece for a children's playground. When the land came up for sale in 1984, it could not be split and with the help of a £7500 grant from Rural Aid and £500 from the Show and Fair, the whole area was

Manaton Parish Council 1999. From left: Janet Kennedy, Jean Baldwin; Stan Fitton, Brian Moss; Brian Warne; and Frank Smith. Clare Boughey, also a PC member, is not in the photograph.

bought for the parish to enjoy. Later, the Dartmoor National Park Authority agreed to manage the woodland and a court was built in the field for a variety of games, although in practice only tennis has been played.

More recently, the Green management was passed to the Parish Council although it remained in the care of the Charity Commission. There was a protracted argument with Devon County Council over the maintenance of the road to the church running beside the Green, but eventually responsibility was accepted and a new surface was laid by the Highways Department.

In 1980, an Emergency Committee was set up and its members attended information meetings, made maps of the area's facilities, learnt First Aid and generally prepared the village for a state of emergency should one come. With the ending of the Cold War there seemed no need and the Committee was disbanded in 1993. The data were given to the Parish Council for safe-keeping and could still be of use in an emergency.

During the 1970s and 80s there was an explosion of building in Manaton which caused alarm at the changes being wrought. Where possible, the Parish Council advised against planning permission, but its views were often overruled by the DNPA and Teignbridge District Council. There were also many extensions to existing houses to be monitored and breaches of boundaries and rights of way to be argued through solicitors for years.

Various planning applications for building private houses exercised the emotions of parishioners and several public meetings were held. The planned extensions at Becky Falls generated much ill-feeling and a representative from the DNPA had to explain why permission had been granted. Perhaps the greatest furore was created in 1998 by an application to build a large house near Horsham. The Parish Council listened to all views and tried to give a fair and balanced recommendation to the planning authorities. The application was eventually turned down.

For some years the area around the telephone box was considered to be in need of 'enhancement', and with the help of a small contribution towards the cost from the Parish Council, the DNPA built stone kerbs, laid turf and moved the old lamp standard to the notice-boards.

Other initiatives have included the surgery, run on a weekly basis at the Parish Hall by the Moretonhampstead Clinic since 1985; the waste paper collected at Ebworthy and used to provide money for the Church; and information for the

Fire and Rescue Service on the width of access to properties in Manaton. Also, the *Bulletin* was started in 1996 and this has proved a popular and informative publication, particularly for newcomers to the parish.

This brief sketch of the Parish Council's work can give no idea of the amount of paper which falls through the Clerk's letterbox, nor the many committees and meetings of local organisations which are attended by the seven councillors. This lowest tier of Government is closest to the rural population and its views are sought constantly by those in higher places before plans and policies are finalised. The last twenty-five years of the century have seen a gradual increase in this consultative role which has now been added to the Council's continuing position at the hub of parish life.

Chairmen	Clerks
1975 Ray Hugo	J Hurst
1976 Horace Rose	Simon Butler
1978 Vernon Hunt	Kate Warne
1980 Brian Warne	ditto
1981 ditto	Kathleen Perkins
1982 Betty Bindloss	ditto
1984 Horace Rose	Rex Griffiths
1985 Ray Hugo	Pauline Teeling
1987 Penelope Keogh	Jean Baldwin
1989 Ronald Hudson	
1991 Antony Cullen	
1995 Bryan Harper	
1999 Stanley Fitton	

THE WOMEN'S INSTITUTE

On the 9 of January 1930, Miss Leach invited six ladies of the parish to The Mount for discussion on the feasibility of forming an Institute in Manaton. The decision to ask County Headquarters to send a representative to a meeting on the 14 January was taken and at that meeting, held in the Rifle Club and attended by seventeen ladies, the forming of the Manaton Institute was agreed. A committee of eight was chosen and Miss Leach was elected the first President. Tea was then served at a charge of 2d each!

As the months went by, membership increased. In August, a stall at the Manaton Flower Show (charge 5 shillings) made a profit of £2.0s.6d. In September an entertainment committee was formed and games, dancing, singing and acting became a major part of the proceedings. In December, at the first Annual Meeting, the

Manaton WI members at the old Parish Hall c. 1960. 1. Miss Moody; 2. Mrs Griffin; 3. Miss Whitehead; 4. Mrs Hugo; 5. Mrs Armsworth; 6. Mrs Wheeler; 7. Mrs Hall; 8. Mrs Pym; 9. Mrs Kenyon; 10. Betty Perryman; 11. Miss Earle; 12. Mrs Warne; 13. Mrs Lodge; 14. Mrs Longbourne; 15. Mrs Endacott; 16. Miss Haines; 17. Mrs Lentern; 18. Mrs Rowland; 19. Mrs Smith; 20. Mrs Kinsey; 21. Miss James; 22. Miss May Towning.

Manaton WI members in 1953 performing in 'A Victorian Musical Evening'. Miss Wadland, the former Manaton schoolteacher, is second from left.

Treasurer reported a balance of £2.3s.4d! The following year the Institute had grown to fifty-two and the idea of building a hut was discussed. An estimate of £39 was obtained, but the Parish Hall Committee quickly made an offer to reduce the fees and it was decided that the Parish Hall should be the future venue.

Miss Earle became the second President and Mrs Hunt the third, remaining in the post for sixteen years! During the 1930s, outings by charabanc to Plymouth, Newquay, Preston, Ilfracombe and Westward Ho! were undertaken, and garden parties in the summer were enjoyed. There were visits to Seale Hayne, Buckfast Abbey and Dartington, and social evenings were used for enjoyment as well as raising funds. The regular monthly meetings continued, with topics including basketry, bottling of fruit, sweet-making, dyeing, cross-stitch rugs, quilting, loose covers, beekeeping, first aid, growing vegetables, dairywork and dress-making. These rural interests were interrupted in January 1938 by a talk on Air Raid Precautions with demonstrations of gas-masks and clothing to be worn in gas attacks.

The outbreak of war is not mentioned in the records, but there was a change from evening meetings to afternoons due to the lighting restrictions. Before long, however, talks changed to topics such as wartime dishes, vegetables to feed the family, how to help to win the war, and keeping pigs and poultry. Knitting became the occupation for all the members, and working parties to make garments for hospitals and the armed services were set up. Marmalade was made and sold to buy wool and, by June, 1940, one hundred and sixty-four garments had been made. War Savings Certificates were bought with five guineas taken from the funds, and these were not cashed for many years.

In 1941, a co-operative fruit preservation scheme was set up by the Government, and Manaton applied to be a centre. Two hundredweights of sugar were ordered and jam making began in the Rifle Club although there is no record of how much was made. Wortleberries were gathered on Black Hill – fifty-one pounds in 1941, but only twelve pounds in 1942 due to inclement weather. The profits were put into the wool fund for yet more knitting. Manaton also became a centre for gathering foxglove leaves which were then taken to Newton Abbot for drying. Speakers were reduced to alternate months, with knitting parties at the other meetings, although some members knitted throughout them all.

There is, unfortunately, a gap in the meeting records from 1942 to 1951, although it was recorded that after the war one hundred and two garments, many for babies and children, were knitted for liberated Europe by an average of forty members.

From 1951, with Mrs Apletre as President, the numbers steadily rose and in 1958 reached fifty-six. There was a monthly competition and mystery parcel, and the Speakers' topics became more general in nature. Outings were re-instated, with visits to Weymouth and the Bath & West Show. In 1953, Manaton was hostess for a Group Meeting, and the entertainment was a playlet called 'A Victorian Musical Evening' of which a photograph exists.

Mrs Endacott became the next President, followed by Mrs Smith and Mrs Rowland. The years went by using the same format as before, but one highlight was a visit to the mediaeval village excavations at Houndtor in August 1964. In November 1964 the Parish Hall was destroyed in a storm and meetings were held at the Kestor until the new hall was built. The Institute decided to give curtains and fund-raising enabled cherry-red curtains to be installed in 1967. These lasted 20 years when they were replaced by a gift from May Towning.

During the 1970s, with Mrs Griffin and then Miss Towning as President, the WI in Manaton became concerned with environmental issues such as hedge cutting and reinstatement, the spraying of bracken and gorse, and the controversial request not to pick wild flowers. A car pool was instituted to take villagers without cars to the moors and seaside, but due to problems with insurance it was later reduced to emergencies only. This became the Red Cross Service which continued until very recent times and is now independent.

A market stall on the Green every two weeks during the summer months was begun in 1973 and this ran for some years until it became the Village Stall. The WI continued to fund-raise by running the stall once a year. Other village issues with which the WI was concerned included building of the Amber Tor flats, the siting of the public telephone in its present position, and in particular, requesting the Parish Council to build a bus shelter at the lower end of the village.

Despite the continuing role of the WI at the centre of village life, the numbers steadily declined. Many older members died and others left to live elsewhere. By 1980, only twenty-seven were on the roll. The Speakers' topics widened

Right: *Manaton WI members displaying the banner celebrating 75 years of the WI in 1995.*

Below: *The Manaton Parish map; a collage of embroidered and painted images associated with the parish.*

further, a typical selection being Antarctica, supermarkets, public speaking, travel in the Middle East, birds of prey, antiques and national parks, although flower arranging, crafts and cookery were still regularly booked. Fund-raising for charities was a continuing concern, but when the National Federation of Women's Institutes became a charity itself in the early 1990s, this was no longer possible, except for local ones. Many members lamented the passing of an important part of WI life.

After alternating between Mrs Smith and Miss Towning once more, the Presidency passed to Mrs Morris in 1982. Except for two years under Mrs Bearne, she remained until the sixtieth birthday of Manaton WI in 1990. This was celebrated by staging an exhibition of crafts in the Parish Hall with examples of spinning, quilting, dress-making, embroidery, tapestry, floral art and painting produced by members.

During the last ten years it was discovered that catering for parties was an excellent way to fund-raise. A lunch and tea for English Nature lifted

the bank balance to an unprecedented level, and catering for other WIs and organisations, together with cream teas in the summer, became an enjoyable and profitable part of the year's work.

In 1992, Mrs Baldwin followed Miss Towning's third term of office, and remained until 1997. In 1995, the seventy-fifth Anniversary of the founding of the Devon Federation occurred and a whole year of events was planned. A banner was carried by various means from institute to institute throughout the county over several months, and Manaton received it from Lustleigh WI who walked across the Cleave. Widecombe WI was to be the next recipient, so a party from Manaton walked across in paired relays, those not walking riding in a decorated car.

There was a 'Midsummer Miscellany' of events at Stover School during 1995, one of which was a collection of parish maps. Manaton's map was begun 18 months before the exhibition, with help from other people in the village as it was meant to be a parish project. The finished map, showing the parish surrounded by embroidered paintings depicting places, houses, animals and plants, now hangs in the Parish Hall for future generations to see. 1995 was also the fiftieth anniversary of VE day. The WI catered for a lunch in the suitably decorated Parish Hall while the Royal British Legion arranged the drinks. A very enjoyable time was had by all.

The present members of Manaton WI number twenty-one, but due to healthy funds, the standard of the varied Speakers remains high. With regular trips both near and far, catering for the Show and Fair teas as well as other groups, sharing Christmas lunch with husbands and friends, staging exhibitons and entering competitions with other institutes, and socialising at parties, the original purposes of education, friendship and fun are as relevant as ever. Mrs Fitton, the President since 1997, can lead the WI with confidence into the next millennium.

THE ROYAL BRITISH LEGION

A meeting of thirteen ex-servicemen was held on the 10 February 1928 in the Assembly Room of the Kestor Inn, during which the Rev. J Kitson proposed that a branch of the British Legion be formed in Manaton. The proposal was seconded by Mr S. Harvey and carried unanimously. A membership fee of 2s.6d. was agreed. Colonel C. Francis was elected as President, Major Rev. J Woodhouse as Chairman, Rev. J. Kitson as vice-Chairman, and Mr S. Scarr as Secretary. At the meeting it was proposed that men other than ex-service personnel could be asked to join the Legion as honorary members.

The next meeting on the 10 March that year was also held in the Kestor, during which the branch was inaugurated. Some seven names were proposed as vice-Presidents including the Rt Hon.

Members of the British Legion, churchmen and churchgoers, commemorate the fallen on Remembrance Day 1998, standing before the memorial to those Manaton men who gave their lives in two World Wars.

Viscount Hambleden. Rules and bye-laws were read out and adopted, and each person was issued with a membership card.

The meeting during April made arrangements to celebrate Empire Day (long since disappeared). The meeting at the end of May was held in St Winifred's Room, during which a Benevolent Fund and Committee were set up and also an Entertainments Committee. The organisation of a supper to commemorate Armistice Day, which had been held in previous years, was taken over by the Legion.

The annual commemoration of Armistice Day with wreath-laying at the village memorial was organised, the wreath being made by ex-servicemen at the British Legion Poppy Factory. The Entertainments Committee organised dances and whist drives during the course of each year which helped to raise funds to support the Benevolent Fund and to donate to Legion charities.

There do not appear to have been any meetings between September 1938 and October 1945, although a page missing from the minutes perhaps explains this break. At the October 1945 meeting the membership was 15 and the subscription was still 2s.6d. In November 1946, Major Woodhouse presented a standard to the branch and in 1947 J. Endicott became the Standard Bearer.

In October 1948, Major Woodhouse resigned as President and Brigadier Welchman was elected in his place. A vote of thanks was given to Major Woodhouse for all his work for the branch since its inception, and all members raised their glasses in his honour.

The regular pattern of whist drives, dances, annual dinner (or buffet supper) and Remembrance Day Commemoration continued until the late 1980s. Whist drives and dances then ceased to be popular and were discontinued. Cream teas at weekends during the summer months took over for fund-raising.

In 1971 the British Legion was granted its Royal prefix and became the Royal British Legion.

In May 1995, the 50th Anniversary of V.E. Day was celebrated in the Parish Hall with a lunch and an evening dance to 1940s music. The event was arranged in conjunction with the Manaton WI and was both successful and enjoyable.

Manaton Branch has a present membership of 26 and its finances are in a healthy state. The efforts of a small team in providing cream teas enables us to donate between £300 and £400 each year to be shared between three residential homes run by the Legion.

The first poppy collection began in 1921 and for many years this task in Manaton has been the responsibility of Penny Keogh, and a band of helpers. During that time the amount raised has steadily increased. In 1998 the total collected house-to-house was £478 and £160 was given at the memorial service, making £638 in all. This, together with £400 from the cream teas represents a very generous response from a small moorland village.

The roll of Manaton Branch Chairmen is as follows:

1928 Major Rev. J. Woodhouse
1948 Brigadier G. de V. Welchman
1968 Lt-Colonel G. Wilkinson
1974 R. Hugo
1976 H. F. Pearce

Our present Chairman has held the office for the last 23 years and is still going strong.

THE PARISH HALL

On the 5 October 1928 a social meeting and dance was held in the galvanised iron hut known as St Winifred's Room, or the Iron Room, which was used as the church hall. The large number of people present gave proof of the need in the parish for larger accommodation and a building committee was set up in 1929 to plan ahead.

During 1930, a parcel of land on which the hut stood was leased to the parish from the glebelands of Manaton Rectory for 21 years, at an annual rental of £1.

Unfortunately the details of these early days are not known as the minutes of the Parish Hall Management Committee before January 1981 are missing. However, some correspondence relating to the lease was kept and from this we know that the Rev. J. Kitson was on the committee and the Rev. J. Woodhouse was the Secretary/Treasurer.

In January 1930, requests for tenders to extend and renovate the Iron Room were sent out to five local builders by R.A. Rodgers (Architect & Surveyor) acting for the committee. The contract was eventually awarded to C. A. Jeffery of Manaton, with the proviso that he undertook to complete the work by Easter under penalty of a suitable fine.

Entertainment was organised during the course of the following months to raise money for the building fund, and the Hall was officially opened on the 15 May 1930 by Mrs Kitson. From a comtemporary Parish Magazine it was reported

A crowded Parish Hall on opening day 1966.

that 'the opening ceremony which was largely attended, was followed by a social entertainment provided by local talent. The evening finished with a dance attended by over 100 people and carried on to the small hours of the next day.' The final charges for the lease of the land and hut were received in early December 1930 and totalled 12 guineas which the Treasurer considered to be excessive!

On the 17 and 18 June 1940, the last British troops were evacuated from France via the Cherbourg peninsula when France capitulated. Some 156 000 troops, including 20 000 Poles, were landed in South West ports, mainly Plymouth. Much larger vessels were used than in the earlier Dunkirk evacuation and there were many casualties when some of these ships were sunk. The troops were dispersed to resting billets until they could be catered for properly. Some of these soldiers were accommodated in Manaton at Town Barton, Ebworthy and the Church Cottages. The Parish Hall was used as a mess hall during this turbulent period.

In December 1951 the lease expired and a conveyance was drawn up by the Church Commissioners, selling the land for £25 to Trustees Margaret Sayers, Helen Duckworth Hunt, Brigadier Godfrey de Vere Welchman and Samuel Scarr. In June 1953, a new Trust regarding the running of the Parish Hall was prepared, specifying the purposes for which it could be used and that the general management and control of the premises be vested in a Committee of Management governed by a listed set of rules. This was in accordance with the requirements of the Charity Commissioners.

During November 1964, the Hall was irreparably damaged by a tree from Manaton Gate falling on it. Committee meetings for the next 2 years were held in the Kestor Inn. Plans for a new hall were drawn up by N. Rodgers and submitted during April 1965. The building specifications were presented during January 1966. Money for the new building was raised by public subscription and there is a photograph of a large thermometer outside the Kestor indicating the rising level of collected money. The total cost was in the region of £7000 and Group Captain P. Walker officially opened the new building.

During 1968, Brigadier Welchman died and a memorial table and chair in English oak, with an inscription, were commissioned from Herbert Read of Exeter at a cost of £89.10s. for use in the committee room. The Brigadier had played a very active role in the community life of Manaton over many years and the money was raised by public subscription.

The maintenance of the Hall is the responsibility of the Management Committee and over the years a number of improvements have been made such as double-glazing, insulation of the roof and water pipes, periodic redecoration inside and out, and refurbishment of the floors. The work is financed by grants from Rural Aid and by hiring for various activities and functions such as fortnightly whist drives, twice weekly badminton, art and yoga classes, theatre productions, occasional dances and parties, voting for elections both national and local, and meetings of various kinds such as the WI.

Other sources of income include the sale of cream teas on Saturday, Sunday and Monday during the summer months and an annual jumble sale. This enables the Committee to maintain the Hall in good order so that it can continue to form a venue for village activities.

15 - Sports and Pastimes

Hunting is probably the oldest sport in the parish. The Normans defined great areas of the country as out of bounds to all but the King and his appointed subjects as far as the chase was concerned, while the term 'Dartmoor Forest' refres not to a wooded area but to a tract specifically reserved for the hunt. In past times the quarry would have included wolves and wild boar, as well as deer.

Countrymen saw recreational hunting and shooting for the pot pretty much as the same thing, with rabbits (see page 60), hare and wildfowl being in greater abundance than now. Rook pie was not an uncommon country dish.

Trout and salmon were in plentiful supply as witnessed by the accounts of the Hunt family of Foxworthy (and tales of local poachers!). These days only the smallest native brown trout occupy the Bovey, while the spring and autumn run of sea trout and salmon are much reduced. Otters were a favourite quarry in the last century, as were 'fitches' (polecats), both hunted with hounds.

These sports, along with fox-hunting, are comparatively recent developments in the country calendar. Of the photographs provided for use in this book a considerable number show the hunt in progress – a reflection of how significant this activity was in the life of the parish.

THE SOUTH DEVON HUNT

The history of the South Devon Hunt for the first one hundred years of its existence is well documented in Edward J. F. Tozer's book which, written in 1919, records that George Templar of Stover sold 'ten couples of hounds to the Belvoir Hunt in

Hounds and huntsmen in the rocks above Ebworthy in the late 1930s.

Left: *The South Devon Hunt meets on Manaton Green in the 1920s.*

Below: *The South Devon Hunt on Easdon Tor c.1930.*

YARNER HOUSE.

There was a slight blue haze when the South Devons met at Yarner House on Tuesday, where they were hospitably entertained by Mrs. Lee, and the chances of a scent seemed all too remote. However, the reverse, happily, proved to be the case, and a brilliant hunt with a kill in the open and a 5¼ mile point was enjoyed from the big Yarner woodland. The draw commenced above the iron mines, and, before long, a fox was roused opposite the Keeper's Cottage. Instead of beating about the wood, he elected to leave at once for Shewte Gorse. Leaving this, hounds kept Reddaford Thatch on their left as they crossed the road to the Soldridge Gorse. They stuck to their fox grandly here, and, after ten minutes' close hunting, forced him to quit. He now retraced his steps to Yarner Wood, passed the mine chimney, and crossed the lower drive above the cascade. A sharp left turn on his part brought hounds back over the stream, and crossing the main drive, they broke the covert fence on to the moor after 45 minutes. Scaling Haytor Down the pack inclined right towards Black Hill, swung left as if for the Rubbie Heap, and finally dropped into the Leighon Valley by Smallacombe Rocks. The stream was negotiated above the fishponds, hounds then bearing right for Greator Rocks. Finding the big earths stopped, their stout pilot continued to Hound Tor, and from this time forward was evidently beginning to feel the pace. After a short double he crossed the head of Houndtor Combe and led his pursuers past Jane's Grave to Cripdon Down, where they swung left into Heatree. There was many a twist and turn in the plantation before hounds came out into the meadows by Heathercombe Cottages, and they brought a first-rate hunt to a successful conclusion as they pulled their fox down in the kitchen-garden of the Forest Fox Farm. Time: 1 hour 50 minutes. Only four were up at the finish, besides the Hunt staff, Mr. P. Carew, Miss Betty Kitson, Captain A. H. Wheeler and Mr. Roger Leach. The last-named received the mask, while the brush was handed to Miss Kitson.

GIMCRACK.

Above: *Newscutting reporting an exciting chase across the parish c.1940.*

Right: *Paulie James – shooting in the fields near Latchel c. 1935.*

1810'. Thus Templar was the first recognised Master of the South Devon Hunt and began a tradition which has lasted for nearly two hundred years. Originally the 'country' hunted stretched from Cheriton Fitzpayne in the north to Prawle Point in the south, and from Okehampton in the west to Exmouth in the East.

The spread of urbanisation and the break up of many large estates has seen a reduction in the size and type of country hunted, and the majority of meets are held in and around moorland parishes. The Green has been a traditional meeting place (see photographs on page 44 and 144) and a large number of Manaton parishioners have been keen supporters throughout the history of the Hunt. Washington Singer, son of the famous American entrepreneur, not only lived in the village, at Leighon, but was Master of the Hunt from 1901 until ill health forced him to resign in 1907.

The First World war saw the requisition of many hunt horses by the army for active service, many perhaps to perish along with Manaton men in the mud of Flanders and the Somme. The Whitley family, then of Barton Pines and Primley, did much to sustain the hunt during that war and, many years later, Claude Whitley of Hedge Barton farm held the mastership for over 30 years.

The Dartmoor countryside has always attracted huntsmen from outside the area who are enchanted by the beauty of the wide open spaces and delighted by the opportunity to see hounds working from afar.

Present parishioner members of the South Devon Hunt include, Dr S. Lake (Chairman) and Mrs T. Lake, Miss S. Smith, Miss F. P. James, Mrs A. Howarth, Mr P. Ripman, Miss S. Rich, Miss G. Everitt, Mr and Mrs H. Whitley. Several meets are held within the parish each year in addition to the annual meet at Manaton Green; the latter being well supported by local people.

Whilst the future for fox hunting would appear to be short-lived, the past near two hundred years of this very traditional English country sport will long be remembered.

MANATON RIFLE CLUB

The Manaton Rifle Club is one of the oldest established parish clubs or institutions, being formed on 26 May 1908 at a public meeting held in the School Room, Manaton. Some 14 persons formed its first executive committee with a further 17 adults and 5 youths enrolled as additional members. The annual subscription was set at 2s.6d. Ammunition was sold at five shots for one penny.

With such local dignitories as the Rector, the writer John Galsworthy, Mr Kitson, other local landowners and workers in support the club soon had a 100 yard outdoor range.

Two Martini-Henry .22 calibre rifles were purchased at a cost of £1.6s.6d. each and 5000 rounds of ammunition at 11s.6d. per thousand. Affiliation to the National Rifle Association and approval of the range by Captain Law of the Devon Regiment, British Army, were completed by June of that year.

Plans for an indoor 25 yard range in the school grounds were soon in hand with John Galsworthy donating £20 for materials and labour. Silas Harvey, the local carpenter and undertaker agreed to build the club room and a range with two firing points.

In the early days the range was lit by both oil and acetylene lamps, with a coke stove for heating. The tale is told of local lads climbing on to the roof and blocking the chimney causing much distress to those meeting in the room below.

The popularity of the club as a meeting place is well recorded throughout the First World War with regular deliveries of newspapers (donated by the Galsworthy family), and use of its facilities for Whist Drives, meetings of such organisations as the Parish Council, Labourers Union, the War Memorial Committee, and the Royal Horticultural Society.

By 1919 the club had built a skittle alley within the indoor range after protracted negotiations with the Reverend Kitson of the Old School over the gifting of six feet of land to the club. Between the wars the club was used as a meeting room by the local cricket and football clubs and at one time by the local Rural District Council. Even the plight of the club wireless (radio) was mentioned in the records when it failed to work and 'in light of the fact that most members now (1935) own their own wireless,' the donor was asked to remove it.

The cost (£9) of a replacement rifle for the old Martini-Henrys indicated rising costs since 1908. By the beginning of the Second World War the Manaton Women's Institute was using the club for the distribution of wool to Red Cross knitting parties who were making comforters for the armed forces. The indoor range continued to be operated by civilian club members, but with increasing use by the Home Guard and by servicemen billeted in the village.

Wilfred Creber served for a long period as club secretary both before, during and in the immediate post war period. From mid 1947 the club

Left: Manaton Rifle Club c. 1966. Back row l-r: Phil Warne; Brian Snell; A. Millard; Norman Warne; ?; Brian Warne. Front row: Wilf Creber; Paulie James; Mrs Mitchell; Miss Sampson (later Mrs Lyn Warne); F. Dymond.

Manaton Yoga Club in the Parish Hall, October 1999. Back row l-r: Mel Veal (teacher); Antonia Hoggett; Britt Merrison; Rob Steemson; Audrey Cullen. Middle row: Rosemary Whitton; Betty Wilson; Carol Fisher; Liz Bates; ?. Front row: ?, Janet Wellingham, Anna Butler, Yvonne Crout.

suffered falling membership and eventually failed to meet the rifle range safety standards, ceasing to operate for some time.

An interesting story related by Francis Germon tells of the discovery by his father of a badly holed watering can that he had previously hung in good order in a garden shed at the end of the range. It appears that members' shots were passing through the butts, penetrating the garden shed and making a colander of the watering can. Fortunately nobody was in the shed at the time.

In the early 1950s a well attended meeting decided to carry out renovation of the club facilities and it was at this point that the current president, Miss F. P. (Paulie) James, was first mentioned.

Brigadier Welchman became the driving force behind the club and a benefactor in that he donated a rifle. Charlie Cotton and Colonel Wadham helped in revitalising the club and increasing membership, supported by Miss James (Treasurer), Mrs Greenaway, Fred Dymond and Brian Moss. The club continued to meet at the original venue surviving fluctuating membership and collapse of the range roof – rebuilt by members of the club – until in 1966 it was presented with a trophy for fifty years' membership of the NSRA.

In more recent years much is owed to the support of the Warne family who have been regular members of the club (see photo above). Brian Warne was secretary and later Chairman of the club, retiring in 1997. Today the club continues to shoot in the Devon County Winter League and the Exeter Summer League. Membership is small in comparison to the large support at its inauguration in 1908 and current membership fees at £25 and ammunition at 5 pence per round reflect large changes in the near ninety years of the club's existence.

MANATON BADMINTON CLUB

This is one of the longer-lived of all Manaton's sporting activities, with members coming and going over the years, but always active. The Parish Hall provides sufficient room for a single court, with the low roof line requiring the development of skills peculiar to that venue.

MANATON GAMES COURT

For many years, Sally Doe had been of the opinion that a tennis court would be a desirable addition to the sporting facilities in Manaton, particularly for the children. She collected a group of like-minded people together, and in November 1987 a public meeting was called to see if the project would find support. The Parish Council agreed to back the idea and the next 18 months were devoted to raising money from grants, donations and events.

The site of the court was the first problem to be solved, as the Church Field was the choice of many people. However, there were problems with underground water and flying cricket balls, and the decision was made to ask for a lease on part of Mellowmead Field from the Parish Council.

The next problem was Planning Permission which would only be granted if the hedge at the side of the road running down from the entrance to the field was levelled to improve visibility and a hard-standing for 10 cars was built. A tarma-cadam court by Courtstall was chosen as not only cheaper than a Playdek type, but also more serviceable in Manaton's weather conditions.

Rural Aid granted £5000 for the project, the Sports Council £1500, and the Devon Playing Fields Association £500, but the Sports Council insisted that the court must be equipped for netball and volleyball as well as tennis, and that it should be known as a 'games' court - hence the name of the association.

Meanwhile, generous donations were acquired by the fund (one for £500!), and a number of events were held which involved a wide selection of parishioners. First, the children held a sponsored walk in Mellowmead Field, and this was followed by a skittles evening in the Kestor, a bridge afternoon and a square dance in the Parish Hall, and a sponsored ride and walk out to Challacombe and back to Houndtor.

Christmas cards bearing photographs of Manaton were sold in the shop, and a cleverly knitted family of dolls was also sold. By the spring of 1989, a total of £2500 had been raised, and this was sufficient – just – to build the court, have the hedge levelled, and build the hard-standing.

The problems were not over yet, as there was a suggestion that 5-a-side football would be required on the court. This would entail boarding around the netting to strengthen it, and it was beyond the means of the fund. A compromise was reached when it was agreed to sink Metposts around the edge of the court so that boarding could be installed at a later date if there was a demand.

At last everything was ready. The grants, each with a different time limit on them, were in place, the contractors were ready to begin, enough money had been collected, Trustees had been found and a 28-year lease signed.

Then the Government announced that, from 1 April 1989, VAT would be charged on sports facilities built by voluntary bodies. This bombshell rocked the project to its foundations as

£1200 more would be required, and by the time that was raised the grants would have been lost. The Parish Council came to the rescue by agreeing to pay all the bills with money given to it by the Games Court Association. As the land already belonged to the Parish Council and the court would belong to it as well, the VAT could be claimed back and the hardstanding built with that money later.

So in August 1989, the ground was levelled and prepared by Brian Warne, the court was laid and rolled, and the Metposts and netting were installed. The court was painted with lines in white for tennis and yellow for netball, and the tennis net was put in place. Later, the hard-standing was built, equipment for netball and volleyball were purchased, and Sally gave a hut, which had been in her garden, for storage.

The Grand Opening Ceremony was held on 2 September, and the Chairman of the Parish Council, Ron Hudson, cut the ribbon across the gate. Refreshments were provided for the large number of people who came, including the Chairman of the Rural Aid Committee, and the first games were played. Enrolments that day totalled 76, and lists of those interested in games other than tennis were circulated. However, since then there has been no demand and apart from a few games of volleyball, tennis has been the only game played.

The Association is still run by virtually the same committee which saw the project through: Pauline Evans, Maggie Kapff, Jean and Michael Baldwin, Sally Doe, Anna Butler and Colin Stewart, while Clare Boughey is the Parish

Ron Hudson cuts the tape at the official opening of the Games Court, September 1989.

The cast of The Hedge *included from those living in Manaton at the time: Penny Keogh as Bramble, Norman Littler as Authority, Gena Evans as Woman from the Ministry, Jan Goddard as Barbed Wire, Mairi Hunt as Birch, Julia Oliver as Sheep, Kate Oliver, George Oliver, Abigail Clapp and Vicki Newton as Lambs, Alison Hastie as Small Business, David Evans as Holly, Pauline Evans as Femina Leathergaiterus, Mike Baker as Homo Leathergaiterus, Mike Malseed as Law and Order, Laura Newton as Peace, Adam Perkins as Fox and Katie Perkins as Butterfly.*

Council representative. The number of members in its heyday was 94, but unfortunately interest has lessened recently and the number is down to 60. This is still impressive, and it is hoped that newcomers to the village will continue to use this excellent and most attractive facility which took so much effort to build.

MANATON AND EAST DARTMOOR THEATRE

By no means all the recreational activities in the village involve sport and Manaton has quite a tradition of concerts and theatrical events. Various groups, including the WI, have staged plays, whilst visiting theatre groups have performed at the Parish Hall and on the Green.

MED theatre was born out of the aspirations of playwright and poet, Mark Beeson, who grew up in Manaton and who has lived at Easdon for many years. The theatre had its roots in a play called *The Badgers*, written by Mark and performed by local young people in a barn at Easdon Farm in 1980. The core of this group was again involved when Mark Beeson initiated the performance of a village community play, *The Hedge*, in Manaton Parish Hall in April 1984, in collaboration with Phil Oliver and members of his Manaton choir.

Manaton Parish Hall Management Committee provided a grant of £50 on condition that any profits were donated to the Parish Hall. Hessian wings and backdrop had to be hung on a temporarily constructed frame as there is no permanent stage in the hall. This served as a model for all the play sets, until MED Theatre began performing in the round in 1997.

Three more plays followed – *Childe the Hunter, The Swallows,* and *The Green Woman* - until in 1989 the informal Manaton play was formally constituted as the Manaton and East Dartmoor Theatre (MED Theatre) and registered as a charity. Since then, with Mark Beeson as artistic director, twelve community plays, a mini-musical and a children's play have been performed, covering subjects ranging from the future (*The Wilderness* and *The Unknown*) through contemporary times (*The Salmon, Forest Fantasy ,The Bees, Monkey Rock, The Audience, The Therapists* and *The Forest Fire*) to the past (*The Paint Man, The Dragon and the Mermaid, The White Bird of the Oxenhams, The British in Exeter,* and *A History of Dartmoor Theatre*).

Performances mix professionals with amateurs, and adults with children. The plays have been built in Manaton, involving over the years more than sixty different people from the parish alone, and then toured to village halls and occasionally other venues in the Dartmoor area and its vicinity. Performances at Manaton between 1984 and 1997 had refreshments served by members of the Manaton Parish Hall Management Committee, and the Committee has helped the plays in various other ways.

The Dragon and the Mermaid in 1994 involved a cast of more than 40, and was watched by over 400 spectators. MED Theatre has also put on many drama, music and movement workshops, as well as courses on playwriting, some in Manaton, some elsewhere. The organisation, whose aim is to produce theatre for and by Dartmoor people, has worked extensively with teenagers and with children, particularly through the local primary school in Moretonhampstead, where many Dartmoor plays written by the pupils have been performed.

Since 1990 MED Theatre has been funded by various grant-making bodies, in particular the Carnegie United Kingdom Trust and Teignbridge District Council, and locally by the Manaton Show and Fair Committee and the Claude and Margaret Pike Woodlands Trust. In 1998 the organisation obtained more substantial funding from the European Regional Development Fund along with matching funding for a three-year project called Performing Dartmoor.

MANATON CRICKET CLUB

As with the Rifle Club, Manaton Cricket Club owes much to the influence of John Galsworthy and his contemporaries. He obviously cared a great deal about his cricket, even at village level, writing in a letter to London a triumphal account of how Manaton had overcome their local rivals Moretonhampstead. Some things don't change!

The exact date of the club's founding is unknown but an account book survives from 1921 detailing the subscriptions received. A number of familiar names appear including Galsworthy, various Kitsons, Lord Hambelden and Washington Singer, along with Sam Scarr, Silas Harvey, Leonard Skerrett and the Vallances. All this was before the purchase of the Church Field

Above: *A photograph from a photo album of Leighon. Manaton cricketers at Bovey Tracey in the mid 1920s.*

Right: *A page from the Manaton CC treasurer's notebook, which runs from 1921 to 1962. This, the first entry, indicates that this was when the club was founded. It contains the names of many men who have played for Manaton over that period, along with details of revenue and expenditure.*

A photograph dated August 1925 from Paulie James 'Manaton CC and other players'. 1. F. Vallance; 2. Mr Ferguson; 3. Mr Savil; 4. J. Douglas Kitson; 5. Mr Ferguson; 6. L. Price; 7. T. James; 8. R.C. James (vice-captain); 9. Mr Hammersley; 10. H. Wreford; 11. A. 'Buzz' Kitson; 12. Rev. J.A. Kitson; 13. Bob Kitson; 14. W. Kitson; 15. Major J. Woodhouse; 16. E. Underhill; 17. Mrs Hammersley; 18. Sam Scarr; 19. E.G.T. Lowe (captain); 20. Canon L. Evans; 21. G. Parker; 22. A. Kitson; 23. T. Pattle.

in 1929 when cricket was played at Heatree, although some have said games were also played at Cross Park.

Tom Pollard has a watercolour sketch from the 1920s by the artist Maude Earle, celebrated in her day for her pictures of dogs and horses, passed on to him by his grandmother who lived at Wingstone. It shows John Galsworthy and his spaniel, with a cricket ball lying in the foreground.

An early photograph, taken at Leighon in the 1920s, shows a group of men off to play at Bovey Tracey, resplendent in striped blazers. The earliest photograph known to be of Manaton Cricket Club comes from Paulie James and is dated 1925. The earliest surviving fixture card is from the 1930 season and minute books and scorebooks survive from 1949 onwards.

Manaton was unique in the county for having a concrete wicket, and at one time the village MCC advised its older cousin on the suitability of this novel form of surface. Nowadays most clubs have an artificial wicket

MANATON CRICKET CLUB

Date	Opponents	Ground	Result	Runs for	Runs agst.	Member's Score	Member's Wickets
May 3	Depot Devon Regt.	Home	Won	100	50		
,, 10	Babbacombe II.	Home	Scr.	Rain —			
,, 17	Depot Devon Regt.	Away	Lost	78	105 (9)	10.	0.
,, 24	Chagford	Away	Won	69	55		
,, 27	Kelly College	Away	Lost	105 (9)	139 (9)	2	
,, 31	Newton Abbot Y.M.C.A.	Home	Draw.	47 (4)	—		
June 7	Chudleigh II.	Away	Draw.	95 (6)			
,, 14	Torquay Y.M.C.A.	Home	Draw.	68 (7)	133.		
,, 21	Moretonhampstead	Away	Lost	45	105		
,, 28	Newton YMCA	Home	Won	124 (6)	78		
July 5	Chudleigh II.	Home	Scr.		95		
,, 12	Newton Secondary School	Home	Scr.				
,, 19							
,, 26							
Aug 2	Sports						
,, 4	Chagford						
,, 9	Babbacombe II. ...	Home	Lost				
,, 16	Torquay Y.M.C.A.	Away	Lost	11	150		
,, 20	Canon L. H. Evans' XI.	Away	Won	69	99		
,, 23	Moretonhampstead	Home	Scr.	77 (4)	98		
,, 30	Dartington ...	Home					
Sept 6	Dartington						

Left: Fixture card from 1930.

Right: Manaton CC playing at Torquay YMCA, possibly in the away fixture on the card above which they won narrowly by one run. Known players are (back row): Bob Kitson, far left; F. Vallance, 3rd from left; Sam Scarr, far right; (front row): A.B. Kitson, 2nd from left; E.G.T Lowe 3rd from left; E. Underhill, far right.

of some kind so Manaton could be said to have been fifty years ahead of its time. The truth, however, is that the wicket was born of necessity. Following the purchase of the Church Field in 1929, the club met to discuss the creation of a grass wicket, as the minutes of a meeting held at the Kestor Hotel on 18 August 1948 record. Captain J. J. Hallett 'believed the only solution as far as the pitch was concerned was to lay a concrete or tarmac slab and have a matting wicket'. Mr J. Edwards objected to this proposal on the grounds that it would be a handicap to have con-

crete in the middle of a playing field and that the bowlers would be likely to 'dig graves' at either end. After much discussion it was agreed unanimously that the club should construct a turf wicket as soon as the field became available.

However, a year later, with a season in which no home games were played, a concrete wicket was built over which coconut matting was laid, and the rest, as they say, is history.

The club continued until the early 1960s with the treasurer's notebook detailing subs up to the season of 1962. Then, through lack of players, the

MANATON CRICKET CLUB

Left: *Cricket in the 1940s.*

Below: *A photograph that appeared in the* Times *in the 1940s, summing up the appeal of Manaton's ground. There are few better views in cricket.*

Manaton C.C. advise M.C.C.
EXPERIMENTS WITH CONCRETE WICKET
"BEST EVER" SEASON

Tiny Manaton Cricket Club have been asked for their views on the subject of concrete wickets by the mighty M.C.C.

This small moorland hamlet has been doing great things in the interests of cricket and cricketers this season by being the first village club, locally, to play their matches on a concrete wicket.

The pros and cons of the experiment will be listed in a full report to the M.C.C. at the end of the season.

Col. G. A. Wadham, the popular hon secretary of the Manaton Club explained that it all started at the beginning of th   n when they found that

cricket, the Colonel maintains that the majority are not. "Anybody who plays on them is always a little fearful that the ball is going to fly up suddenly and hit them. A batsman never knows what is going to happen on some of these grass pitches. At Manaton, we wanted something that was going to be fairly reasonable. On concrete the ball comes through true and at a respectable height, and a spin-bowler must obtain results by his skill rather than rely upon the odd dandelion."

Better coaching benefits for cricketers is anoth   in emp'

A cutting from the South Devon Times of 1949 which refers to the occasion on which the MCC asked Manaton for its opinion on the artificial wicket. Note the trenchant observation about bowlers 'relying on the odd dandelion'. At the time a concrete and matting wicket was a rarity in this country, although games, including first class matches, were regularly played on this surface in India and South Africa.

Pages from the treasurer's notebook dated 1957. They record subscriptions from the inimitable Gaywood brothers. Richard, Mike and Ken Gaywood were stalwarts of Manaton CC in this period, and became a major force in local cricket over several decades.

club ceased to function. It was to remain in abeyance until 1976 when one of the driest summers on record inspired locals to think of re-establishing a cricket team.

Those instrumental in this revival were Simon Butler, Jim and Nick Crout (who had started playing in the 1950s), Brian Warne, Mick Moreton, Eddie Walker and Jim Harries. The field was by now a cow pasture although the concrete slab survived, as did the coconut matting, now used as a squirrel's nest, in the tea-shed that had survived intact. The first game was played on 29 April 1977 against Wheatons of Exeter and 23 games were played in all that year, Manaton victorious in 15 of them. Players at this time included Dave Thomas, Tom Pollard, Miles and Simon Partridge, Dave Amery and Terry Turner. Winnie Walker was the official scorer for many of the early seasons, John Frost official club umpire.

Manaton CC 1950, outside the old wooden pavilion and tea shed. It was the latter building, with its lift-up front, that survived until the club was reformed in 1976. The gentleman in the background with the trilby is Clarence Stacey.

MANATON CRICKET CLUB

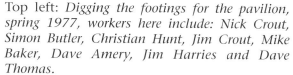

Top left: *Digging the footings for the pavilion, spring 1977, workers here include: Nick Crout, Simon Butler, Christian Hunt, Jim Crout, Mike Baker, Dave Amery, Jim Harries and Dave Thomas.*

Top right: *Sam Butler emerging from the pavilion.*

Above: *Roofing begins, summer 1977.*

Left: *Opening ceremony - the ribbon is cut by Clive Gunnell. Jim Crout looks on. The clock originally came from Newton Abbot racecourse.*

Left: *Former Manaton players at the opening of the new pavilion. They include Clarence Stacey, Charlie Crout, and Frank Vallance.*

MANATON CRICKET CLUB

Left: *A Manaton Ladies versus Ilsington Ladies match in 1977, raising funds for the club. At bat is Alison Bean (née Snell), Anna Butler backing up.*

Below: *Celebrating the opening of the pavilion in 1978 – Manaton CC v. a Celebrity XV from Westward Television. MCC members include: John Frost (umpire), Dave Amery, John Hutchings, Simon Butler, Phil Oliver, Dave Thomas, Mel Goddard, Mike Baker, Nick Crout, Cyril Giles, Tom Pollard and Jim Crout.*

Manaton CC 1977. Back row standing l-r: Mick Moreton; Simon Partirdge; Jim Harries; Dave Amery; Tom Pollard; Dave Thomas. Front row: Andy Martin (Seale-Hayne Student); Miles Partridge; Jim Crout; Simon Butler; Nick Crout; Mike Baker.

Manaton CC 1978. Back row standing l-r: *John Frost (umpire); John Hutchings; Dave Amery; Mel Goddard; Andrew Martin (bearded); Eddie Walker; Tom Pollard; Jim Crout.* Front row: *Dave Thomas; Simon Butler; Cyril Giles; Phil Oliver; Mark Harries.* Children l-r: *Sam Butler; Anne-Marie Crout; George Oliver.*

Manaton CC 1979. Back row standing l-r: *John Frost (umpire); Nick Crout; Jim Crout; Simon Butler; Dave Amery; Mel Goddard; Dave Thomas; Steve Miners.* Front row: *Mark Harries; Jim Harries; Cyril Giles; Eddie Walker; Mike Baker; Terry Turner; Carl Allerfeldt. Mike Baker was famous for arriving on his Triumph motorbike with his dog, Nelly, sitting on the petrol tank. 'Which one's steering?' was a common remark.*

Manaton CC 1980. Back row standing l-r: *Dick Taylor (Kestor landlord); Jim Crout; Dave Amery; Andrew Martin; Simon Butler; Cyril Giles; Gordon Hooper;* Front row: *Mike Baker; Phil Oliver; Eddie Walker; Tom Pollard; Peter Austin. Children: George Oliver and Sam Butler. Eddie Walker was almost solely responsible for the building of the original children's play area on the field, and worked tirelessly for the MCC in its early years. His efforts were rewarded by his being voted 'Teignbridge Sports Personality of the Year' for the best 'backroom' worker.*

THE BOOK OF MANATON

The following January (1977) saw work beginning on the new pavilion for which a grant of £4700 had been obtained from Rural Aid, the remaining 50% of the costs being raised by the club. Jim Crout trained a motley band of workers, including a dentist, a journalist, and several farmers, in the art of mixing concrete and laying blocks and during that year the pavilion gradually took shape. In May 1978, at a grand opening attended by a huge crowd, and players from past and present, the pavilion was officially opened. A year or two later the old coconut matting gave way to a full size astro-turf wicket.

At its height Manaton became one of the strongest village sides in Devon, with the fiery concrete wicket matching the temperament of a number of its fast bowlers. Not every team has entirely happy memories of their visit! However, Manaton enjoyed great success in the South Devon Village League, winning the trophy three times, and usually participating in the league finals.

The beauty of the ground, and the reputation of its unmatched teas, brought many touring sides to the club, some of whom have continued to visit year after year. With the Kestor as 'Official MCC HQ' many a night has been spent celebrating, or commiserating over games won and lost.

In common with many village teams, Manaton suffers from lack of fresh young talent. Many of its current players have been with the club since 1976 and are now not in their first flush of youth. Young players tend to move from the area, either to find work or to attend college, leaving the club with a shortage of players. However, all those who have participated, over seventy years, can be proud to have provided yet another cohesive force in the community, bringing together people of different backgrounds and ages to participate in a common enjoyable aim.

Above left: *Manaton CC indoor team narrowly beat Chudleigh and Bovey Tracey in a nail-biting final to win the Indoor Cricket cup in 1985. Pictured standing l-r: Eddie Walker (President); Mel Goddard; Jim Crout; Simon Butler; Dave Thomas (umpire); Winnie Walker (scorer). Front row: Dave Amery; Tom Pollard; Pete Bartlett.*

Last ball title win

A SPECTACULAR batting assault, in which they scored 53 runs off the last three overs, saw Manaton snatch a last-ball victory against favourites Bovey Tracey and win the Teignbridge Six-A-Side Indoor Cricket Championship at the Broadmeadow Sports Centre, Teignmouth.

After beating holders Chudleigh off the last ball in their first match, Manaton were set to score a daunting 134 in 12 overs by Bovey in the round-robin play-offs.

An unbeaten 34 by Tom Pollard and Dave

Amery's hard-hitting 30 not out carried them to victory and lifted the Stonelake Trophy at the end of their first season in the competition.

Final Scores:
Chudleigh 96-5 (S. Grayson 27; S. Butler 2-15). Manaton 96-4 (P. Bartlett 23) — Manaton won on fewer wickets lost.
Bovey Tracey 133-2 (B. Shaw 28no, S. Mills 26no, K. Butcher 22), Manaton 134-4 (T. Pollard 34no, D. Amery 30no, S. Butler 19) — Manaton won by two wickets.
Bovey Tracey 88 (B. Shaw 21, K. Butcher 21), Chudleigh 89-3 (A. Scott 27).
Final positions — 1. Manaton; 2. Chudleigh; 3. Bovey Tracey.

Left: *Manaton Captain in 1985, Jim Crout holds up the league cup which Manaton won that year along with the league title shield. Jim has played for Manaton in each year of its existence since 1950, and intends to play at least one game in the year 2000 to celebrate his Golden jubilee!*

Manaton CC 1987. Back row standing l-r: *Tom Amery (President); Dave Amery and his daughters Hannah and Vicky; Martin Hann; Paul Foot; Graham Rees; John Eddison; Jim Crout; Howard Basham;* Sitting on bench l-r: *Bob Bowes; Mel Goddard and his son Charlie; Simon Butler; Winnie Walker.* Sitting front: *Eddie Walker; Steve Martin; Sadie Butler and Luke Beeson.*

Right: *Manaton CC 1995.* Back row standing l-r: *Gordon Hooper; Graham Rees; Mark ?; Samuel Butler;* Middle row: *Bob Bowes; Howard Basham; John Butler; Simon Butler;* Front row: *Paul Hooper; Brain Male; Harry Butler.*

Manaton CC 1999. Back row standing l-r: *Mark Wakefield; Jim Crout (wearing a Manaton 2000 tee-shirt); Graham Deasy; Simon Butler; Richard Thorns; Howard Basham.* Front row: *Luke Wakefield; Brian Male; Cyril Giles; Bob Bowes (Captain); Mel Goddard; Harry Butler.*

16 - Events and Celebrations

The Church Field on Show and Fair day, taken from the church tower. Inset top: *Horticultural Show Challenge Cup presented by Miss Lancaster Lucas in 1932, won by J Endacott 1932/33, J. Skerrett 1934, and L. Skerrett 1935/7.* Inset bottom: *The Sports Cup presented by Mr and Mrs Walter Kitson, won 1922/24 by L. Skerrett.*

THE SHOW AND FAIR

The Manaton Show and Fair is now a well-established landmark in the village calendar and it might seem that it had a long tradition behind it, but this is not entirely true, at least in its present form.

It is known that there has been a horticultural show in Manaton on a regular basis for probably 60 or 70 years. This used to be run by a Flower Show Committee and was held on Mill Field, just west of Hayne Cross. This was very much a traditional village horticultural show displayed in a marquee with open classes and classes for cottagers. Cottagers were defined as those working for a weekly wage, in other words who were not professional gardeners and who would have to tend their gardens in the evenings and at weekends. The standard was nevertheless high and the competition keen, to the extent in fact that on one occasion at least, members of the committee went round inspecting gardens to see that all entries had been grown in Manaton and complied with the rules of the Show! On hearing of this, two leading competitors apparently declined to have their gardens inspected and withdrew their entries!

One of the trends over the past 40 or 50 years, noticed in Manaton as well as elsewhere, has been the decline in the growing of vegetables. But in the years between the Wars and even for a time after 1945 there were many keen vegetable gardeners such as Charlie Crout, Pat Perryman, Lewis Hern and Bill Hutchings, and the quality and number of entries for the vegetable classes in particular was much higher than today.

Along with the horticultural marquee on Mill Field in past years, used to go a few tradesmen's stalls and an afternoon of gymkhana and sports events, organised for some time by Charles Perryman. There was a variety of sports, not only for children, but for adults as well, such as a tug-of-war, high jumping and pole vaulting competitions (see page 80). There was also a Manaton-

Left: *Bill Burrell and his son dressed up for the 'Fayre' in 1968.*

Below: *Classic cars on the green, 1993.*

Top left: *The plant stall at Manaton Fayre and Market, 1969. Betty Smith with the help of Susan Wheeler and May Towning, selling to the Rector, Robin Taylor, with Stella and young Debbie. Will Hannam stands in attendance.*

Left: *Bill Howe off to the Show with a prize potato c. 1935.*

Manaton Show and Fare Committee meeting at the Kestor to plan the 1999 Show. From left: Susan Smith, Janet Kennedy, Richard Thorns, Lyn Fitton, Andrew Taylor, Colin Stewart, John Ducker, Stan Fitton, and David Mason.

Manaton Show 1999- top left: MC for the day Colonel Robert Perkins. Top right: Penny Keogh on the Prize Draw stall. Bottom left: Brain Warne tossing the sheaf. Bottom right: Alan White and Mairi Hunt preparing the barbecue for the evening dance held in the marquee.

style triathlon relay, open to non-villagers as well, in which the first leg was raced on bicycles, the second run, and the third leg on horseback. Tom Heath and friends were for a long time the team to beat! As well as these there was a horse and pony gymkhana, with the emphasis on races and competitions which provided much entertainment for the visitors and no doubt profit for the bookmakers who organised a lively betting market on most events.

Gate money together with a house-to-house collection towards the Show prize money seem to have ensured that the show and gymkhana by and large covered its costs.

During the Second World War the Show was discontinued but thanks to the efforts of Wilfred Creber, who became the Show secretary in 1945 and held the post for about 25 years, it was revived when peace returned. He was supported by a committee which included at various times Jack Skerrett, Pat Perryman, Lilian Lentern, Doris Brown, Ann Pascoe, and Paulie James.

The War, however, marked the end of the equine sports (which were for a year or two in the late 1970s revived as a gymkhana by Jenny Harries) and since it had been these which had originally taken the whole event to Mill Field, the

Show subsequently moved into the heart of the village and ever since has used the Church Field.

The move to the Church Field also marked a further move away from an extreme emphasis on vegetables in the marquee and the introduction of more classes for flowers and cooking. A Ladies' Challenge cup was awarded for these, to match the Men's Challenge cup awarded for the vegetable classes, based on the belief, true perhaps then but scarcely sustainable today, that ladies don't grow vegetables and men don't grow flowers or cook! Anyone who questions this should ask a regular winner of the Men's Challenge cup, Paulie James!

It was in the 1960s, quite independently of the Horticultural Show, that the Parochial Church Council began to look at ways of raising funds for maintaining the church fabric, and this led to a Village Fayre and Market being held in June, 1967. Since there was a wish to differentiate this event from the annual Horticultural Show the choice of stalls was chosen with care; there was an auction, teas in the Parish Hall and above all, the helpers at the stalls all wore Victorian costumes - hence the 'Fayre'! The event was deemed a success, yielding the Church a net profit of £310.18s.9d, and everyone thought it should be

Manaton Show 1999 – top left: *Jim Crout and colleagues on the Manaton 2000 stall;* Top right: *David Shilston and Francis Germon take time out for a cuppa (Nigel Ford in background);* Bottom left: *The finish of the children's race;* Bottom right: *Jim Goddard mans the book stall.*

repeated. Similar events were therefore held in 1968 and 1969.

It was clear that many of the same people were involved in both events and, with the Show losing money, by 1970 the possibility of combining the Show with the Church's Fayre and Market was being openly discussed. At a public meeting on 26 November 1969, chaired by the Rector, Robin Taylor, general principles were agreed and it was decided that from 1970 the Show and the Fayre should combine, sharing the expenses initially with any proceeds going to build up a reserve fund and to make contributions, if possible, to the Church fabric, the Parish Hall, the Village Green, the Recreation Field and the Rifle Club. They were nothing if not optimistic in those days!

The first combined Manaton Show and Fair thus took place on 22 August 1970 and since then there has been just one annual village event.

The Show and Fair now takes place on the second Saturday of August each year. The centre of activity and entertainment is the Church Field but the church itself, the Village Green and the Parish Hall are all also now used.

Entertainment is now based on a main arena in which a variety of displays have appeared, from pipe bands to handbell ringers, from axe men to morris dancers, from falcons to parachutists.

The Show and Fair has also extended into the church itself. Initially a few items from the Church archives were put out for people to look at, but in the early 1980s David and Pauline Evans began to put on larger exhibitions, a sequence which was taken up by Maggie and Peter Kapff –Earth, Air, Fire and Water, East of Suez, and then in 1998 'Old Manaton' which was a major part of the build-up to the book you are now reading!

On the sporting front, the children's sports remain but for those wanting something a bit more challenging, and picking up the tradition set by the Mile Race of pre-war years (1st prize £5!) the Bowerman's Nose race became a well-known and popular event. Over the past thirty or forty years the Show and Fair has developed and its scale has increased, but its character hasn't changed. The primary aim is to organise an afternoon which will be enjoyed by those attending, as well as by all those who help to run it.

Fancy dress: Manaton men setting off for Moreton carnival in the 1920s. L-r: George Crout, Marwood Melhuish, Arthur Brown, Jack Skerrett and Sid Perryman.

EMPIRE DAY IN MANATON – 24 MAY 1929

The following extract comes from Manaton's *Church Magazine* of June 1929:

Empire Day was observed in due form: the school children attended Church in the morning when the object in observing the day was explained to them, that it was a day not of self-glorification or a spirit of boastfulness but of thanksgiving to God for His goodness to us as a nation and of remembrance of our responsibility to Him for the possession of so great an Empire.

In the afternoon the children gave a pageant of Empire in the schoolyard which was excellently rendered and much enjoyed by spectators and performers alike. The children did great credit to the trouble and care taken by Mrs Prowse and Miss Follett in producing the pageant. Medals were presented by Mr Champernowne to the children who had written the best essays on the Empire, the two first being won by Ivy Wreford and Kenneth Dixon repectively. The children and their mothers were afterwards entertained by the Manaton branch of

the British Legion to Tea in St Winifred's Room. The arrangements were carried out by Mr S. Scarr, the Secretary of the branch; thanks to his indefatigable efforts, the willing assistance of many helpers and the generosity of those who gave quantities of cream, cake and other delicacies, a most excellent tea was provided, which was thoroughly appreciated by all who partook of it.

THE CORONATION OF KING GEORGE VI

The photograph of the Green in 1937 shows it decked out with bunting and flags to celebrate the coronation of King George VI (see page 44). A group of villagers formed themselves into a band and played up and down the village from the Kestor to the Green for a week (see over)!

THE CORONATION OF QUEEN ELIZABETH II

The celebrations for the coronation of Queen Elizabeth II on the 2 June 1953 were planned by a committee which first met six months before. It comprised the Chairman, Brigadier Welchman,

The Manaton minstrels outside the shop on the Green in 1937. This impromptu band were said to have marched up and down from the Green to the Kestor every day for a week in order to celebrate the Coronation of King George VI. They include Reg Harvey, Bill Hutchings, Francis Heath, Jack Heath (from Mill Farm, father to Francis and Tom); Len Crout, Tom Marsh (from Hound Tor Farm); Les Prowse (son of Mrs Prowse the school-teacher), and Lewis Hern.

with Mr Edy as Secretary, Mr Harris as Treasurer, and Mrs Endacott, Miss Earle, Miss Haines, Mrs Wheeler, Mr Cotton, Mr Roberts and Colonel Wadham. Various ideas were put forward and suggestions for permanent memorials of four bus shelters, one to be ready in time for the day, and a portrait of the Queen were made. It was agreed that the over-seventies should have a souvenir and the children would receive commemoration medals as prizes. Suggestions for the day were a bonfire, children's races and a large tent on the Green sufficient for 100 people to have tea at one sitting.

Colonel Wadham was in charge of the children's races and a schedule in age groups for boys and girls was drawn up. The races were to be on the Green if the grass could be made suitable, with the obstacle race laid out on the Church Field. It was agreed that prizes of the new Elizabethan coinage should be given in addition to the medals.

The bus shelter estimate from Mr Tickner was accepted and he was told to go ahead with drawing up the plans. It was decided to have a commemorative plaque affixed to the finished shelter.

By the 14 May, the foundation had been laid, but the timber had still not arrived and neither had the design been approved by the planning authorities. However, by the 29 May the wood had been delivered – some of it unsound and having to be replaced – planning permission was given, and the shelter was ready for Coronation Day.

Meanwhile, the money rolled in from various fund-raising events, and by the 15 April had reached £127.11s.6d. The budget comprised medals £13, hire of tent £17, teas £40, Queen's portrait £5, and bus shelter £50, making a total of £125, but beer, cider and decorations were still required. By the 29 May the fund had risen to £148.4s.6d, which included donations from the British Legion and Cricket Club and it was thought that all expenses could be covered.

It was decided that the souvenir for the over-seventies should be a tea caddy containing half a pound of tea. Two and a half dozen were ordered and these were distributed privately by the Chairman who had paid for them himself. The Women's Institute provided the children's mugs and eight dozen were ordered as it was agreed that visiting children attending the celebrations could have them as well. After much deliberation it was agreed to purchase an uncoloured portrait of the Queen at £4.12s.

The preparation for the bonfire on Manaton Rocks began on the 25 April. A trailer would take brushwood as far as possible and the final ascent would be by relay. Villagers were asked to bundle up material for the fire so that it could be collected and the bonfire was carefully built by Arthur Brown, Lewis Hern and Sid Perryman, ready for the lighting on Coronation night.

Decorations for the Green were procured by Mrs Wheeler for £2, and fairy lights were lent by the W.I. The grass was cut and rolled, the tent was erected and seats and benches were placed inside so that all was ready for the great day.

The programme began with a religious service in the tent followed by the National Anthem. The children's races came next and the prizes were presented in the tent by Mrs Welchman. Eighty mugs were then given out by Mrs Endacott to all the children present. Tea for about 250 was followed by a cricket match between mixed teams on the Church Field until it was time to light the bonfire at 10 o'clock. Music from records was played throughout the festivities.

Two weeks after the Coronation, a public meeting was held to decide on the distribution of the surplus £12.2s.9d. As there was a coronation baby Pascoe, it was agreed to purchase a silver spoon. With the remainder, a litter basket for the shelter was obtained, and as the Parish Council would be taking over the maintenance, all surplus cash was handed over to help the precept. Unfortunately, the other bus shelters had to be abandoned due to lack of funds, and the one on the Green remains, together with the portrait of the Queen in the Parish Hall's committee room, as the permanent memorial.

THE SILVER JUBILEE

Twenty-five years after the Queen's accession to the throne a celebration on similar lines to that of the Coronation was held in Manaton. The Government thought that the weather would be more suitable in the summer, so the Silver Jubilee was held on 7 June 1977, with bonfires lit the evening before. Again, a committee was formed, but time had moved on and the members were from a different generation. The Chairman was

Mr Rose, Vice-chairman the Rev. Sherley-Price, Secretary Simon Butler, Treasurers Dr and Mrs Littler, and other members were Brian Warne, Mrs Stabb, Mrs Rose, Susan Smith and Anna Butler. Yvonne Crout and Mike Baker were co-opted later.

A house-to-house collection initially brought in £196.45 which was not thought to be sufficient, so a further appeal was made to bring the funds up to £209.75. A whist drive was held which brought in another £30. Jubilee crowns were purchased for the winners of the races, tankards for a Bowerman's Nose race, and mugs for all the children under the age of 16. Other expenses were the children's tea and the evening supper which was to be attended by 163 parishioners and a number of visitors. Mrs Crout estimated that £165 would cover the costs of the buffet and visitors would pay £1 towards the cost of their meal. Beer, cider and lemonade were purchased from the Kestor, allowing one pint for each person, and orange juice was obtained for distribution from the cricket pavilion during the afternoon.

Flags and bunting were hung around the Green, and programmes were taken to every household in the parish. On the eve of Jubilee Day, a great bonfire was lit on Hayne Down within sight of the village to coincide with a chain of bonfires which was kindled throughout the West Country at 10 o'clock.

On Jubilee Day itself, the bells were rung before the start of the church service which consisted of suitable prayers and hymns, and Mr Rose took the reading. The ladies' team for the cricket match was organised by Mrs Littler, but Mike Baker had not been able to persuade men other than those in the cricket team to play for the men. The children's races, organised by Mr Taylor, consisted of egg and spoon, sack, obstacle, tyre, 50 yard sprint, wheelbarrow and 3-legged, and visiting children were allowed to enter. The Fancy Hat Contest was open to both boys and girls and was judged by Mrs Stabb and Mrs Wheeler. Mrs Rose and Mrs Butler presented crowns to the three best hats and winners of the races. Mugs were presented to the children after tea by the Rector and Mrs Sherley-Price.

The Bowerman's Nose race was organised by Simon Butler and Mike Baker, while Susan Smith provided flags to mark the course of the race and a bus was used to take the competitors to the start. Tankards were presented to the first man and first woman home.

17 - Lore, Legend and Local Tales

Dartmoor abounds with stories of ghosts, fairies, whisht hounds and the devil and so it is not surprising that Manaton should have a share of these. In this book we have already heard of the penchant of the people of Manaton to carry their dead three times around the churchyard cross before burial – almost certainly a custom derived from pagan times. Other stories, such as the tale of the Spanish mother and her daughter who lived at Horsham (see page 101), also have a ring of truth about them.

However, many of the legends associated with the parish have their parallels in other parts of the country and ghosts and fairies have a way of transferring themselves from one place to another, especially if that place happens to be as evocative as Hound Tor or Bowerman's Nose.

The troop of ghostly knights in Horsham Cleave, though now well-established in the literature of Dartmoor, may well be a recent addition to the folklore scene. Jay's Grave, a prehistoric site, has a more convincing and poignant story attached to it.

JAY'S GRAVE

In the eighteenth century Kitty Jay, a young orphaned servant girl, became pregnant. Her lover abandoned her and to escape the shame of carrying a child out of wedlock with no family to help her, she hanged herself. In common with practice at the time, she could not be buried in consecrated ground, and was interred at the point

Jay's Grave today.

where the parish boundaries of Widecombe, North Bovey and Manaton meet so that her spirit would be unable to find its way back to any places she had formerly known.

In 1860 the grave was disturbed by a roadmender who, it is said, found the bones of a young woman. They were reburied at the same place in a coffin. Since then the grave always has flowers on it, but no one admits to knowing who puts them there.

John Galsworthy's short story *The Apple Orchard* is said to be based on the story of Kitty Jay, whilst the tale is included in numerous books, plays, and a TV film.

THE LEGEND OF BOWERMAN'S NOSE

Many years ago a man known as Bowerman the Hunter lived on the eastern part of the moor. He was a big and powerful man who owned a pack of large and fierce hounds which he enjoyed hunting over the moors. It was said that he was afraid of nothing, not even the Devil himself, but he was popular with the poor people of the moor to whom he was generous.

At that time there were witches who held their meetings in secluded places on the moors and terrorised local people who were afraid of them. The witches disliked Bowerman and were a little afraid of him because of his great strength and his pack of fierce hounds who went everywhere with him.

One evening Bowerman was out following the scent of a hare with his pack. Just as they nearly caught it the hare ran into a narrow valley, closely followed by the hounds and Bowerman himself. This valley was one where the witches used to hold their Sabbaths, and they suddenly found themselves interrupted by the hunt. Bowerman laughed, the dogs barked and the chase continued, leaving the witches screaming with rage. Once they had settled down they plotted their revenge. One of the witches had the power to turn herself into a hare. She did this and went to where she knew that Bowerman and the hounds would find her. The pack found her and gave chase. The witch gave Bowerman and his hounds a chase such as they had never experienced before until they were almost exhausted, then she sprung her trap. The witch, disguised as a hare, almost let herself be caught, but suddenly turned round the side of a tor where the other witches were hidden. The exhausted hunter found himself surrounded by the evil witches who cast a powerful spell, turning Bowerman and his hounds to stone where they stood. It is still possible to see the stone figure that was Bowerman with his stone hounds scattered around him and sometimes, when the night is dark, misty and moonless, local people say you can hear Bowerman and his pack following their quarry.

THE WHISHT HOUNDS

At one time it was believed that Dartmoor was hunted over at night by a black hunter with black fire-breathing hounds. They were known as the whisht hounds or wish hounds, and on stormy nights could be heard in full cry with the occasional blast of the hunter's horn. This story is told by Sabine Baring-Gould:

One night a moorman was riding home from Widecombe. There had been a fair, he had made some money and had taken something to keep out the frost as the night promised to be cold and wet. The horse knew the way better than his master and had crossed the ridge of Hameldown approaching a circle of upright stones. Suddenly there was a sound that startled the man – a horn blew and a pack of black dogs swept past him without a sound.

The moorman was not frightened, he had drunk too much, so when a black hunter came up to him he shouted 'Hey! Huntsman, what sport? Give us some of your game.'

'Take that,' replied the hunter, and threw something which the man caught. Then the black hunter rode on. The night was so dark that the man could not see what was in the bundle and he continued home thinking it seemed too big to be a hare and too small to be a deer. So as soon as he arrived home he called for a lantern only to find that the game hunted by the Black Rider was his own baby, dead and cold.

HOUNDTOR WOOD EARTHWORKS

Though not directly associated with ghosts, the Old Manaton Road is an atmospheric place. Just off the road is a footpath signed to Lustleigh, via the Cleave. Here there can be found some earthworks, known by local children in the 1920s and 30s as the Roman Fort, although in fact this is a sister site to the Hunter's Tor Iron Age Fort across the river. The ramparts are still visible but the whole area is quite overgrown now.

The area was once used as a rifle range by Major Woodhouse between the wars. Participants would lie on the earthworks and fire out across the Bovey Valley. This practice was stopped when it was pointed out that it could be quite dangerous.

Major Woodhouse lived in Water House. When he came out of the Army he went into the Church and was the parson at Manaton for many years. It is said that he was a very good soldier, but not a very good parson. His sermons went on for a very long time!

John Frost recalls that Major Woodhouse would hit the local boys with his riding stick: 'Mind you, we were in his orchard at the time...'

GREAT HOUND TOR FOLK LORE

Eric Hemery records that a schoolmaster on a visit to Great Hound Tor had a seizure and started to talk in Hebrew. He died three days later.

On a clear night in the late 1960s the north side of the tor was bathed in moonlight. A passing motorist saw a man in cavalier's costume step into the road and walk for some distance ahead of him, vanishing as suddenly as he had appeared.

In the *Transactions of the Devonshire Association*, 1972, Ruth Tongue reports: 'My daughter used to ride everywhere on Dartmoor. One evening she came back and said: "I was up by Hound Tor and suddenly a huge black dog came out of the rocks. The pony didn't like it, but I thought he was lost, so I called him, and he followed all the way home, about ten yards off. Just as I got at our yard he disappeared. I was looking right at him. He was huge."'

THE GREATOR ROCKS GHOST

A young lady from Great Hound Tor farm and her lover from Greator Rocks farm used to meet regularly here. They would discuss their plans for the future, their wedding, how many children they wanted, how they would earn a living and generally enjoy each other's company.

The young man was unexpectedly called up into the army and sent abroad before he was able to tell the young lady. He was killed and never returned home. She continued to visit Greator rocks to look for him until her death. She is still said to be found looking around the rocks in a state of distress for her missing lover.

Hound Tor rocks, from a postcard of the 1920s. In fiction this dramatic landscape is associated with the Hound of the Baskervilles and in more recent times the elusive Dartmoor Beast has been sighted close by. The 'beast' which has been blamed for killing sheep is thought perhaps to be a puma or a similarly large member of the cat family, released into the wild.

THE GREATER FARM GHOST

This ruined farm (see page 110) is still visited by one of its long gone inhabitants and if you happen to be at the right place at the right time, you may see him.

In 1997 a man working on the Leighon estate walked from the track through the woods into the old farmyard and saw, standing in the entrance to the barn, a man. He thought that it was an oddly dressed rambler, wearing a longish smock and cloth leggings. 'Who are you and what are you doing here?' he asked. The man made no reply, but turned and walked into the barn. The workman followed but when he entered the barn he found it was completely empty, and there was no sign that anyone had been there.

FREELANDS TOWER

This strange structure standing on the tor above Latchel Plantation, and now almost hidden by the trees, often gives rise to comment and speculation. Captain Bearne who lived at Freelands provided the following information.

The tower is a sizeable structure, about 35 feet high and 12 feet in diameter at the base. It has an internal oak staircase (now ruinous) to provide access to the top. It seems probable that it was built around 1900 as it does not appear on Ordnance Survey maps earlier than this.

It was apparently built by the 'Old Captain' (presumed to be a Master Mariner) and is situated on the Freelands boundary with the plantation, on land then owned by Mr Harvey of Freelands.

It was known locally as White's Tower, because it was said to have been built by 'Daddy' White.

It was used as an astronomical observatory, and records of observations made from the site have been seen by a local member of the British Astronomical Society. The Tower was capped with a characteristic hemispherical dome, which remained intact until around the time of the Second World War. There was no requirement for the telescope to be mounted so high above the ground for use in observing the sky, so it must be that the tower was also used as a lookout or viewing platform. The views are supposed to be spectacular.

During the Second World War, the Home Guard used the Tower as a lookout post. Below the Tower, just behind High Bank, is a small brick building with a curved corrugated iron roof, now derelict. It is thought that this could have been the Home Guard ammunition store.

Before the war local children used to play in and around the tower. It is believed that a heavy snowfall damaged some of the glass and that once the weather was able to get in, the rest came down soon after. Since that time it has not been maintained and it is likely to fall further into ruin.

In the 1930s there was no policeman based in Manaton, the responsible officer was based in Lustleigh and would routinely cycle to Manaton as part of his round. Around 1936 a local youth was caught trespassing inside the tower by the owner and was locked in. The policeman was called from Lustleigh on his bike but by the time the policeman arrived the trespasser had escaped without penalty!

The view from Bowerman's Nose across to Easdon Tor and beyond illustrates some of the variety of landscapes present in the parish. From upland moor to ancient woodland valleys and farmland, it provides a wide range of habitats for wildlife and a range of micro-climates.

Left: *Becky Falls never looks better than when the rocks are cascaded with icicles.*

Above: *The Great Blizzard of 1947. The Clements delivering newspapers in their Austin 7.*

18 - Wildlife and Wild Weather

While Manaton's human history can be measured in mere centuries, its landscape and wildlife have evolved over countless millennia. Hemmed in by landscape which remains unchanged since before the village's early settlers came here, our man-made environment is still dominated by the natural one, not vice versa. In southern Britain this is very rare indeed.

What creatures would have been roaming Dartmoor before our village existed? Thanks to a freak of geology we can see 125 000 years into the past when - under a plateau nine miles to the south of Manaton - the roof of a cave collapsed to form a pit which could have inspired Pooh Bear's Heffalump Trap. Bones recovered show that bison, rhinoceros, hippopotamus and straight-tusked elephant blundered into the hole in remarkable numbers, while spotted hyenas and lions jumped into the pit to feast on the carnage and were unable to get out again.

Fast forwarding to the modern era, what wildlife would Manaton's early human inhabitants have been living alongside? Bears were here for the first few centuries AD, but were gone long before the Norman conquest. Wolves survived much longer: they were still around at the time St Winifred's Church was being built, despite having bounties placed on their heads to speed up their extinction. Wild boar would last have been seen (and eaten) around 1200.

Various wild creatures were 'managed' for food in the Middle Ages, for example deer and fish. Fish, most notably sea trout, were channelled into large man-made ponds called stews, and caught on the medieval Church's 'no meat' days (three out of every seven). Barnacle geese (believed to hatch out from barnacles rather than eggs!) could also be brought up from the coast and eaten on meatless days, as they were considered to be fish!

Manaton people a thousand years ago would never have seen a rabbit. These exotic Mediterranean animals were imported post-conquest by Norman gourmets. A far cry from their hardened twentieth-century descendants, the early arrivals were too feeble even to dig their own burrows - special 'buries' were built to encourage them. Place names incorporating the word 'warren' indicate the sites of early commercial rabbit farms, a local example being Soussons Warren.

Red squirrels weren't farmed but they were hunted, and considered as a delicacy fit for a king. Outcompeted by grey squirrels (imported from the USA by misguided Victorians), they disappeared from Devon during the present century.

Black rats were arriving on ships from the East throughout the Middle Ages, bringing bubonic plague with them. They are now virtually extinct. Other recent winners and losers include villainous brown rats, Russian stowaways which first jumped ship here in the eighteenth century; and the blameless pine martens and red kites, gratuitously exterminated by gamekeepers and others within the last century or so.

THE RIVER BOVEY

What connects Manaton with Sticklepath, on the northern edge of the moor? The answer is slightly alarming. One night in 1955, that village was shocked out of its slumber by an earth tremor originating on the Sticklepath Fault - a great geological crack which runs right across Devon from north-west to south-east. Manaton is perched a few hundred feet above the same fault, known locally as the Cleave - the valley of the River Bovey.

The Cleave is the eastern boundary of Manaton Parish. In spate after heavy rain or snow, the Bovey rips through the deep and densely wooded valley at an awesome rate. It cascades down a number of waterfalls every bit as impressive (if not so accessible) as the more celebrated Becky Falls. At Horsham Steps, where an expanse of

Sea trout.

huge moss-covered boulders clogs the valley floor, the river actually disappears for a hundred yards or more: peering down from the tops of the rocks you can see the water swirling through the cracks and channels ten feet below.

Johnny the otter - a pet at Leighon during the 1930s.

As well as being part of Dartmoor National Park, the Bovey Valley is designated a National Nature Reserve because of the wealth of mosses, lichens and parasitic ferns found on the rocks and trees. These plants are highly sensitive to air pollution, and their abundance here demonstrates the air quality in the valley.

Water quality in the Bovey – as in all Devon rivers – has improved significantly towards the end of the twentieth century. This is good news for dippers, whose remarkable feeding technique is to hunt while walking upstream, under water, in the fastest-flowing reaches of the river. It is equally welcome for kingfishers: they rely on seeing their prey from above and are generally seen in the calmer stretches above Foxworthy.

Otters had been drifting towards pollution-fuelled extinction in the 1970s, but Devon is now England's otter stronghold. Although rarely seen these animals are easy to track, as their footprints, droppings and dens are very distinctive. At the time of writing, Manaton's section of the River Bovey is something of an otter paradise: the whole four-mile stretch shows evidence of constant activity and there is at least one breeding holt in the parish.

Mink are another story. Introduced from America in the 1920s, their first UK break-out was from a fur farm on the nearby River Teign. Since then they have been menacing native wildlife across wider and wider areas of the country. Although still much in evidence on the River Bovey, they may be on the decline due to the resurgent otter population. Otters are two to three times longer than mink and many times their weight; better adapted to the water environment, when food is limited otters easily out-compete the invaders. But whether ousted mink populations die out or just quit the river in favour of drier hunting grounds is still unknown.

THE BECKA BROOK

Manaton village lies between the River Bovey and Becka Brook. The rivers meet at the parish's eastern tip, while the source of the Becka (near Holwell Down) marks Manaton's southernmost point. What it lacks in length Becka Brook makes up for in interest, as the Dartmoor explorer William Crossing enthused in 1905:

> *No stream on Dartmoor with so short a course will compare with it in beauty. From its source to the point where it joins the Bovey, the distance is not much over four miles, and yet within this it flows by some remarkably fine tors, passes through a beautifully wooded valley, and at one point tumbles over a wilderness of boulders, and forms the well-known Becky Falls.*

It can be an impressively forceful stream too. Manaton residents of the late 1930s remember with awe the terrific flash flood which caused the Becka Brook to burst its banks, sweep away a bridge, and move so many large boulders downstream that the whole character and appearance of Becky Falls changed quite radically. The water level rose so high that a gamekeeper at the Leighon estate found pheasant hutches lodged ten feet up in the trees.

The Falls have been a popular attraction for summer tourists since Victorian times, but are arguably at their best on sub-zero winter days when the boulders are glazed over and the cascades are frozen into glittering curtains of icicles.

FARMS AND GARDENS

From the Becka-Bovey confluence to the top of Hameldown, Manaton's altitude varies from 80 to 530 metres above sea level. Between the valleys and the open moor lies a broad band of woods and farmland. In this more populated area, there is increased interaction between humans and their fellow mammals which can generate a good deal of friction. Foxes and badgers, stoats and weasels, roe deer and rabbits, moles and various rodents – all visit Manaton's gardens and farms regularly. Welcomed enthusiastically by some, they are just as likely to have people howling for their blood because of uprooted gardens, damaged trees or anticipated attacks on livestock.

Not all of our wild neighbours court such controversy. Dormice are nationally scarce but locally common: one of Manaton's many largely unknown nocturnal inhabitants, they lead a

Dormouse

blameless existence high up in the tree canopy. Spectacular hawk moths may also be lured into Manaton gardens, some blindingly colourful and others as large as the bats which pursue them. The nightjar, a rare African visitor whose weird call resembles an over-revving car engine, breeds here regularly. Tawny owls are numerous and their territorial screeching contests sometimes seem to encompass the whole of the parish.

In May and June the dawn chorus is at its loudest and most melodious, but is so ridiculously early that most people miss it. At other times of year the birds perform at a more civilised hour but with considerably less vigour. The parish boasts an impressive variety of resident and migrant birds, and you can easily see and hear at least forty different species from the average Manaton window in the course of a year.

The rulers of the roost, the Royal Family of the Manaton bird world, are undoubtedly the buzzards. Unconcerned with lesser feathered mortals, they shrug off the mob attacks of crows and magpies. On a clear day with good updrafts you can sometimes see half a dozen buzzards stacked and circling higher and higher, mewing to each other. Occasionally one drops like a rock towards a fleeing rabbit, but generally these birds seem more concerned with the sheer thrill of surfing the thermals than with the humdrum pursuit of food.

OPEN MOORLAND

Dartmoor is the stump of a mountain system formed by an upheaval of the earth's crust millions of years ago. The softer rocks above gradually wore away, leaving the underlying volcanic granite on the surface. In some places, rock was left bare of vegetation and weathered into a fantastic variety of shapes we can still see today - the tors.

Above the church, Manaton Rocks (once known as Manaton Tor) presents a smoothly rounded appearance. So too does Hay Tor, which dominates the skyline in many parts of the Parish. On the other hand Hound Tor is a spectacularly ragged, broken mass of granite stacks and boulders and Bowerman's Nose has been moulded into a shape so bizarre and unnatural that in earlier centuries it was assumed to have been a religious monument created by Druids or other pagan ancestors.

The vast blanket bogs which cover much of central Dartmoor do not reach into Manaton. However, we have extensive areas of drier moorland – for example Black Hill, Hound Tor, Hayne Down and Easdon Tor. Hameldown is one of the finest expanses of heather on Dartmoor and boasts a small population of red grouse, while in spring Holwell is noted for the eerie calls of curlew in one of their few Devon breeding sites. In the wild west of the parish, Challacombe's marshy pastures are the main UK stronghold of the bog hoverfly, an insect so obscure that it was believed to be extinct in this country until the early 1990s.

Further west still, a square mile of Soussons Down was planted up with spruce in the 1920s. Only six miles from Manaton church as the crow flies, it takes a good half hour to drive to Soussons: it is the scarcity of roads towards the centre of the moor which gives it such a wild feel and makes exploration on foot all the more exciting. The plantation has attracted crossbills and siskins, two colourful Nordic finches. Siskins, strictly winter visitors to England until recently, now breed prolifically in Manaton: in early summer they can be tempted to bird tables in flocks of twenty or more.

MOORLAND FIRES

Much of the open moorland is grazed by sheep, ponies and cattle. Because sheep prefer young heather to older, woodier plants, controlled burning (swaling) has become popular over the last two centuries. Properly managed at the right time of year, a fast-moving fire kills woody stems without damaging plant roots and encourages a new growth of succulent green shoots to emerge. Unfortunately, across much of the Moor swaling is too frequent and badly timed, with the result that the heather weakens and bracken is encouraged to spread.

Striking the right balance is very hard to achieve. In any event it is vital that we guard against such conflagrations as that which swept across Trendlebere Down in 1997, destroying four square miles of moorland wildlife habitat and threatening the existence of rare flora and fauna, some of which will take decades to recover.

Left: *The hurricane of January 1990 brought down thousands of trees in the county, including this huge beech completely blocking the road at Neadon farm.*

Below: *March 1978. It took four days before this car at Freelands was eventually dug out.*

WEATHER

As the buzzard (or blizzard) flies a mere five miles separate Manaton from Bovey Tracey, but the nine hundred foot difference in altitude can put us in a different, and sometimes inaccessible world. On the highest ground snow is reckoned to fall on 20 to 25 days of the year, and although it does not always settle there are days every year or two when the roads are only passable for four-wheel-drives. In some years – for example 1891, 1947 and 1976 – snow drifts up to twenty feet deep have cut off the village for days on end. Veterans of the 1947 white-out recall that volunteers would ride into Moretonhampstead on horseback each day and bring back provisions for the whole community.

March 1947 witnessed a legendary Dartmoor ammil. An ammil (Devonian for 'glazed frost') happens when dew forms and then the temperature suddenly drops below freezing point. Twigs and grasses, gates and fences are sheathed in layers of clear ice. This is a fairly common occurrence on Manaton's higher ground, in fact the name Hameldown may be a corruption of 'Ammil Down'. Whereas ammils usually melt away after a few hours, 1947's was freakish and lasted for days: whole trees were frozen solid and a witness wrote that the tors looked 'like mighty glaciers'.

High winds and thunderstorms regularly batter houses in more exposed parts of the village. In the 1980s two properties lying a good 200 metres apart were struck by lightning simultaneously, resulting in extensive property damage and some

miraculous escapes from personal injury. Another storm in 1999 saw lightning hit a Ridge Road telephone pole; the charge bolting down the wires was so explosive that it took the telephone company two weeks to repair the damage. In one house, a chunk of telecom shrapnel was blasted twenty feet from its wall and into the next room.

But our good weather can be just as spectacular as the bad. Early mornings often see the village basking in moorland sunshine, while below us Bovey and the Teign estuary are submerged under a rolling sea of white cloud. Evening light throws up different colours from the moor at every season. The crystal clear night sky, free of light pollution (away from the single street lamp!) is an astronomer's dream, and the distant roar we hear after dark is not traffic but the river barrelling through the Cleave. This is one corner of Britain where it is still easy to forget which era we live in. The millennium is not just a time to reflect on the extraordinary developments of the last thousand years - it is also a chance to celebrate those things which, just as remarkably, remain unchanged.

19 - Lest We Forget

It is appropriate that this book, which is published to celebrate the end of a millennium, should conclude with a chapter on those people of Manaton who gave their lives during the wars of the twentieth century. It is easy to pass by the memorial in the churchyard without a glance at the names of those who marched off to war and never returned. It is easier still to look back on those conflicts and to dismiss them as the result of empire building, poor political judgement, or jingosim. But hindsight is not a privilege allowed to those who die in war. We, who now share the land upon which they strode as young men, owe our future, in part, to them.

MANATON AND THE WARS

It is inevitable that any mention of war should immediately bring to mind the great European conflicts of 1914–1918 and 1939–1945 in which Manaton parishioners made great sacrifices on the battlefield, at sea and in the air. However, other conflicts touched the Parish albeit in a minor but interesting way.

The English Civil war between Cromwell and the Monarchy saw much action in the South West of England, with the battle nearest to Manaton being fought at Heathfield. There is a curious structure in the grounds of Manaton Gate that is thought to have been a Civil War gun battery, but it is difficult to find any logical reason for its location some six miles from Bovey Tracey and remote from any major communication route or possible encampment. A further curiosity is the river pebble stone floor in the entrance hall to Great Hound Tor farm which is said to have been laid by French prisoners of the Napoleonic Wars on parole from Dartmoor prison (see page 106).

1914–1918

No one living in the Parish can recall the events of the Great War but the memorial in the churchyard pays silent tribute to those who gave their lives as a result of that conflict. One who did return was Jack Perryman. Badly injured and invalided from the army he was trained as a bootmaker/repairer and started his business at

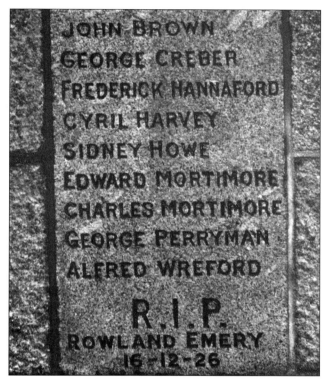

Names on the churchyard war memorial of those Manaton men who fell in the Great War 1914-18.

Blissmoor where his son Pat was born. As previously mentioned, the remoteness of the cottage limited trade so he moved to 1 Mellowmead.

Little photographic evidence remains but the 1919 Armistice Dinner held at the old Kestor Assembly rooms built by James Harvey, reminds us of the local men who served their country during that conflict. For a number of years the dinner was financed by Major Woodhouse.

1939–1945

For over 200 years large areas of Dartmoor have been used for military training with the area south of Okehampton being the main place for both peace time and wartime exercises. During the Second World War training by both British and American troops took place on moorland around Manaton. Manoeuvres near Hedge Barton Farm resulted in the death of a local worker, Reddaway, who is thought to have disturbed

Left: *Dartmoor has a long association with the military, not least through the use of its open landscape as a training area. This postcard is of unidentified troops leaving a stone compound, complete with sentry boxes. The postcard was sent from Throwleigh in 1905 to R.H. Creber of Deal. The message reads 'wish you and yours to come next Tuesday to see the country and have a little rabitting, perhaps Amos would come too. Please let us know by return.'*

Above: *Manaton men's outing in the 1920s. A number of these men would have experienced the warfare of 1914-18, while the younger ones present would be likely to see action in the 1939-45 conflict. The decimation of a generation of young men on the battlefields of Europe had a profound effect upon the communities in rural areas, not least as a high proportion of men did not return. Taking the population of Manaton at this time as around 300, and assuming half of these were women, and half the men were too young or too old for military service, the names appearing on the 1914-18 memorial, represent a devastating toll.*

Right: *The war memorial shortly after its completion in the 1920s.*

The 1919 Armistice Dinner held at the Kestor Assembly rooms.

Manaton men who fell in the war of 1939-45.

discarded live munition. With a detachment of men and trucks around Leighon a large field gun carried out firing practice causing large craters on the east side of Hound Tor. Soldiers were billeted in local houses (Ebworthy for example) and the old Village Hall was used as a military kitchen for troops. The Home Guard met in the Rifle Club and carried out live firing on both the indoor and outdoor ranges. A hut on the top of Easdon Tor served as both a look-out and communications post as did the old observatory tower at Freelands.

Both men and women responded to the call to arms in 1939. The Miss Browns joined the Womens Auxiliary Air Force (WAAF) from 1942–1946. Ruby (Florence), serving at RAF Predannick and RAF Bicester, received a Mention in Despatches, while Doris served at Torquay and Regents Park.

The Manaton Home Guard was part of the 14th Moorside Battalion which comprised over 1100 men. The Manaton Company included: Eric James, Jim Ash, Frank Beer, Arthur Brown, Mr Cowling, Langford Crout, Roy Greenaway, Jeff Greenaway, Sgt. R. C. James, Will Crout, Lewis Hern, John Kitson, Alec Kitson, Sid Perryman. Gilbert Shilston, Alban Shilston, Jack Skerrett,

Above: *Jim Hern serving as RAF aircrew was killed in WWII.*

Above right: *Unknown evacuee children at Leighon, the dog is being held by a child called Olive.*

Centre right: *Poles set up in the Second World War to deter glider-borne troop landings can still be seen.* Centre: *Ruby Brown in her WAAF uniform.* Above: *Penny Keogh (right) and fellow members of the Women's Land Army.* Above right: *Doris Brown also served with the WAAF from 1942-46.*

In the years when our Country was in mortal danger

Arthur William Brown.

who served *From: 19.6.40 to 31.12.44*

gave generously of his time and powers to make himself ready for her defence by force of arms and with his life if need be.

George R.I.

THE HOME GUARD

Above left: *An evocative picture of Land Girls in Manaton during the early 1940s. Penny Keogh is standing in the front row, second from right.* Above right: *Arthur Brown's Home Guard certificate.* Above left: *The Morgan-Giles family, owners of M-G Ltd, a shipyard in Teignmouth, where fast launches were built during the Second World War. The family lived at Shaldon and spent many holiday periods during the summer in Manaton. The photograph (1929) outside of Heemstede, now Mill House, shows: 2nd left seated, Morgan Morgan-Giles later to become Admiral Sir Morgan Morgan-Giles, MP for Winchester; 3rd left, Hebe, his sister; 4th from left, Mrs Moin; 5th left, Nina Finch; 6th left seated, Michael Morgan-Giles, brother; Lady standing Gladys Bowden, mother's help; far left, Jack Gaskin, driver of the lorry. The family would bring clothes, bedding, food and pets in the lorry. The family pony and trap would board a train in Newton Abbot for the journey to Bovey Tracey and then be driven up the old Manaton road to the village. In the early 1930s the family bought Swallerton Gate and lived in it during the summer months only, travelling to the cottage in a Bull-nose Morris. The children would operate the moor gate between Hound Tor and Swinedown for coppers.*

Harold Wreford and H. Cobbett. Commanding Officers were Captain Wheeler, Colonel Cotgrave and Captain Longbourne.

Members of the ARP and Special Constables were Wilfred Creber, Charles Perryman and Frank Coniam. At the Battalion Stand Down Parade on the 3 December 1944 the farewell address was given by Colonel P. I. Newton with each man receiving a certificate of service signed by King George VI. The local Women's Land Army was organised by Joyce Carew of Beckhams and a group of girls were billeted at Ivy Cottage (Church Cottage) under the supervision of Penny Ripman (now Penny Keogh).

The village war memorial records those from the Parish who fought and fell, whilst others

returned. Each year members of the Manaton Branch British Legion parade on Armistice Sunday to pay their respects to those who fell in the two major wars (see photograph on page 164). A more lighthearted but still signicant remembrance took place on the 50th anniversary of V.E. Day when several parishioners raised the Union flag on the top of Manaton Rocks

50th ANNIVERSARY OF V.E. DAY – 8 MAY 1995

The Women's Institute agreed that the 50th Anniversary of V.E. Day should be suitably celebrated in Manaton and that the Royal British Legion should be asked to share the organisation of the festivities. It was decided that a lunch in

Hameldown in 1991 during the ceremony in which the Aircrew Association erected a plaque on the existing stone memorial on which were inscribed the initials of an RAF aircrew who died there in 1941. The plaque reads: 'On 22nd March 1941 a RAF bomber of 49 Squadron, Scampton, crashed returning from operations over France and 4 crew were lost. This memorial commemorates their selfless courage and that of fellow airmen who perished on Dartmoor 1939-45. Their sacrifice helped us to maintain freedom.'

the Parish Hall, followed by a dance in the evening, should be arranged.

Decorations for the Hall were red, white and blue bunting which was draped around the walls, caught up at intervals by bunches of red, white and blue balloons. A large Union Jack – actually a bedspread! – was hung on the wall at the end nearest to the door, and some facsimiles of wartime posters were fixed around the room between the windows. There was also a display of wartime memorabilia in the form of old newspaper cuttings and pictures. Trestle tables were arranged across the length of the room, covered with damask patterned banqueting roll and decorated with posies, again in red, white and blue.

The Parish Council gave a grant of £50 towards the costs and this enabled children of parishioners to have a free meal. Everyone else paid £3. The food was cold turkey breast and ham, together with salads, followed by home-made apple pie, trifle and cream, and wine.

Members of the Royal British Legion helped with putting up the decorations and preparing the tables and later ran the bar when parishioners began to arrive.

After the meal, the Chairman of the Parish Council, Major A. Cullen, gave a short speech, followed by the Chairman of the Royal British Legion, Mr F. Pearce. After that, the Parish Map, which had recently been finished and framed in time for the day, was unveiled by Major Cullen to great applause.

It was a very happy occasion at which some eighty members of the village were brought together in a wave of nostalgia. There was rousing singing after the meal to a selection of wartime songs, accompanied on the piano by Alan Jeffs. A smaller number of people returned in the evening to dance to records of 1940's music, to eat and drink remains from the afternoon's meal and to complete a most convivial and enjoyable day.

Hoisting the Union Flag on Manaton Rocks to celebrate the 50th anniversary of VE Day. L-r: Jim Crout; David Mason; Steve Miners, Ray Hugo, Stan Fitton and Brian Warne.

Subscribers

Dave and Jo Alderton, The Forge, Manaton

Margaret Andrews, Lower Weddicott Farm, Chagford, Devon

Mrs Suzanne Ashleigh-Thomas, Shrewsbury

Martin Aspinall, Landlord, Kestor Inn, Manaton

Mr and Mrs M. Baker, 5 Mellowmead, Manaton

Michael and Jean Baldwin, Pembereley, Manaton

Kay Balmforth, Where the Woozle Wasn't, Manaton

Julie Banahan, Rockfield, Manaton

Alison Bean, Moorcrest, Manaton

Captain N. Bearne R.N., Kingswear, Dartmouth, Devon

Becky Falls, (Mr J. Harding), Manaton

Revd John and Dr Hazel Bell, Kingsnympton, Umberleigh, Devon

Mrs Joan Bell, Bristol

Reg and Betty Bellamy, York/Postbridge, Devon

Peg Bentley, Oxford

John D. Bewsher, Paignton, Devon

Nick and Sylvie Beyts, Moor House, Manaton

Phyllis Bickham (née Webber), Moretonhampstead, Devon

Margery Elizabeth Bindloss J.P., Bovey Tracey, Devon

C. H. Bolton, Kilmington, Axminster, Devon

W. Boughey, Ebworthy, Manaton

Benedict and Karen Brennan, Swallerton Gate, Devon

Mrs Karen Brennan, Wattisham, Suffolk

Mrs Susan Brewer (Wheeler), formerly of Manaton

V. D. M. Brown, Ivy Cottage, Manaton

Mr T. Bunney, Warsash, Hampshire

W. E. Burrell, Malaga, Spain

K. J. Burrow, Bucks Cross, Bideford, Devon

Anna Butler, Roseweek, Penrice, St Austell, Cornwall

John Butler and family, Edmonton, Alberta, Canada

Lydia Ann Butler, London

Sadie Butler, Albuquerque, New Mexico, USA

Samuel Butler, Islington, London NW1

Simon, Anna and Harry Butler, Little Neadon, Manaton

Jean Carne, Mousehole, Penzance, Cornwall

Marion Carpenter (née Breeze), Bovey Tracey, formerly of Manaton

Ros and Steven Carr, Barne Farm, Moretonhampstead, Devon

Miss Mary Chandler, Lytham, Lancashire

Jim Churchward, Ilsington, Devon

Barbara Clarke (née Mortimore), Buckfastleigh

Mrs A. Cleave (née Winsor), Sigford

Ian Clements, formerly of Oversley, Manaton

Mr S. and Mrs P. Clements (née Cowling), formerly of Manaton

Ella Corbett, Manaton

R. C. Cornish, Liverton, Newton Abbot, Devon

Mr and Mrs N. R. Cowling, Widecombe-in-the-Moor, Devon

Derrick Cowling, Winkleigh, Devon

John and Jean Criggall, formerly of Amber House, Manaton

Joyce Cross, Moretonhampstead, Devon

Anne-Marie Crout, Mellowmead, Manaton

Charles A. Crout, Moretonhampstead, Devon

Jim and Yvonne Crout, Mellowmead, Manaton

Antony L. and Audrey D. Cullen, Leighon, Manaton

Mrs B. Cullum (née Jones), Leominster, Herefordshire

Denis and Pamela Daley, Hunters Wood, Manaton

Mrs Lynn Dann, Widecombe-in-the-Moor, Devon

Dartmoor National Park Authority, Devon

Mrs P. Davies, Payhembury, Honiton, Devon

Peter Daw, Tavistock, Devon

Heather S. M. Delaney, Deal Lodge, Manaton

Sally Doe, Hayne, Manaton

John Dommett, Rock Cottage, Manaton

E., E., and F. Donne, Manaton

Richard Donne, Sidmouth, Devon

Mr D. J. Dymond, Bovey Tracey, Devon

J. M. Ellingworth, Wells, Somerset

David Endacott, ex Bovey Tracey, Devon

Mr R. W. Evans, Bournemouth

The Revd. and Mrs D. A. N. Evans, High Bank, Manaton

Michael Eveleigh, Tipton St John, Sidmouth, Devon

Richard, Rosalind and Oliver Field, Plymouth, Devon

Mrs M. Flowers, Axminster, Devon

Mr and Mrs W. Foster, Tavistock, Devon

Andrew Frost, Callington, Cornwall

Mrs Gladys Gardner, Exwick, Exeter, Devon

F. P. Germon, formerly of Manaton

Mr and Mrs G. W. Gilliam, Ringmore, Kingsbridge, Devon

Mrs Sue G. Glover, Shipney, Bognor Regis, Sussex

Heidi Gould (née Perryman), Roborough, Plymouth, Devon

Derek J. Greenaway, Hill Farm House, Liverton

Dr. Tom and Mrs Elisabeth Greeves, Tavistock, Devon

Stella Grimsey, Overton, Hants.

Gavin Grimsey, Bovey Tracey, Devon

Mrs Mary Ham, Sandygate, Newton Abbot, Devon

Mr P. Hamilton-Leggatt BSc, Tavistock, Devon

Glenn M. Hannigan, Tavistock, Devon

Bryan and Jane Harper, Swallerton Gate, Manaton

Mr and Mrs J. R. Harries, Topsham, formerly of Manaton

Mr and Mrs Harris, Okehampton, Devon

THE BOOK OF MANATON

Mrs D. M. Harris, Sidmouth, Devon
Peter and Mary Head, Gratnor, Manaton
Francis E. Heath, Bovey Tracey, Devon
Robert Hern, Lustleigh, Devon
James and Diane Hern, Liverton, Devon
Judith Hervey (Nosworthy, Harvey), Australia
Jane Hewitt and Julian Tope, Mill House, Manaton
Gwen Hines, Manaton
Antonia Hoggett, Furze Park, Manaton
William (Bill) Howe, Kenilworth, Warwick
Mrs R. K. Hudson, London SW17
Mr R. V. and Mrs M. Hugo, Cherry Trees, Manaton
Bob, Frannie and Marlee Hunka, Los Angeles, USA
Mrs E. Hunt, Neadon, Manaton
Tom, Mairi, Ben and Daisy Hunt, Neadon, Manaton
Miss Pauline James, Latchel, Manaton
Mr Hugh James, Teddington, Middlesex
Mr Robert James, Steeple Bumpstead, Suffolk
Mr Patrick James, Goonhaven, Cornwall
Mr Andrew James, Bloomsbury, London
Wing Cdr Tim James, Latchel, Manaton
Major Ralph James, Latchel, Manaton
Dr Charles James, Ringmoor, Devon
Mike and Brenda Jeffery, Moretonhampstead, Devon
Charles F. P. Jewell, Fernstone, Manaton
Margaret and Peter Kapff, Wingstone, Manaton
Gareth and Charlotte Keene, Buttermead, Manaton
Janet Kennedy and Andrew Taylor, Moorlands, Manaton
Penelope Keogh, Deal Farm, Manaton
Mrs C. M. Kilminster, Hazlemere, Bucks.
Colin C. Kilvington, Stoke, Plymouth, Devon
Miss. P. King, Newton Abbot, Devon
Thomas E. King, Clyst St. Mary, Devon
Dr and Mrs S. G. Lake, Beckaford Farm, Manaton
Celia Leaman, British Columbia, Canada
Miss. J. Lee, Tavistock, Devon
Jonathan T. C. Lowe, Newent, Glos.
Mrs Joanne Maber, New Zealand
Andrew R. Manaton, Butterleigh, Devon
Olwen B. Manaton, Honiton, Devon
Jack Manaton, Yetminster, Dorset
Mr Tym Manley, Hampstead, London
Mr Stephen Manley, Wembworthy, Devon
Mrs Katharine Manley, Latchel, Manaton
Douglas Marsh, Chagford, Devon
Mrs D. R. Mason, Clifton, Bristol
Mr M. P. McElheron, Kingskerswell, Devon
Alasdair J. McEwen Mason, Mill Farm, Manaton
Katie L. McEwen Mason, Mill Farm, Manaton
Christina J. McEwen Mason, Mill Farm, Manaton
Joyce and David J. McEwen Mason, Mill Farm, Manaton
Brian Mead, Fardel, Cornwood, Devon
Britt, Ida and Thea Merrison, Freelands, Manaton
Jim and Diane Miller, Melbourne, Australia
Tina (née Crout) and Ian Morgan, Exeter

Rear Admiral Sir M. Morgan-Giles, Winchester (formerly of Manaton)
Robin Morgan-Giles, Porthmadog, Gwynedd, Wales
Steve Morris, Manaton
Mrs H. Moss, Cherhill, Manaton
Barbara Mugford, Bovey Tracey, Devon
Roger and Sandra Mules, Manaton Gate, Manaton
J. N. and M. E. Munk, Blue Haze, Manaton
S. C. Needham, Widecombe-in-the-Moor, Devon
Captain Brian and Mrs Joan Newton (née Shakespeare), Moorcrest, Manaton
Stephen G. Nosworthy, Exmouth, Devon
Mr N. J. Osborne, Westbury, Wiltshire
C. Otho-Briggs, Blissmoor, Manaton
Mr and Mrs K. Owen, Owens Book Centre, Tavistock, Devon
Mike and Jane Passmore, Exeter, Devon
Andrew Passmore, Exeter, Devon
Freddie Pearce, Manaton
Kathleen and Robert Perkins, Town Barton, Manaton
Doreen Perkins, Pinchbeck, Lincs
Kate S. M. Perkins, South Knighton, Leicester
Mr and Mrs R. M. Perry, Plymouth, Devon
Mrs E. Perryman, Manaton
Frank Perryman, Buckfastleigh, Devon
Pat Perryman, Bovey Tracey, Devon
Richard, Sally, Dickon and Molly Perryman, South Fordgate, Manaton
David Perryman, Buckland-in-the-Moor, Ashburton, Devon
Claude Pike, Heathercombe, Manaton
Mark and Hilary Pilkington, Ullacombe Farm, Haytor, Devon
Gerald and Valerie Pilkington, Lounston, Ilsington, Devon
Tom Pollard, Beetor Farm, North Bovey (born at Wingstone, Manaton, 1947)
Audrey Prizeman, Plymouth, Devon
June M. Puttick, Eastbourne, Sussex
Mr and Mrs D. W. Puttick, Eastbourne, Sussex
Ken Rickard, Lydford, Devon
Peter Ripman, Manaton
Mr and Mrs G. M. Roberts, Manaton
Jill and David Rogers, Water Cottages, Manaton
Mr and Mrs Rolfe, Lower Dimson, Devon
Mr and Mrs Rolfe, Tamerton Foliot, Plymouth, Devon
Mrs A. J. Rowley, Brunel Park, Torquay, Devon
Don and Joyce Rowley, formerly of Manaton
Mrs Jenny Sanders, Tavistock, Devon
Mrs S. A. Sanders, Bickington, Newton Abbot, Devon
Tim Sandles, Denbury, Newton Abbot, Devon
Alison and Mark Shannon, Yeadon, Leeds
Janet Shilston, Cherry Tree Cottage, Moretonhampstead, Devon
Mrs B. Shilston, Chudleigh, Newton Abbot, Devon

Christopher G. W. Simmons, Hayes, Bromley, Kent
Jane Sims, Deal, Kent
Leonard Skerrett, Broadclyst, Exeter, Devon
Eric Skerrett, Teignmouth, Devon
Cyril Skerrett, Dawlish, Devon
Mrs M. Skerrett, Nailsea, Bristol
Margaret Skerrett, Moretonhampstead, Devon
Mrs D. Skipper, Tunbridge Wells, Kent
Doreen and Frank Smith, Manaton
John E. Smith, Turnchapel, Plymouth, Devon
S.A.M. (Susan) Smith, Cross Park, Manaton
Alan Smith, Epsom, Surrey
Hugh Somerville, Newton Abbot, Devon
Bob and Liz Spurrell, Amber House, Manaton
Colin and Mary Stewart, Green Loaning, Manaton
Frances Stewart and Stephen Saunders, Foxworthy,
    Manaton
Robert Stone, Barnstaple, Devon
The Rev. J. Robin C. Taylor, Hadleigh, Suffolk
Jeane Taylor, Long Tor, Lustleigh
Max and Rosie Taylor, Moorlands, Manaton
Vanessa (née Crout) and Andrew Taylor, Torquay
Pauline Teeling, Torlands, Manaton
Mrs P. Theobald (née German), Haslemere, Surrey
Kay (née Crout) and Colin Thomas, Hamilton,
    Ontario, Canada
Mrs Michelle Thomas (née Morgan-Giles), Newton
    Abbot, Devon
Richard, Jenny, Tracy, Joshua and Naomi Thorns,
    The Post House, Manaton
Ruth Thrower and Geraldine Craig (née Kitson),
    Somerset/Surrey

Dr and Mrs E. N. Tiratsoo, Water, Manaton
Amelia Tope, Ashburton, Devon
Mrs Hebe Tremain (née Giles), Torrington, Devon
The Turner Family, Barracott, Manaton
Kieron F. Unwin, Christow, Exeter, Devon
Anne Vallings (née Wadham), Newton Abbot,
    Devon
Mr and Mrs R. A. Vane, Lincoln
Mel Veal, Greystones, Manaton
Mr G. Waldron, Plymouth, Devon
Eddie and Winnie Walker, Wayfarers, Manaton
John F. W. Walling, Newton Abbot, Devon
Christine Walton, Moretonhampstead, Devon
Miss Ruth Warne, Southcott, Manaton
Warne Family, Southcott, Manaton
Alan Watson, Exeter, Devon
Gideon Webber, Moretonhampstead, Devon
Mr and Mrs Douglas Webster, Freelands, Manaton
John and Janet Wellingham, Jays, Manaton
Neville and Valerie Wheeler, Little Rocks, Manaton
Mr Stuart Wheeler, formerly of Manaton
Michael George Wiles, Haytor, Devon
Robert David Willcocks, Ipplepen, Newton Abbot,
    Devon
Brenda Williams, Paignton, Devon
Carl and Diane Wills, 5 Amber Tor, Manaton
Eric and Betty Wilson, Rockend, Manaton
Val and Stephen Woods, Portchester, Hants.
Nick Wotton (Walking Guide), Ogwell, Newton
    Abbot, Devon
Roger Wrayford, Preston, Lancs.
Mrs R. Wurtzburg, Bovey Tracey, Devon

Also available in the Halsgrove Community History Series:

Widecombe-in-the-Moor – Stephen Woods
The Book of Grampound with Creed – Amy Bane and Mary Oliver
Lanner: A Cornish Mining Parish – Sharron Schwartz and Roger Parker
The Book of Cornwood and Lutton – compiled by the People of the Parish
Postbridge: The Heart of Dartmoor – Reg Bellamy
The Book of Bampton – Caroline Seward
The Ellacombe Book – Sydney R. Langmead
The Book of Lamerton – The Lamerton Parish History Group
The Book of Loddiswell, Heart of the South Hams – The Loddiswell Parish History Group
The Book of Manaton – The Manaton Parish Book Group
The Book of Meavy – Pauline Hemery
The Book of North Newton – J.C. Robins and K.C. Robins
The Book of Plymtree, The Parish and Its People – compiled and edited by Tony Eames
The Book of Porlock – Dennis Corner
The Book of Stithians, The Changing Face of a Cornish Parish – Stithians Parish History Group
The Book of Torbay, A Century of Celebration – Frank Pearce
The Book of Trusham: A Parish Patchwork – Alice Cameron
Clearbrook - Pauline Hemery
The Book of Werrington – Joan Rendell MBE
Widecombe–in–the-Moor Revisited – Stephen Woods
Woodbury, The Twentieth Century Revisited – Roger Stokes

Forthcoming titles in the Halsgrove Community History Series:

The Book of Silverton
The Book of Bickleigh
The Ilsington Book
The Book of Helston
The Book of South Zeal
The Lustleigh Book

Further information:
If you would like to find out more about having your parish featured in this series, please write to
The Editor, Community History Series, Halsgrove House, Lower Moor Way, Tiverton Business Park,
Tiverton, Devon, EXI6 6SS, tel: 01884 243242 or visit us at http://www.halsgrove.com
If you are interested in a particular photograph in this volume,
it may be possible to supply a copy of the image.